Cisco Software Access

Jason Gooley, CCIE No. 38759

Roddie Hasan, CCIE No. 7472

Srilatha Vemula, CCIE No. 33670

Cisco Press

Cisco Software-Defined Access

Jason Gooley

Roddie Hasan

Srilatha Vemula

Copyright© 2021 Cisco Systems, Inc.

Published by:
Cisco Press
Hoboken, NJ

1 2020

Library of Congress Control Number: 2020938615

ISBN-13: 978-0-13-644838-9

ISBN-10: 0-13-644838-0

Warning and Disclaimer

This book is designed to provide information about Cisco Software-Defined Access (Cisco SD-Access). Every effort has been made to make this book as complete and as accurate as possible, but no warranty or fitness is implied.

The information is provided on an "as is" basis. The authors, Cisco Press, and Cisco Systems, Inc. shall have neither liability nor responsibility to any person or entity with respect to any loss or damages arising from the information contained in this book or from the use of the discs or programs that may accompany it.

The opinions expressed in this book belong to the author and are not necessarily those of Cisco Systems, Inc.

Trademark Acknowledgments

All terms mentioned in this book that are known to be trademarks or service marks have been appropriately capitalized. Cisco Press or Cisco Systems, Inc., cannot attest to the accuracy of this information. Use of a term in this book should not be regarded as affecting the validity of any trademark or service mark.

Special Sales

For information about buying this title in bulk quantities, or for special sales opportunities (which may include electronic versions; custom cover designs; and content particular to your business, training goals, marketing focus, or branding interests), please contact our corporate sales department at corpsales@pearsoned.com or (800) 382-3419.

For government sales inquiries, please contact governmentsales@pearsoned.com.

For questions about sales outside the U.S., please contact intlcs@pearson.com.

Feedback Information

At Cisco Press, our goal is to create in-depth technical books of the highest quality and value. Each book is crafted with care and precision, undergoing rigorous development that involves the unique expertise of members from the professional technical community.

Readers' feedback is a natural continuation of this process. If you have any comments regarding how we could improve the quality of this book, or otherwise alter it to better suit your needs, you can contact us through email at feedback@ciscopress.com. Please make sure to include the book title and ISBN in your message.

We greatly appreciate your assistance.

Editor-in-Chief: Mark Taub

Alliances Manager, Cisco Press: Arezou Gol

Director, ITP Product Management: Brett Bartow

Managing Editor: Sandra Schroeder

Development Editor: Marianne Bartow

Senior Project Editor: Tonya Simpson

Copy Editor: Bill McManus

Technical Editors: Dax Mickelson, Nicole Wajer

Editorial Assistant: Cindy Teeters

Book Designer: Chuti Pratsertsith

Composition: codeMantra

Indexer: Timothy Wright

Proofreader: Gill Editorial Services

Americas Headquarters
Cisco Systems, Inc.
San Jose, CA

Asia Pacific Headquarters
Cisco Systems (USA) Pte. Ltd.
Singapore

Europe Headquarters
Cisco Systems International BV Amsterdam,
The Netherlands

Cisco has more than 200 offices worldwide. Addresses, phone numbers, and fax numbers are listed on the Cisco Website at **www.cisco.com/go/offices.**

Cisco and the Cisco logo are trademarks or registered trademarks of Cisco and/or its affiliates in the U.S. and other countries. To view a list of Cisco trademarks, go to this URL: www.cisco.com/go/trademarks. Third party trademarks mentioned are the property of their respective owners. The use of the word partner does not imply a partnership relationship between Cisco and any other company. (1110R)

About the Authors

Jason Gooley, CCIE No. 38759 (RS and SP), is a very enthusiastic and spontaneous person who has more than 25 years of experience in the industry. Currently, Jason works as a technical evangelist for the Worldwide Enterprise Networking sales team at Cisco Systems. Jason is very passionate about helping others in the industry succeed. In addition to being a Cisco Press author, Jason is a distinguished speaker at CiscoLive, contributes to the development of the Cisco CCIE and DevNet exams, provides training for Learning@Cisco, is an active CCIE mentor, is a committee member for the Cisco Continuing Education Program (CE), and is a program committee member of the Chicago Network Operators Group (CHI-NOG), www.chinog.org. Jason also hosts a show called MetalDevOps. Jason can be found at www.MetalDevOps.com, @MetalDevOps, and @Jason_Gooley on all social media platforms.

Roddie Hasan, CCIE No. 7472 (RS), is a technical solutions architect for Cisco Systems and has 29 years of networking experience. He has been with Cisco for more than 12 years and is a subject matter expert on enterprise networks. His role is supporting customers and account teams globally, with a focus on Cisco DNA Center and Cisco Software-Defined Access. He also specializes in technologies such as MPLS, Enterprise BGP, and SD-WAN. Prior to joining Cisco, Roddie worked in the U.S. federal government and service provider verticals. Roddie blogs at www.ccie.tv and can be found on Twitter at @eiddor.

Srilatha Vemula, CCIE No. 33670 (SEC), is a technical solutions architect for the Worldwide Enterprise Networking Sales team at Cisco Systems. There, she works with account teams and systems engineers to help Cisco customers adopt Cisco DNA Center, Cisco SD-Access, Cisco Identity Services Engine, and Cisco TrustSec. Srilatha has served in multiple roles at Cisco, including technical consulting engineer and security solutions architect. She led the design and implementation of security projects using Cisco flagship security products for key U.S. financial customers.

About the Technical Reviewers

Dax Mickelson has been working in network engineering for more than 20 years. Most of this time has been spent building training material and labs for Cisco. Dax has obtained many industry certifications over the years, including Cisco Certified Internetwork Expert Written (CCIE Written); Cisco Certified Network Associate (CCNA); Cisco IP Telephony Support Specialist (CIPT); Cisco Certified Network Professional (CCNP); Cisco Certified Academy Instructor (CCAI); Linux Certified Instructor (LCI); Linux Certified Administrator (LCA); Mitel 3300 ICP Installation and Maintenance Certified (this includes several periphery certifications like teleworker); NEC IPKII Basic, Advanced, and IP Certified; Oracle Certified Professional (OCP/DBO); Certified Novell Administrator (CNA); Cradle Point Network Associate and Professional (CPCNA and CPCNP).

Nicole Wajer graduated with a degree in computer science from the Amsterdam University of Applied Sciences and specializes in security, Cisco DNA, the Internet of Things (IoT), and IPv6. She has a global role for the security aspects of Cisco SDA-Access and SD-WAN on the Enterprise Networking team as a technical solutions architect (IBN security).

Nicole's career with Cisco started in routing and switching and network security, but fighting spam and malware turned out to be in her "Cisco DNA" since her first day on the Internet, so a move to content security was an obvious progression. Nicole then joined the Enterprise Networking team to continue her security passion and progress with Cisco DNA Center.

Dedications

Jason Gooley:

This book is dedicated to my wife, Jamie, and my children, Kaleigh and Jaxon. I love you all more than anything! I also want to dedicate this book to my father and brother for always having my back. In addition, this book is dedicated to all the people who have supported me over the years and all the candidates who are studying or trying to improve themselves through education.

Roddie Hasan:

To my mother, Sylvia: You taught me the phrase "to make a long story short." I dedicate this to you, whose story ended up being too short. I miss you, Mom.

Srilatha Vemula:

This book is dedicated to my parents, Adiseshu and Lakshmi, and my sisters for your love and support. Your sacrifices and lessons opened up doors to opportunities in my life that wouldn't have been possible without you. Throughout the years of my personal and professional life, I learned a lot from friends, co-workers, and mentors who have made me a better person. I would also like to dedicate this book to those who have had a positive influence in my life.

Acknowledgments

Jason:

Thank you to Brett and Marianne Bartow as well as everyone else involved at Cisco Press. Not only do you make sure the books are top notch, you make me a better author!

Thank you to my team, Worldwide Enterprise Networking Sales at Cisco, for always supporting me through all the awesome projects I am fortunate enough to be a part of. #TeamGSD

Thank you to all the people who follow me on my journey, whether through social media or in person. You are much appreciated!

Roddie:

Thank you to Brett, Marianne, and all the staff at Cisco Press for putting up with my nonsense as I struggled to transition from an in-person communication style to a writing one. I learned a lot during this process thanks to your expertise and guidance.

Thank you to Jason Gooley for setting up this project for us, for your patience with chapter delay after chapter delay, and for being an amazing co-author along with Srilatha Vemula.

Thank you to all the amazing and sharp people at Cisco that I have worked with for the past 12 years for helping me grow in this field and helping get me to a point where I was ready to write a book.

And finally, and most importantly: Thank you to my wife, Erin, and kids, Sousan and Brian, for supporting me throughout my career and understanding when I had to go do "nerd stuff."

Srilatha:

Thank you, Cisco Press, especially Brett and Marianne Bartow, for your help and guidance through my first book. Thank you to the technical editors, Nicole Wajer and Dax Mickelson, for reviewing our work and making the book better. Thank you to my friend, mentor, and a fellow author Vivek Santuka for your guidance throughout the years.

Thank you to my co-authors Jason Gooley and Roddie Hasan for the collaboration and making this fun.

Thank you to my team and Cisco for taking a chance on me. I am grateful for the opportunity to work for Cisco.

Contents at a Glance

Introduction   xvii

Chapter 1   Today's Networks and the Drivers for Change   1

Chapter 2   Introduction to Cisco Software-Defined Access   21

Chapter 3   Introduction to Cisco DNA Center   59

Chapter 4   Cisco Software-Defined Access Fundamentals   81

Chapter 5   Cisco Identity Services Engine with Cisco DNA Center   111

Chapter 6   Cisco Software-Defined Access Operation and Troubleshooting   167

Chapter 7   Advanced Cisco Software-Defined Access Topics   195

Chapter 8   Advanced Cisco DNA Center   255

Chapter 9   Cisco DNA Assurance   285

Glossary   307

Index   313

Reader Services

Register your copy at www.ciscopress.com/title/9780136448389 for convenient access to downloads, updates, and corrections as they become available. To start the registration process, go to www.ciscopress.com/register and log in or create an account*. Enter the product ISBN 9780136448389 and click Submit. When the process is complete, you will find any available bonus content under Registered Products.

*Be sure to check the box that you would like to hear from us to receive exclusive discounts on future editions of this product.

Contents

Introduction   xvii

Chapter 1   Today's Networks and the Drivers for Change   1

Networks of Today   1

Common Business and IT Trends   4

Common Desired Benefits   5

High-Level Design Considerations   6

Cisco Digital Network Architecture   10

Past Solutions to Today's Problems   12

    Spanning-Tree and Layer 2–Based Networks   13

Introduction to Multidomain   16

    Cloud Trends and Adoption   18

Summary   20

Chapter 2   Introduction to Cisco Software-Defined Access   21

Challenges with Today's Networks   22

Software-Defined Networking   22

Cisco Software-Defined Access   23

    Cisco Campus Fabric Architecture   24

    Campus Fabric Fundamentals   25

    Cisco SD-Access Roles   27

Network Access Control   30

    Why Network Access Control?   31

Introduction to Cisco Identity Services Engine   32

    Overview of Cisco Identity Services Engine   32

    Cisco ISE Features   34

    Secure Access   34

    Device Administration   37

    Guest Access   38

    Profiling   40

    Bring Your Own Device   45

    Compliance   46

    Integrations with pxGrid   48

Cisco ISE Design Considerations   50

    Cisco ISE Architecture   50

Cisco ISE Deployment Options   51

Standalone Deployment   51

Distributed Deployment   51

Dedicated Distributed Deployment   52

Segmentation with Cisco TrustSec   54

Cisco TrustSec Functions   54

Classification   55

Propagation   55

Enforcement   57

Summary   58

Chapter 3   Introduction to Cisco DNA Center   59

Network Planning and Deployment Trends   59

History of Automation Tools   60

Cisco DNA Center Overview   62

Design and Visualization of the Network   64

Site Design and Layout   64

Network Settings   69

Wireless Deployments   70

Network Discovery and Inventory   72

Discovery Tool   72

Inventory   74

Device Configuration and Provisioning   77

Summary   79

Chapter 4   Cisco Software-Defined Access Fundamentals   81

Network Topologies   81

Cisco Software-Defined Access Underlay   82

Manual Underlay   83

Automated Underlay: LAN Automation   84

Wireless LAN Controllers and Access Points in Cisco Software-Defined
Access   89

Shared Services   90

Transit Networks   91

IP-Based Transit   91

SD-Access Transit   92

Fabric Creation   92

Fabric Location   93

Fabric VNs   94

Fabric Device Roles   94

Control Plane   95

Fabric Borders   96

Border Automation   98

Border and Control Plane Collocation   99

Fabric Edge Nodes   100

Intermediate Nodes   103

External Connectivity   104

Fusion Router   104

Host Onboarding   105

Authentication Templates   105

VN to IP Pool Mapping   106

SSID to IP Pool Mapping   108

Switchport Override   109

Summary   110

References in This Chapter   110

Chapter 5   Cisco Identity Services Engine with Cisco DNA Center   111

Policy Management in Cisco DNA Center with Cisco ISE   112

Integration of Cisco DNA Center and ISE   113

Certificates in Cisco DNA Center   113

Certificates on Cisco Identity Services Engine   115

Cisco ISE and Cisco DNA Center Integration Process   116

Group-Based Access Control   122

Segmentation with Third-Party RADIUS Server   126

Secure Host Onboarding in Enterprise Networks   128

Endpoint Host Modes in 802.1X   128

Single-Host Mode   128

Multi-Host Mode   128

Multi-Domain Mode   129

Multi-Auth Mode   129

802.1X Phased Deployment   130

Why a Phased Approach?   131

Phase I: Monitor Mode (Visibility Mode)   132

Phase II: Low-Impact Mode   133

Phase II: Closed Mode   134

Host Onboarding with Cisco DNA Center   136

No Authentication Template   137

Open Authentication Template   138

Closed Authentication   140

Easy Connect   141

Security in Cisco Software-Defined Access Network   144

Macro-Segmentation in Cisco SD-Access   144

Micro-Segmentation in Cisco SD-Access   145

Policy Set Overview in Cisco ISE   146

Segmentation Policy Construction in Cisco SD-Access   148

Corporate Network Access Use Case   149

Guest Access Use Case   159

Segmentation Outside the Fabric   164

Summary   164

References in This Chapter   165

Chapter 6   Cisco Software-Defined Access Operation and Troubleshooting   167

Cisco SD-Access Under the Covers   167

Fabric Encapsulation   167

LISP   168

VXLAN   171

MTU Considerations   172

Host Operation and Packet Flow in Cisco SD-Access   172

DHCP in Cisco SD-Access   172

Wired Host Onboarding and Registration   175

Wired Host Operation   176

Intra-Subnet Traffic in the Fabric   176

Inter-Subnet Traffic in the Fabric   179

Traffic to Destinations Outside of the Fabric   180

Wireless Host Operation   180

Initial Onboarding and Registration   180

Cisco SD-Access Troubleshooting   181

Fabric Edge   182

Fabric Control Plane   186

Authentication/Policy Troubleshooting   188

Authentication   188

Policy   190

Scalable Group Tags   191

Summary   193

References in This Chapter   193

Chapter 7   Advanced Cisco Software-Defined Access Topics   195

Cisco Software-Defined Access Extension to IoT   196

Types of Extended Nodes   198

Extended Nodes   198

Policy Extended Nodes   198

Configuration of Extended Nodes   200

Onboarding the Extended Node   203

Packet Walk of Extended Cisco SD-Access Use Cases   205

*Use Case: Hosts in Fabric Communicating with Hosts Connected
     Outside the Fabric   205*

*Use Case: Traffic from a Client Connected to a Policy Extended
     Node   206*

Use Case: Traffic to a Client Connected to a Policy Extended Node   207

Use Case: Traffic Flow Within a Policy Extended Node   207

Multicast in Cisco SD-Access   208

Multicast Overview   209

IP Multicast Delivery Modes   210

Multicast Flows in Cisco SD-Access   210

Scenario 1: Multicast in PIM ASM with Head-End Replication
     (Fabric RP)   211

Scenario 2: Multicast in PIM SSM with Head-End Replication   213

Scenario 3: Cisco SD-Access Fabric Native Multicast   214

Cisco SD-Access Multicast Configuration in Cisco DNA Center   216

Layer 2 Flooding in Cisco SD-Access   218

Layer 2 Flooding Operation   219

Layer 2 Border in Cisco SD-Access   221

Layer 2 Intersite   224

Layer 2 Intersite Design and Traffic Flow   224

Fabric in a Box in Cisco SD-Access   227

Cisco SD-Access for Distributed Campus Deployments   228

Types of Transit   229

IP Transit   229

Fabric Multisite or Multidomain with IP Transit   230

Cisco SD-Access Transit   232

Cisco SD-WAN Transit   237

Policy Deployment Models in Cisco SD-Access Distributed
     Deployment   238

Cisco SD-Access Design Considerations 240

Latency Considerations 240

Cisco SD-Access Design Approach 241

Very Small Site 241

Small Site 242

Medium Site 243

Large Site 243

Single-Site Design Versus Multisite Design 244

Cisco SD-Access Component Considerations 245

Underlay Network 246

Underlay Network Design Considerations 246

Overlay Network 247

Overlay Fabric Design Considerations 247

Fabric Control Plane Node Design Considerations 248

Fabric Border Node Design Considerations 248

Infrastructure Services Design Considerations 249

Fabric Wireless Integration Design Considerations 249

Wireless Over-the-Top Centralized Wireless Option Design Considerations 250

Mixed SD-Access Wireless and Centralized Wireless Option Design Considerations 250

Wireless Guest Deployment Considerations 250

Security Policy Design Considerations 251

Cisco SD-Access Policy Extension to Cisco ACI 252

Summary 254

References in This Chapter 254

Chapter 8 Advanced Cisco DNA Center 255

Cisco DNA Center Architecture and Connectivity 256

Hardware and Scale 256

Network Connectivity 256

High Availability and Clustering with Cisco DNA Center 258

Software Image Management 259

Image Repository 261

Golden Image 262

Upgrading Devices 263

Cisco DNA Center Templates 266

Template Creation 267

Template Assignment and Network Profiles   269

Deploying Templates   270

Plug and Play   272

Onboarding Templates   273

PnP Agent   275

Claiming a Device   276

Cisco DNA Center Tools   280

Topology   280

Command Runner   281

Security Advisories   283

Summary   284

References in This Chapter   284

Chapter 9   Cisco DNA Assurance   285

Assurance Benefits   285

Challenges of Traditional Implementations   285

Cisco DNA Analytics   286

Cisco DNA Assurance Architecture   287

Cisco DNA Assurance Data Collection Points   289

Streaming Telemetry   290

Network Time Travel   292

Health Dashboards   292

Overall Health Dashboard   293

Network Health Dashboard   294

Cisco SD-Access Fabric Network Health   296

Client Health Dashboard   297

Application Health Dashboard   299

Cisco DNA Assurance Tools   300

Intelligent Capture   300

Anomaly Capture   301

Path Trace   303

Sensor Tests   303

Cisco AI Network Analytics   304

Summary   306

References in This Chapter   306

Glossary   307

Index   313

Icons Used in This Book

Workgroup Switch   Multilayer Switch   Branch   Nodes

Wireless Access   Multilayer Switch   Cisco ISE   Fabric Wireless
Point   Controller

IoT Security   Rapid Threat   Security Service   Cisco WSA
                  Containment (RTC)

DDI   Cisco DNA Center   File Servers

Command Syntax Conventions

The conventions used to present command syntax in this book are the same conventions used in the IOS Command Reference. The Command Reference describes these conventions as follows:

- **Boldface** indicates commands and keywords that are entered literally as shown. In actual configuration examples and output (not general command syntax), boldface indicates commands that are manually input by the user (such as a **show** command).

- *Italic* indicates arguments for which you supply actual values.

- Vertical bars (|) separate alternative, mutually exclusive elements.

- Square brackets ([ ]) indicate an optional element.

- Braces ({ }) indicate a required choice.

- Braces within brackets ([{ }]) indicate a required choice within an optional element.

Introduction

This book was written to address the technical benefits and features of Cisco Software-Defined Access (Cisco SD-Access). This book is designed to deliver a use-case-based approach to implementing and adopting Cisco SD-Access in your organization. In addition, readers will learn when and where to leverage Cisco SD-Access instead of a typical three-tier campus network design. Readers will also learn the key functionality of a campus fabric architecture, such as Layer 3 routed access and the elimination of Spanning Tree Protocol.

Goals and Methods

The goal of this book is to illustrate how to implement Cisco SD-Access. Understanding the fundamental building blocks of a campus fabric architecture and how to design a software-defined campus will help readers determine the unique value that the Cisco SD-Access solution can bring to their organization.

This book can also help candidates prepare for the Cisco SD-Access portions of the Implementing Cisco Enterprise Network Core Technologies (ENCOR 350-401) certification exam, which is part of the CCNP Enterprise, CCIE Enterprise Infrastructure, CCIE Enterprise Wireless, and Cisco Certified Specialist – Enterprise Core certifications.

Who Should Read This Book?

The target audience for this book is network professionals who want to learn how to design, implement, and adopt Cisco SD-Access in their environment. This book also is designed to help readers learn how to manage and operate their campus network by leveraging Cisco DNA Center.

Candidates who are looking to learn about Cisco SD-Access as it relates to the ENCOR 350-401 exam will also find the necessary best practices and use case information valuable.

How This Book Is Organized

Although you could choose to read this book cover to cover, it is designed to be flexible and allow you to easily move between chapters and sections of chapters to cover just the material that you need more experience with. Chapter 1 provides an overview of network automation, which is at the pinnacle of most conversations these days. Chapter 1 also covers some of the most common benefits of using automation in the campus networking environment. The dichotomy of using network automation is continuing to maintain and operate the network in a manual fashion. Chapters 2 through 9 are the core chapters and can be read in any order. If you do intend to read them all, the order in the book is an excellent sequence to follow.

Book Structure

The book is organized into nine chapters:

- **Chapter 1, "Today's Networks and the Drivers for Change":** This chapter covers the most common trends and challenges seen in the campus area of the network. This chapter also describes some of the benefits and key capabilities of automation in general, as well as the associated return on investment in terms of time and risk.

- **Chapter 2, "Introduction to Cisco Software-Defined Access":** This chapter discusses the need for software-defined networking, emphasizes the importance of security in IT networks, introduces network access control, and describes the value of segmentation using Cisco TrustSec and Cisco Identity Services Engine.

- **Chapter 3, "Introduction to Cisco DNA Center":** This chapter covers network planning and deployment trends, past and present, provides a brief history of automation tools, and introduces Cisco DNA Center and its core concepts.

- **Chapter 4, "Cisco Software-Defined Access Fundamentals":** This chapter introduces the basics of Cisco Software-Defined Access design, components, and best practices, along with the typical workflow to build and deploy a Cisco SD-Access fabric.

- **Chapter 5, "Cisco Identity Services Engine with Cisco DNA Center":** This chapter describes the integration of Cisco DNA Center and Cisco ISE, explains onboarding different types of endpoints securely using a phased approach, and examines the value of macro-segmentation and micro-segmentation and their use cases in Cisco SD-Access.

- **Chapter 6, "Cisco Software-Defined Access Operation and Troubleshooting":** This chapter goes deeper under the covers of Cisco SD-Access to explain the underlying technologies in the solution along with common fabric troubleshooting steps and examples.

- **Chapter 7, "Advanced Cisco Software-Defined Access Topics":** This chapter discusses multicast flows, Layer 2 flooding, and the extension of the Internet of Things (IoT) into Cisco SD-Access networks. It also includes various design considerations for Cisco SD-Access deployments and extending the policy to WAN and data center networks.

- **Chapter 8, "Advanced Cisco DNA Center":** This chapter discusses the deployment options for Cisco DNA Center itself, along with the various tools and solutions that are available independent of Cisco SD-Access.

- **Chapter 9, "Cisco DNA Assurance":** This chapter introduces the analytics offered by Cisco DNA Assurance, which include analytics regarding the health of clients, network devices, and applications. Assurance goes into detail with operational workflows and leverges a proactive approach to troubleshooting. Sensor-driven tests, insights offered by artificial intelligence and machine learning (AI/ML), as well as integration with third-party services such as ServiceNow for event tracking are useful for the IT operations team.

Chapter 1

Today's Networks and the Drivers for Change

This chapter covers the following topics:

- **Networks of Today:** This section covers the technologies that are driving changes in the networks of today.

- **Common Business and IT Trends:** This section covers the most common trends that are having a considerable impact on the network.

- **Common Desired Benefits:** This section examines the benefits and desired outcomes that organizations are looking for from a solution.

- **High-Level Design Considerations:** This section covers various aspects of network design and things that affect the deployment and operations of networks today.

- **Cisco Digital Network Architecture:** This section examines from a high level the benefits and drivers of Cisco DNA.

- **Past Solutions to Today's Problems:** This section covers the technologies used in the past and the challenges associated with them.

- **Introduction to Multidomain:** This section covers the value and benefits of a multidomain environment.

- **Cloud Trends and Adoption:** This section covers the trends and challenges of cloud adoption.

Networks of Today

The IT industry is constantly changing and evolving. As time goes on, there is an ever-increasing number of technologies putting a strain on the network. New paradigms are formed as others are being shifted away from. New advances are being developed and adopted within the networking realm. These advances are being developed to provide faster innovation and the ability to adopt relevant technologies in a simplified way.

This requires the need for more intelligence and the capability to leverage the data from connected and distributed environments such as the campus, branch, data center, and WAN. Doing so allows for the use of data in interesting and more powerful ways than ever seen in the past. Some of the advances driving these outcomes are

- Artificial intelligence (AI)
- Machine learning (ML)
- Cloud services
- Virtualization
- Internet of Things (IoT)

The influx of these technologies is putting a strain on the IT operations staff. This strain comes in the form of requiring more robust planning, agreed-upon relevant use cases, and detailed adoption journey materials for easy consumption. All these requirements are becoming critical to success. Another area of importance is the deployment and day-to-day operations of these technologies as well as how they fit within the network environment. Disruption to typical operations is more immanent with regard to some of these technologies and how they will be consumed by the business. Other advances in technology are being adopted to reduce cost of operations and to reduce complexity. Every network, to some degree, has inherent complexity. Having tools that can help manage this complexity is becoming a necessity these days.

Automation is something that many in the IT industry are striving for, because the networks of today are becoming more and more complicated. Often organizations are operating with a lean IT staff and a flat or diminishing IT budget and are struggling to find ways to increase the output of what the network can do for the business. Another driver for the adoption of these technologies is to improve the overall user experience within the environment. This includes enabling users to have the flexibility and capability to access any business-critical application from anywhere in the network and ensuring that they have an exceptional experience when doing so. In addition to improving user experience, the IT operations staff is searching for ways to simplify the operations of the network.

There are many inherent risks associated with manually configuring networks. There is risk in the form of not being able to move fast enough when deploying new applications or services to the network. Risk could also be seen as misconfigurations that could cause an outage or suboptimal network performance, resulting in impacting business operations and potentially causing financial repercussions. Finally, there is the risk that the business itself is relying on the network for some business-critical services and that they might not be available due to the IT operations staff not being able to keep up with the demand of the business from a scale perspective. According to a Cisco Technical Assistance Center (TAC) survey taken in 2016, 95 percent of Cisco customers are performing configuration and deployment tasks manually in their networks. The survey also stated that 70 percent of TAC cases created are related to misconfigurations. This means that typos or incorrectly used commands are the culprit for a majority of issues seen in the network environment. This is where automation shines. Having the capability to signify the intent of the change that needs to be made, such as deploying quality of service (QoS) across the network, and then having the network automatically configure it properly, is an excellent example of automation. This accomplishes configuring services or features with great speed and is a tremendous value to the business. Simplifying operations and reducing human error ultimately reduces risk.

A simple analogy for network automation would be to think of an automobile. The reason most people use an automobile is to meet a specific desired outcome. In this case, it would be to get from point A to point B. An automobile is operated as a holistic system, not a collection of parts that make up that system, as depicted in Figure 1-1. For example, the dashboard provides the driver all the necessary information regarding how the vehicle is operating and the current state of the vehicle. When the driver wants to use the vehicle, certain operational steps are required to do so. The driver simply signifies the intent to drive the car by putting it in gear and using the system to get from point A to point B.

Figure 1-1   *Automobile as a System (Image Courtesy of Bubaone/Getty Images)*

Why can't networks be thought of in the same way? Thinking of a network as a collection of devices, such as routers, switches, and wireless components, is what the IT industry has been doing for over 30 years. The shift in mindset to look at the network as a holistic system is a more recent concept that stems from the advent of network controllers—the splitting of role and functionality from one another. The most common description of this is separating the control plane from the data plane. Having a controller that sits on top of the rest of the devices, so to speak, gives the advantage of taking a step back and operating the network as a whole from a centralized management point. This is analogous to operating an automobile from the driver's seat versus trying to manage the automobile from all the pieces and components that it is derived from. To put this in more familiar terms, think of the command-line interface (CLI). The CLI is not designed to make massive-scale configuration changes to multiple devices at the same time. Traditional methods of managing and maintaining the network aren't sufficient to keep up with the pace and demands of the networks of today. The operations staff needs to be able to move faster and simplify all the operations and configurations that have traditionally gone into networking. Software-defined networking (SDN) and controller capabilities are becoming areas of focus in the industry and are evolving to a point where they can address the challenges faced by IT operations teams. Controllers offer the ability to manage the network as a system, which means policy management can be automated and abstracted. This provides the capability of supporting dynamic policy changes versus its predecessor of manual changes of policy and configurations on a device-by-device basis when something requires a change within the environment.

Common Business and IT Trends

Traditional networking infrastructure was deployed when the security perimeter was well defined. Most applications were low bandwidth, and most content and applications resided in centralized corporate data centers. Today, enterprises have very different requirements. High-bandwidth, real-time, and big-data applications are pushing capacity limits of the network. In some cases, the majority of traffic is destined for the Internet or public cloud, and the security perimeter as it existed in the past is quickly disappearing. This is due to surge in bring your own devices (BYOD), cloud computing, and IoT. The downside and risks of staying status quo are significant, and technological innovation has failed to comprehensively address the problem. There has been a huge increase in the use of Software as a Service (SaaS) and Infrastructure as a Service (IaaS) offerings. It seems as if more applications are moving to the cloud each day. The adoption of solutions like Microsoft Office 365, Google Apps, Salesforce.com (SFDC), and other SaaS-based productivity and business applications is putting a strain on the network. This includes keeping the applications performing to the best of their ability in order to ensure that users have the best possible experience. The following list contains some of the most common trends occurring in the IT industry:

- Applications are moving to the cloud (private and public).
- Mobile devices, BYOD, and guest access are straining the IT staff.
- High-bandwidth applications are putting pressure on the network.
- Wireless-first connectivity is becoming the new normal.
- Demand for security and segmentation everywhere makes manual operations difficult.
- IoT devices often require access to the IT network.

The number of mobile devices in the campus and remote environments that are accessing these applications and the Internet as a result of BYOD and guest services is rapidly increasing. The additional load of traffic resulting from all of these devices, as well as trends such as IoT, is putting an additional strain on the network—especially in the wireless LAN. In addition to everything mentioned, interactive video has finally become the new voice from a popularity perspective. Converging voice and data services was an important transition. However, when it comes to video, today's networks not only have to account for optimized QoS handling for video applications, but also need to address the high-bandwidth, latency-sensitive applications that users are demanding. Traditionally, supporting these technologies was not easy, and implementing them required many manual configurations prior to deployment. This also led to additional complexity in the network environment.

With the business and IT trends covered thus far still in mind, it is important to translate these trends into real challenges that organizations are facing and put them into IT vernacular. As mentioned previously, the network is encountering pressure like never before. This is forcing IT teams to look for ways to alleviate that pressure. Organizations are also looking for ways to improve the overall user and application experience with what they currently own while also driving cost down. Lack of control over visibility and application performance, and keeping up with the ever-growing security attack surface are also contributing to organizations looking for a better way forward. In addition, organizational silos have caused many organizations to not be able to achieve the benefits from some of these newer technologies. Breaking down silos to work toward a common goal for the business as a whole is required for the business to take full advantage of what some of these software-defined advancements have to offer.

Common Desired Benefits

This section covers some of the most common benefits that organizations are looking for from their campus network. Designing and deploying the next-generation campus network is about taking advantage of some very useful benefits and the impact that they have on the network environment and overall user experience. Each of the benefits discussed is listed here:

- Prioritize and secure traffic with granular control
- Reduce costs and lower operational complexity
- Simplify troubleshooting with root cause analysis
- Provide a consistent high-quality user experience
- Implement end-to-end security and segmentation
- Deploy devices faster

Networks of today cannot scale at the speed necessary to address the changing needs that organizations require. Hardware-centric networks are traditionally more expensive and have fixed capacity. They are also more difficult to support due to the box-by-box configuration approach, siloed management tools, and lack of automated provisioning. Conflicting policies between domains and different configurations between services make today's networks inflexible, static, expensive, and cumbersome to maintain. This leads to the network being more prone to misconfigurations and security vulnerabilities. It is important to shift from connectivity-centric architecture to application- or service-centric infrastructure that focuses on user experience and simplicity.

The solution required to support today's cloud-enabled enterprise needs to be complete and comprehensive. It should be based on the software-defined approach mentioned earlier by leveraging the controller concept. The solution must also include a robust set of capabilities that reduces cost and complexity and promotes business continuity and rapid innovation. These capabilities should include the separation of the management plane, control plane, and data plane, which provides more horizontal scaling capabilities and the security of knowing where the data is at all times.

The solution should provide various consumption models, such as some components being hosted in the cloud and some components being managed on premises, with complete redundancy between the two. The solution must also provide a complete set of network visibility and troubleshooting tools that are accessible from a single place. Having this type of solution would assist in providing the following business outcomes and use cases:

- Faster device deployment with no operational interaction

- Complete end-to-end network segmentation for enhanced security and privacy

- Increased LAN performance

- Seamless host mobility

- Better user experience

All of the things mentioned thus far are critical in terms of what organizations are demanding to drive their network to becoming an asset that truly sets the organizations apart from their industry peers. Many organizations rely on the network to function at its best to provide value and competitive differentiation so their organizations can excel. This is what is driving this industry to these types of technologies. This reliance is also why the industry has increased the speed of adoption and deployment of these solutions.

High-Level Design Considerations

Considering the complexity of a majority of the networks out there today, they can be classified in a couple categories such as redundant and nonredundant. Typically, redundancy leads to increased complexity. Often, the simplest of networks do not plan for failures or outages and are commonly single-homed designs with multiple single points of failure. Networks can contain different aspects of redundancy. When speaking strictly of the campus LAN portion of the environment, it may include redundant links, controllers, switches, and access points. Table 1-1 lists some of the common techniques that are introduced when dealing with redundancy.

Table 1-1 *Common Redundancy Techniques*

Redundant Links	Redundant Devices
Administrative distance	Redistribution
Traffic engineering	Loop prevention
Preferred path selection	Preferred path selection
Prefix summarization	Advanced filtering
Filtering	

Many redundancy options are available, such as redundant links, redundant devices, EtherChannel, and so on. Having a visual of what some of these redundancy technologies look like is often helpful. One of these technologies is Cisco Virtual Switching System (VSS), which bonds switches together to look and act like a single switch. This helps put into context how the network will need to be configured and managed to support these types of redundancy options. The following are some of the benefits of VSS technology:

- Simplifies operations

- Boosts nonstop communication

- Maximizes bandwidth utilization

- Lowers latency

Redundancy can take many different forms. VSS is used for much more than just redundancy. It helps with certain scenarios in a campus design, such as removing the need for stretched VLANs and loops in the network. Figure 1-2 showcases an example of a campus environment before and after VSS and depicts the simplification of the topology.

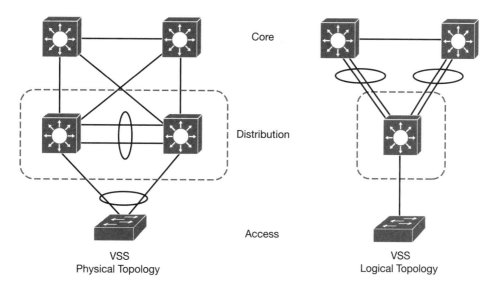

Figure 1-2 *VSS Device- and Link-Based Redundancy Options*

Outside of the complexity associated with redundancy, there are many other aspects of the network that cause complexity within a network environment. Some of these aspects can include things such as securing the network to shield it from malicious behavior, leveraging network segmentation to keep traffic types separate for compliance or governance reasons, and even implementing QoS to ensure optimal application performance and increase users' quality of experience. What further complicates the network is having to manually configure these options. The networks of today are too rigid and need to evolve. The industry is moving from the era of connectivity-centric network delivery models to an era of digital transformation. There is a shift required to transition to a digital transformation model. The shift is from hardware- and device-centric options to open, extensible, software-driven, programmable, and cloud-enabled solutions. Figure 1-3 depicts the transition in a simple summary. Relying more on automation to handle the day-to-day operational tasks and getting back time to focus on how to make the network provide value to the business is crucial to many organizations. This is delivered through policy-driven, automated, and self-optimizing capabilities. This provides closed-loop, automated service assurance that empowers network operations staff to transition from a reactive nature to a more proactive and predictive approach. Freeing up more of the operations staff's time should enable them to focus on more strategic initiatives within the business.

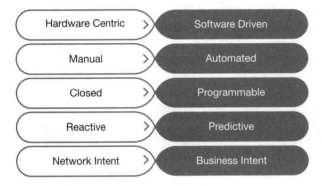

Figure 1-3   *Digital Transformation Transition*

Intent-based networking (IBN) is taking the IT industry by storm. The concept revolves around signifying the intent of the business and automatically translating that intent into the appropriate corresponding networking tasks. This is a circular logic in that it captures the intent of the business and IT staff and then translates that intent into the appropriate policies that are required to support the business. Once the policies are created, the next step is to orchestrate the configuration of the infrastructure. This includes both physical and virtual components. This then kicks off the final step, which is providing assurance, insights, and visibility to ensure the network is functioning properly. Because this is a loop in a sense, the logic uses continuous verification and supplies any corrective actions that are necessary to fix or enhance the network's performance. Figure 1-4 illustrates the intent-based networking model.

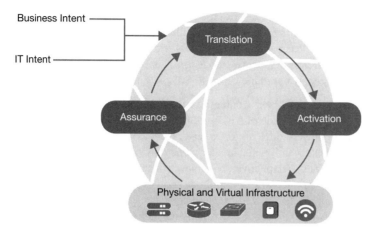

Figure 1-4 *Intent-Based Networking*

Analytics and insights are absolutely critical to networks of today. Typical network management systems (NMSs) do not provide the necessary information to resolve issues in a quick and efficient manner. They are reactive in nature and don't supply the predictive monitoring and alerting that organizations require. Simple Network Management Protocol (SNMP) Traps and SYSLOG messages are valuable but haven't been used as well as they could be. Reactive notifications mean that the issue or fault has already happened and don't prevent any impact to the business. Often, there are false positives or so many alerts that it is difficult to determine what information should be acted upon or ignored completely. Traditionally, the network operations workflow has been similar to the following:

1. Receive an alert or helpdesk ticket.

2. Log in to the device(s) to determine what happened.

3. Spend time troubleshooting.

4. Resolve the issue.

The days are over of hunting around and searching through log files and debugging traffic to determine what the issue is that has caused an outage to the network. The amount of data that runs through these networks and has to be sorted through to chase down an issue is exponentially increasing. This is leading to the manual sifting through information to get to the root cause of an issue being extremely more difficult than ever before. Organizations rely on information relevant to what they are looking for; otherwise, the data is useless. For example, if a user couldn't get on the wireless network last Tuesday at 3 p.m., and the logs are overwritten or filled with non-useful information, how does this help the network operations staff troubleshoot the issue at hand? It doesn't. This wastes time, which is one of the most precious resources for network operations staff. The dichotomy of this is using analytics and insights to help direct network operators to the right place at the right time to take the right action. This is part of what Cisco DNA Assurance does as part of intent-based networking.

Problem isolation is much easier within an intent-based network because the entire network acts as a sensor that provides insights into the failures that are happening in the network. The network also has the capability to have a holistic view of the network from a client perspective. From a wireless perspective alone, this can provide information such as failure reasons, received signal strength indicator (RSSI), and onboarding information.

One of the most time-draining parts of the troubleshooting process is trying to replicate the issue. The previously mentioned issue of a user not being able to get on the network last Tuesday at 3 p.m. would be very difficult to replicate. How would anyone know what possibly was going on last Tuesday at 3 p.m.? In reality, the only traditional way to know what was going on from a wireless perspective was to have constant packet captures and spectrum analyzers running. Due to cost, space, and not knowing where the issue may arise, this is not a practical approach. What if instead there was a solution that could not only act as a DVR for the network but also use streaming telemetry information such as NetFlow, SNMP, and syslog and correlate the issues to notify the network operations staff of what the issue was, when it happened—Even if it happened in the past? Imagine the network providing all this information automatically. Additionally, instead of having Switched Port Analyzer (SPAN) ports configured across the campus with network sniffers plugged in everywhere in hopes of capturing the wireless traffic when there is an issue, imagine the wireless access points could detect the anomaly and automatically run a packet capture locally on the AP that would capture the issue. All these analytics could provide guided remediation steps on how to fix the issue without requiring anyone to chase down all the clues to solve the mystery. Fortunately, that solutions exists: Cisco DNA Assurance can integrate using open APIs to many helpdesk ticketing platforms such as ServiceNOW. The advantage of this is that when an issue happens in the network, Cisco DNA Assurance can automatically detect it and create a helpdesk ticket, add the details of the issue to the ticket as well as a link to the issue in Assurance, along with the guided remediation steps. That means when the on-call support engineer gets the call at 2 a.m., she already has the information on how to fix the issue. Soon, automatic remediation will be available, so the on-call person won't have to wake up at 2 a.m. when the ticket comes in. This is the power of Assurance and intent-based networks.

Cisco Digital Network Architecture

Cisco Digital Network Architecture (DNA) is a collection of different solutions that make up an architecture. It is the Cisco intent-based network. Cisco DNA is composed of four key areas: WAN, campus, data center, and cloud edge. Each area has its own Cisco solutions that integrate with each other: Cisco Software-Defined WAN (Cisco SD-WAN), Cisco Software-Defined Access (Cisco SD-Access), Cisco Application Centric Infrastructure (Cisco ACI), and Cisco Secure Agile Exchange (SAE). Each area is built with security ingrained in each solution. Figure 1-5 illustrates the pillars of Cisco DNA. At the center, Cisco DNA is powered by intent, informed by context, constantly learning, and constantly protecting. This is what translates the business intent into network policy, provides constant visibility into all traffic patterns, leverages machine learning at scale to provide increasing intelligence, and enables the network to see and predict issues and threats so the business can respond faster.

The increased use of cloud services and mobile devices is creating IT blind spots. This industry demands a new holistic approach to security. Security is at the core of Cisco DNA. Cisco offers a full life cycle of on-premises and cloud-hosted solutions to maximize protection for organizations. Because Cisco can focus on all aspects of security, this lowers complexity by reducing to one the number of security vendors required to protect the business. Cisco DNA can turn the entire network into a sensor to detect malicious traffic and anomalies in behavior. Figure 1-6 shows the different areas of security that Cisco provides solutions for.

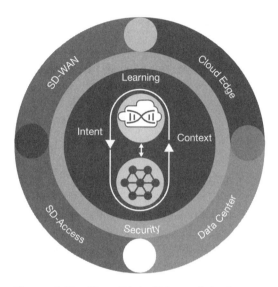

Figure 1-5 *Cisco Digital Network Architecture (DNA)*

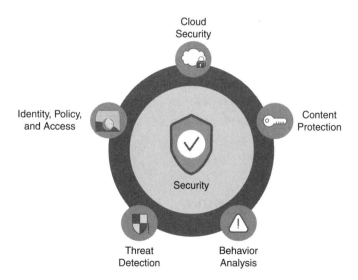

Figure 1-6 *Cisco Security Overview*

Cisco Stealthwatch can baseline the network and provide anomaly detection when something changes. This even includes detecting changes in traffic or user behavior. A great example of this is when a user typically uses an average amount of bandwidth within the network to do her daily job tasks. If all of a sudden the user starts downloading gigabytes' worth of data and sending it to another machine in another country, Stealthwatch considers this an anomaly. This doesn't necessarily mean the user is being malicious or stealing company data; it could be that the user's machine has been compromised and malware is attacking the network. In either case, Stealthwatch would be able to detect this and inform the IT operations staff to take action. Automated network segmentation can address this type of challenge to ensure that the users and networks are in compliance. Taking this innovation a step further, the Cisco Catalyst 9000 Series switches have the capability to detect malware and other malicious threats within encrypted traffic. This is called Cisco Encrypted Traffic Analytics (ETA). This is unique to Cisco and is one of the most advanced forms of security protection available today. Combining this with all the telemetry and visibility that the network can provide, it greatly reduces the risk and potential impact of threats to the network. It is important to note that the power of Cisco DNA is that all of these technologies across all of these pillars work in concert. Security is ingrained in everything Cisco offers; it is not an afterthought or something that rides on top of the network—security *is* the network. Figure 1-7 depicts the Cisco stance on security and how it fits within the network environment. It illustrates that security is just as critical as the network itself. Providing the most robust network that can provide value to the business and enhance users' application experience in a secure and agile fashion is essential to many organizations.

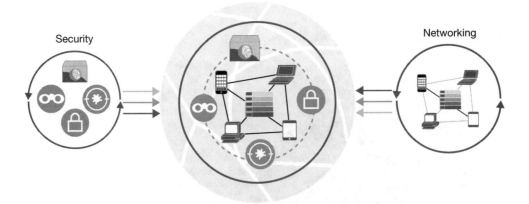

Figure 1-7   *Security in Everything*

Past Solutions to Today's Problems

Over the years, demands on the network have steadily increased, and the IT industry has adapted to these demands. However, this doesn't mean that the industry has adapted quickly or properly. Networks only exist to carry applications and data. The methods of how these applications and data have been handled have also been in constant flux. From a design perspective, the mechanisms implemented in the network ultimately depend on the outcome the business is trying to achieve. This means that the mechanisms aren't always best practice or validated designs. The configurations of these devices are often ad hoc in nature and usually include point-in-time fixes for issues that arise in the network that need to be addressed.

Spanning-Tree and Layer 2–Based Networks

One of the most common technologies that gets a lot of notoriety is Spanning Tree. Spanning Tree was designed to prevent loops in the Layer 2 network. However, it can cause a tremendous amount of problems in the network if not tuned and managed properly. There are many settings and configuration techniques for Spanning Tree as well as multiple versions that provide some variation of what the protocol was designed to do. Table 1-2 lists the many versions or flavors of Spanning Tree and their associated abbreviations.

Table 1-2 *Spanning Tree Versions*

Type of Spanning Tree	Abbreviation
Legacy Spanning Tree Protocol	STP
Per-VLAN Spanning Tree	PVST
Per-VLAN Spanning Tree Plus	PVST+
Rapid Spanning Tree Protocol	RSTP
Rapid Per-VLAN Spanning Tree Plus	RPVST+
Multiple Spanning Tree	MST

Spanning Tree is often used in three-tier campus architectures that rely on Layer 2 distribution and access layers, with routing typically done at the distribution block. This entirely depends on design, of course, but this is the usual place for Spanning Tree. First hop redundancy protocols (FHRPs) are used for each subnet and are configured to provide gateway information for the local subnets and aid in routing the traffic to its destination. The following are examples of first hop redundancy protocols:

- Hot Standby Routing Protocol (HSRP)

- Virtual Router Redundancy Protocol (VRRP)

- Gateway Load Balancing Protocol (GLBP)

Prior to the advent of Layer 3 routed access, Spanning Tree was also primarily used in Layer 2 networks that had stretched VLANs to support mobile wireless users. This was because wireless users required the capability to roam anywhere in the campus and maintain the same Service Set Identifier (SSID), IP address, and security policy. This was necessary due to the reliance on IP addresses and VLANs to dictate which policy or access list was associated to which wired or wireless user. However, there were inherent limitations of Spanning Tree, such as only being able to use half the bandwidth of a pair of redundant links. This is because the other path is in a blocked state. There are, however, many different ways to manipulate this per VLAN or per instance, but this is still the case for Spanning Tree. Other drawbacks are the potential for flooding issues or blocked links causing an outage in the network. This impacts business continuity and disrupts users, making it difficult to get the network back online in a quick fashion. Some Spanning Tree outages can last for hours or days if the issue is not found and remedied.

Figure 1-8 illustrates a typical three-tier campus network architecture design that leverages Spanning Tree and HSRP, showing that there are certain links that are unusable because Spanning Tree blocks links to avoid a looped path within the network.

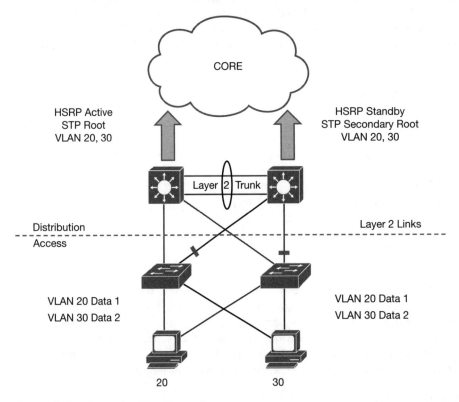

Figure 1-8 *Spanning Tree Example*

With the advent of Layer 3 routed access, Spanning Tree is no longer necessary to prevent loops because there is no longer a Layer 2 network. However, Layer 3 routed access introduced another set of issues that needed to be addressed. There is still the issue of security policy relying on IP addressing. In addition, now that VLANs are not being stretched across the network using trunking, wireless networks have to change how they operate. This means that wireless SSIDs have to map to subnets, and if a user moves from one access point on an SSID and goes to the same SSID in another area of the network on a different access point, it is likely that their IP address would change. This means there has to be another access list on the new subnet with the same settings as the access list on the previous subnet; otherwise, the user's security policy would change. Imagine the overhead of having to configure multiple access lists on multiple subnets. This is how networks were traditionally configured. The amount of manual configuration, potential for misconfiguration, and time wasted are just some of the caveats of this type of network design. Figure 1-9 depicts a Layer 3 routed access network.

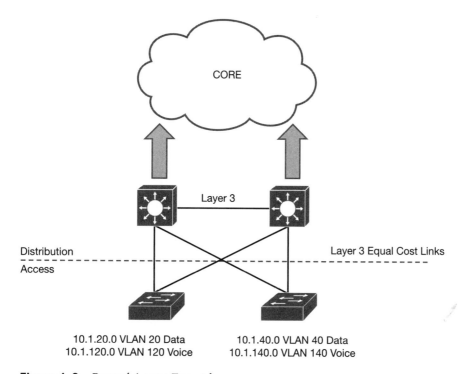

Figure 1-9   *Routed Access Example*

Layer 3 routed access is also very prominent in the data center environment. This is due to all the benefits of moving to a Layer 3 routed access model versus a Layer 2 network. The following is a list of benefits to using a routed access network:

- Increased availability
- Reduced complexity
- Simplified design
- Removal of Spanning Tree

As mentioned earlier in this chapter, real-time and interactive video applications are becoming more mainstream, and organizations expect their users to have the capability to connect from anywhere at any time. The campus network must be available at all times to support this type of business case. Routed access leverages point-to-point links, which not only reduces the amount of time it takes to recover from a direct link failure, but simplifies the design by relying only on a dynamic routing protocol (versus Layer 2 complexities, Spanning Tree, and Layer 3 routing protocols). Coupled with all links in the environment now being active and forwarding traffic, there is a large gain in bandwidth and faster failure detection with point-to-point links versus Layer 2. The industry is demanding networks that include ultra-fast, low-latency, high-bandwidth links that are always available and that are able to scale to meet the demands of the organizations that are using them. Figure 1-10 illustrates the difference between Layer 2– and Layer 3–based campus designs.

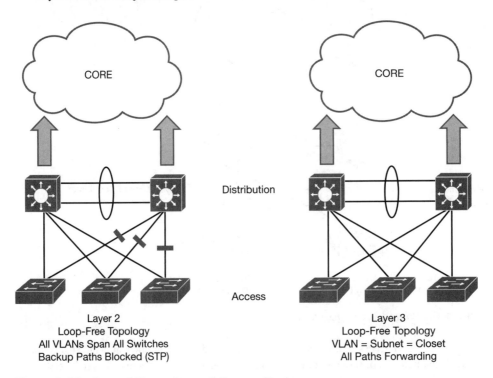

Figure 1-10   *Layer 2 Versus Layer 3 Campus Design*

Introduction to Multidomain

A common trend that is arising in the IT industry is to generate and store data in many areas of the network. Traditionally, a majority of the data for a business was stored in a centralized data center. With the influx of guest access, mobile devices, BYOD, and IoT, data is now being generated remotely in a distributed manner. In response, the industry is shifting from data centers to multiple centers of data. That being said, simple, secure, and highly available connectivity is a must to allow for enhanced user and application experience. The other big piece to multidomain is having a seamless policy that can go across these multiple centers of data. An example of this is policy that extends from the campus environment across the WAN and into the data center and back down to the campus. This provides consistency and deterministic behavior across the multiple domains. Figure 1-11 illustrates a high-level example of sharing policy between a campus branch location and a data center running Cisco Application Centric Infrastructure (ACI).

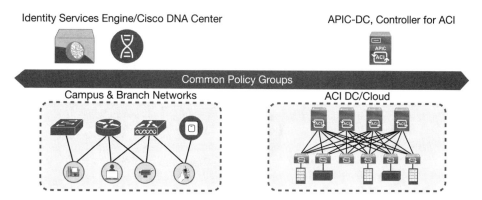

Figure 1-11   *High-level Multidomain Example*

In future evolutions of multidomain, the common policy will extend from the campus across the Cisco Software-Defined WAN (SD-WAN) environment to Cisco ACI running in the data center and back down to the campus, providing end-to-end policy and management across all three domains. This will provide the capability to leverage things like application service-level agreements (SLAs) from the data center to the WAN and back, ensuring that the applications are performing to the best of their ability across the entire network. It will also relieve strain on the WAN and provide a better user experience when using the applications. Figure 1-12 shows a high-level example of what this could look like from an overall topology perspective.

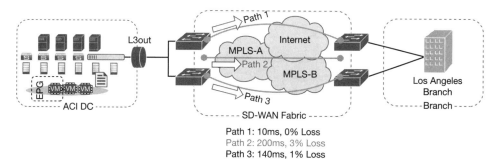

Figure 1-12   *High-level Multidomain with ACI and SD-WAN Example*

Multidomain offers the capability to have the network operate as a holistic system, as mentioned previously in this chapter. This takes intent-based networks to the next level by taking policy across all domains for a seamless application experience. This also implements security everywhere and provides complete granularity in terms of control and operations. Looking at multidomain from another aspect, the Cisco Software-Defined Access solution can share policy with the Cisco SD-WAN solution as well. This is powerful because the policies that control security, segmentation, and application performance can be enforced across the entire network environment. This means that the user and application experience is congruent across the campus LAN and WAN. Tying both domains together is what delivers the capabilities to protect the applications and ensure that the business outcomes organizations are striving for are being met. Figure 1-13 illustrates a high-level multidomain design with Cisco DNA Center, Cisco vManage, Cisco SD-Access, and Cisco SD-WAN.

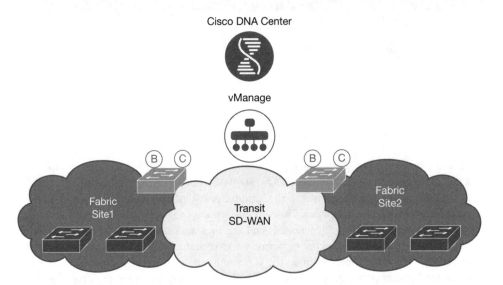

Figure 1-13 *High-level Multidomain with Cisco SD-Access and SD-WAN Example*

Cloud Trends and Adoption

Cloud adoption has been taking the industry by storm. Over the years, the reliance on cloud computing has grown significantly, starting with music, movies, and storage and moving into SaaS and IaaS. Today, there are many aspects of organizations that run in the cloud, such as application development, quality assurance, and production. To make things even more complicated, companies are relying on multiple cloud vendors to operate their business, resulting in unique sets of polices, storage capacity requirements, and overall operations skills on a per-vendor basis. Companies are struggling with things such as shadow IT and backdoor applications in their environment. Shadow IT is when lines of business (LoB) are going to cloud providers on their own, without any knowledge or guidance from the IT departments, and spinning up applications on demand in the cloud. This causes major concerns from a security and privacy perspective. In addition, the potential loss of confidential information or intellectual property could damage the brand and reputation of the business. The risks are significant.

Furthermore, the applications in the cloud, whether legitimate production applications or applications that are currently in development, still require certain levels of priority and treatment to ensure the applications are being delivered properly to the users who consume them. This is where some of the capabilities of the next-generation campus network can help to ensure that the applications are being treated appropriately and the experience for the users is adequate. Figure 1-14 illustrates the demand on the campus LAN and WAN and how cloud applications are becoming critical to the operations of the business. The campus network has the shared responsibility of ensuring that the applications perform to the best of their ability and provide an exceptional user experience. The campus network also has to share the security burden to make sure that the appropriate users are accessing the applications and sharing information in the first place. This is where having a good segmentation and security policy is paramount.

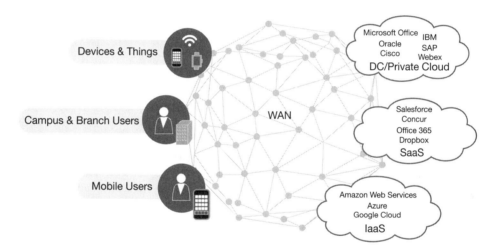

Figure 1-14   *Demand on LAN and WAN for Internet-based Applications*

The majority of the bandwidth that applications consume affects the WAN environment more than the campus LAN. This is due to the WAN links having a more finite amount of bandwidth versus the high-speed bandwidth links seen within a campus environment. Having direct Internet access in a branch can assist with alleviating some of this pressure. By being able to detect application performance through one or more direct Internet access circuits, the branch routers are able to choose the best-performing path based on the application-specific parameters. This helps offset the low-bandwidth WAN transport. If one of the links to the cloud application fails or has degradation in performance, the application can automatically fail over to another direct Internet link. This process is fully automated and requires no interaction from the network operations staff. Figure 1-15 shows this scenario with multiple direct Internet access links.

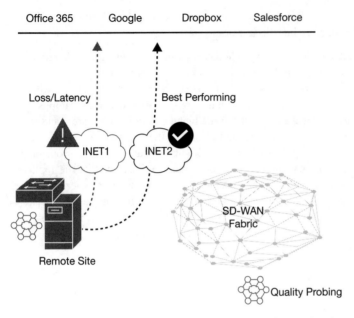

Figure 1-15 *Multiple Direct Internet Access Links to Cloud Applications*

Summary

This chapter provided a high-level overview of how the networks of today are causing challenges for organizations and their operations staff. It also covered the common business and IT trends that the industry is seeing and how they affects the networks of today. The overall benefits desired by organizations and their IT staff lead to the need to rethink the campus environment. Cloud applications and the influx of the amount of data within the network is causing strain on the network. This is causing organizations to look at ways to alleviate the pressure that is being put on the network and the organization as a whole. Security is no longer an afterthought; it is crucial to incorporate security into everything in the environment. This means that from concept to design to implementation, security must be thought of the entire way. The use cases introduced in this chapter will each be covered in depth in the upcoming chapters. Application performance, security, segmentation, improved user experience, redundancy, and resiliency are key drivers that point to an intent-based network infrastructure.

Chapter 2

Introduction to Cisco Software-Defined Access

This chapter covers the following topics:

- **Challenges with Today's Networks:** This section covers the trends and challenges of today's campus networks and how to alleviate them using a fabric architecture.

- **Software-Defined Networking:** This section covers the industry trends that are moving toward a software-defined networking approach to meet the businesses demands.

- **Cisco Software-Defined Access:** This section outlines the components of Cisco SD-Access for campus networks and how using Cisco DNA Center incorporates automation, analytics, networking, and security.

- **Network Access Control:** This section goes into detail of network access control (NAC) and its role in security-driven infrastructure.

- **Introduction to Cisco Identity Services Engine:** This section focuses on Cisco Identity Services Engine (ISE), which is one of the building blocks of Cisco SD-Access. This section also includes a walk-through of all the relevant features of ISE.

- **Cisco ISE Design Considerations:** This section examines design and best practices for deploying a network access control architecture.

- **Segmentation with Cisco TrustSec:** This section provides an overview of Cisco TrustSec (CTS), the components involved, and its significance in modern networks. Cisco TrustSec is an integral piece for Cisco SD-Access to drive toward a business intent–driven network.

Challenges with Today's Networks

Chapter 1, "Today's Networks and the Drivers for Change," provided some of the enterprise trends leading to network transformation through digitization. Major changes have been occurring within the enterprise networking environment, such as the explosion of Internet of Things (IoT) devices, cloud-based applications, bring your own device (BYOD) devices, and cyber security tools. These changes add to the complexity of the network and increase operational expenses for IT. Rapid growth of endpoints has led to more data in the network and an increase in the attack surface, which in turn has increased the average time to detect a security breach to approximately three months. Network security demands have changed; the network needs to adapt to the new business dynamics with constrained IT budgets. Static network designs also make the adoption to the network dynamics challenging. More users and endpoints translates into more VLANs and access control lists (ACLs) and results in more IT hours to implement the changes. With different types of users and endpoints connecting in, segmentation becomes complicated and multiple points in the infrastructure need to be touched for configuration changes. This could lead to manual errors and troubleshooting becoming more difficult as the users roam around the network. As users and devices move around the network, policies may not be consistent, which not only makes finding users when they move around more difficult, but also makes identifying and troubleshooting issues harder. In summary, legacy networks cannot keep up with today's needs. Businesses demand a network that is scalable, secure, programmable, and driven by business requirements. Network digitization can reduce the amount of time spent on manual configurations and reduce the IT overhead of maintaining and operating the network.

Software-Defined Networking

Cisco started the journey toward digitizing networks in 2015 with the vision of creating a network that is flexible and agile. Cisco Digital Network Architecture (Cisco DNA) provides a roadmap to digitization and a path to realize the immediate benefits of network automation, assurance, and security. The ultimate goal is to have an IT network that addresses the challenges of modern networks discussed previously. Security should be embedded into the network with new innovations that leverage simplified and consistent policies. These policies are then mapped into business intent, providing a faster way of implementing changes through a centralized approach. Most importantly, the network should be constantly learning by using analytics, providing visibility and proactively monitoring and reporting issues for the IT operations staff from a centralized management pane.

Software-defined networking makes it possible to design and build networks by decoupling the control and forwarding planes. A separate control plane creates a programmable network environment to abstract the underlaying infrastructure for applications and services. Through abstraction, one can achieve a common network policy, quick implementation of network services, and reduced complexity with a centralized controller. Cisco DNA is an intent-based network binding business context to policy managed by a controller that has a central view of the network domain. Cisco DNA creates a network focused on intent and security that looks like a logical switch for the applications and services. This logical switch can be programmed to meet the demands of business changes with respect to network changes, security policy changes based on mobility, and continuous security threats. Cisco DNA is scalable for future growth, thereby reducing overall IT costs and providing a faster time to market.

Cisco offers multiple controllers to help on the journey toward software-defined networks, including controllers for the campus network, WAN, data center, and cloud:

- **Cisco DNA Center:** The controller used for creating Cisco Software-Defined Access for campus networks.

- **Cisco Software-Defined WAN (SD-WAN):** Powered by Viptela, the controller for WAN networks.

- **Cisco Application Policy Infrastructure Controller (APIC):** The controller for SD-Access for Data Center, which uses Application Centric Infrastructure (ACI).

Figure 2-1 shows an end-to-end software-defined network for the campus, WAN, and data center using the controllers just mentioned.

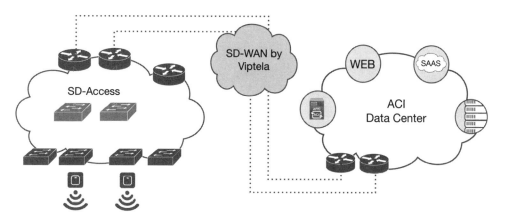

Figure 2-1   *End-to-End Software-Defined Network*

The focus of this book is designing Cisco Software-Defined Access for campus networks using Cisco DNA Center. The following sections go into greater detail about the components, benefits, and features of Cisco SD-Access.

Cisco Software-Defined Access

This section unveils the building blocks of Cisco SD-Access and covers its associated benefits in the campus environment. This section also introduces how Cisco DNA Center makes Cisco SD-Access a reality. Cisco SD-Access is the Cisco digital network evolution transforming traditional campus LAN designs to intent-driven, programmable networks. The two main components of Cisco SD-Access are Cisco Campus Fabric and Cisco DNA

Center. Cisco DNA Center offers automation and assurance to create and monitor the Cisco Campus Fabric. Figure 2-2 shows Cisco SD-Access at a high level. Each component will be discussed as part of the "Cisco SD-Access Roles" section.

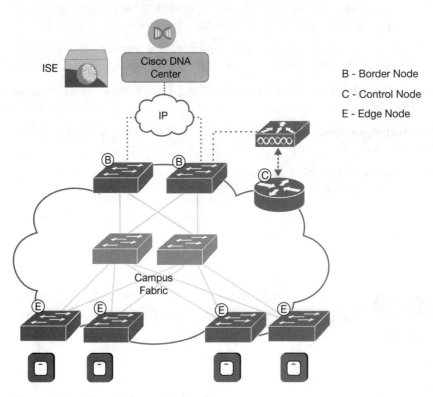

Figure 2-2   *Cisco Software-Defined Access*

Cisco Campus Fabric Architecture

Fabric roles and terminology in Cisco SD-Access are different from the traditional roles in three-tier hierarchical networks. Cisco SD-Access is built on fabric technology implemented for campus networks using overlay networks running on a physical network (underlay network) to create a logical topology. An underlay network is the traditional physical network connecting LAN devices such as routers and switches in the network. An underlay network's main purpose is to provide IP connectivity to enable traffic to traverse from a source to a destination. Because underlay is an IP-based transport mechanism for the traffic, any interior gateway protocol (IGP) can be leveraged.

A fabric is an overlay network. Overlay networks are commonly used in the IT world to virtually connect devices such as Internet Protocol Security (IPsec), Generic Routing Encapsulation (GRE), Dynamic Multipoint Virtual Private Network (DMVPN), Multiprotocol Label Switching (MPLS), Location Identifier Separation Protocol (LISP), and so on. An *overlay network* is a logical topology used to virtually connect devices, built over a topology-independent physical underlay network. Overlay networks separate the forwarding plane from the control plane, providing a network that is flexible, programmable, and easy to scale. The separation of the control plane and data plane helps to simplify the underlay. This allows for faster forwarding while also optimizing packet and network reliability, as the control plane becomes the brain of the network. Cisco SD-Access supports building a fabric using an existing network as the underlay for the centralized controller. Cisco DNA Center has the capability to automate the underlay network. This alleviates the hassle of dealing with bringing up the underlay, making it useful for new implementations or infrastructure growth. An overlay network often uses alternate forwarding attributes in an additional header to provide differentiated services, segmentation, and mobility. These are usually not provided by the underlay. Figure 2-3 illustrates the concept of an overlay and underlay network.

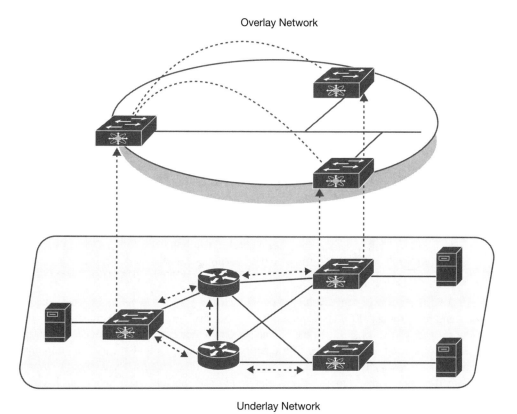

Figure 2-3 *Underlay and Overlay Networks Overview*

Campus Fabric Fundamentals

A Cisco Campus Fabric is composed of a control plane, a data plane, and a policy plane that are required to operate the network infrastructure. The policy plane is provided by

Cisco TrustSec using Cisco Identity Services Engine (ISE), discussed in detail in the later "Network Access Control" section. Cisco SD-Access is the GUI-based approach to create the Cisco Campus Fabric using Cisco DNA Center as the controller for orchestration. Cisco DNA Center integrates multiple systems to orchestrate the Campus LAN, wireless LAN, WAN, and security products such as Cisco ISE. Automation provided by Cisco DNA Center uses the command-line interface (CLI), Network Configuration Protocol (NETCONF)/Yet Another Next Generation (YANG) models, and the RESTful application programming interface (API) to orchestrate the devices in the fabric. To simplify, Cisco SD-Access is a Cisco Campus Fabric (overlay network) managed by Cisco DNA Center.

Cisco Campus Fabric uses the following features and protocols:

■ Control plane based on LISP

■ Data plane based on Virtual Extensible LAN (VXLAN)

■ Policy plane based on Cisco TrustSec

LISP is a routing and addressing architecture developed by Cisco Systems. Cisco Campus Fabric uses LISP as the control plane. Traditional routing protocols depend on IP addresses for both location and identity. LISP separates identity from location and is an on-demand mapping system. When an endpoint connects to a device, the device registers the endpoint identifier (EID) such as IP address, MAC address and its location (e.g., device loopback), also called a Record Locator (RLOC), to a mapping server. The mapping server is similar to DNS in that it contains the identity and location of the total network. When a device needs to send traffic to a destination, it requests the RLOC of the destination address from the mapping server, thereby reducing the number of IP entries in the routing table. LISP is based on a pull model, where the devices do not keep track of all the networks, but instead query the control plane dynamically for the destination traffic location. LISP is used as the control plane in Cisco SD-Access because the LANs have multiple /32 endpoints (in IPv4) or /128 endpoints (in IPv6) and client roaming is handled well by using a pull-based approach such as LISP.

The traditional way of segmenting a network included VLANs, ACLs, and virtual routing and forwarding (VRF). These methods do provide a logical way of segmentation, but they are not scalable due to the limitations on the number of VLANs and access-list entries supported on the devices. The security policy should follow the user or endpoint instead of following the IP address or location. Cisco TrustSec (discussed in detail toward the end of this chapter) provides segmentation by assigning a tag to the endpoint based on its business characteristics, behavior, and role. The tag is called a Scalable Group Tag (SGT). Policies are now applied to SGTs instead of IP addresses, thereby easily translating business intent into policies.

The Cisco SD-Access fabric data plane is based on Virtual Extensible LAN (VXLAN), which is an IETF standard encapsulation (RFC-7348). VXLAN encapsulation is IP/UDP-based, which means it can be forwarded by any IP-based network (legacy or non-Cisco) and it effectively creates the "overlay" aspect of the Cisco SD-Access fabric. VXLAN encapsulation is used (instead of LISP encapsulation) for two main reasons. VXLAN includes the source Layer 2 (Ethernet) header (LISP does not), and it provides special fields for additional information (such as virtual network [VN] ID and group [segment] ID). This technology provides several advantages for Cisco SD-Access, such as support for both Layer 2 and Layer 3 virtual topologies (overlays) and the capability to operate over any IP-based network with built-in network segmentation (VRF/VN) and built-in group-based policy. In Cisco SD-Access, some enhancements to the original VXLAN specifications have been added, most notably the use of scalable group tags (SGTs). This new VXLAN format is currently an IETF draft known as Group Policy Option (or VXLAN-GPO). In short, Cisco Campus Fabric uses VXLAN-GPO as the encapsulation method for the data plane. The advantage of VXLAN-GPO is that the VXLAN header carries VRF and SGT information and retains the Ethernet header, as shown in Figure 2-4. Subsequent mention of VXLAN refers to the VXLAN-GPO version.

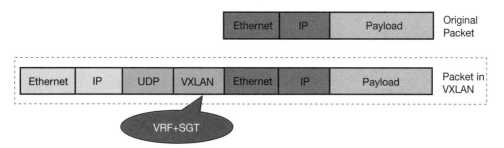

Figure 2-4   *VXLAN Header with VRF and SGT*

The Cisco Campus Fabric uses LISP in the control plane for a destination record locator, VXLAN-GPO as an overlay to encapsulate the original packet, and the underlay to transport the encapsulated packet. As the SGT is carried over in VXLAN, it can be used to enforce policies based on the roles. Cisco SD-Access brings an additional plane called the policy plane, and it uses Cisco TrustSec and ISE that will be discussed in the upcoming section. Cisco ISE maintains the SGT-based policies and pushes them on the network enforcement points. Cisco DNA Center orchestrates the SGT policies on ISE and the enforcement of the policies to the network devices. With SGT-based enforcement, the security policy is attached to the user instead of the location or the IP address of the user. Figure 2-5 illustrates the management of policies from Cisco DNA Center.

Cisco SD-Access Roles

This section provides an overview of Cisco SD-Access components and their roles at a high level. The upcoming chapters discuss the roles in greater detail. Cisco SD-Access consists of Cisco Campus Fabric managed by Cisco DNA Center and Cisco ISE as the policy engine. Figure 2-6 shows the components, their roles, and how they correlate to the campus fabric.

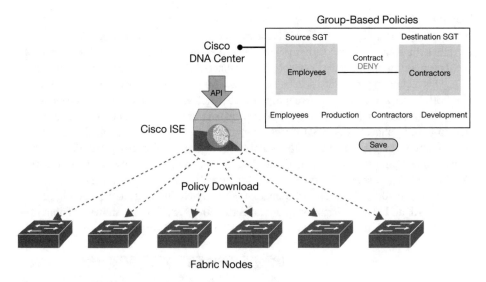

Figure 2-5 *Policy Push from Cisco DNA Center*

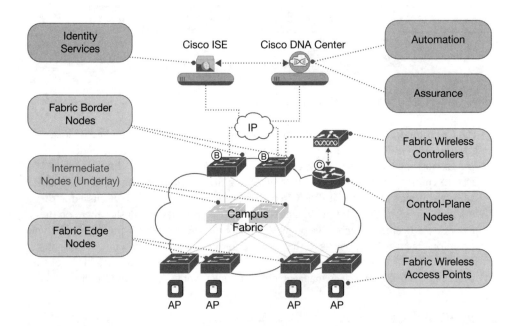

Figure 2-6 *SD-Access Components*

The following is a brief description of each of the Cisco SD-Access components:

■ **Cisco DNA Center:** GUI-based controller that provides intent-based automation for wired and wireless fabric devices. Apart from the fabric automation, Cisco

DNA Center contains an Analytics engine called Cisco DNA Assurance that collects analytics from endpoints, traffic flows, and fabric devices to provide telemetry, powerful insights, and guided remediation actions. Cisco DNA Center supports IPv4 and IPv6 addressing.

- **Cisco Identity Services Engine:** Cisco ISE is an identity-based network access control and policy engine. It dynamically groups the endpoints to Scalable Group Tags for intent-based policy enforcements.

- **Control plane node:** A host database with mapping of endpoint IDs to a location (loopback of the edge device). This control node receives endpoint ID registrations from edge and border nodes. It also resolves the mapping requests received from border and edge nodes to locate destination endpoint IDs. The control plane node is the most important node in the Campus Fabric because it is the brains behind the system and is responsible for maintaining large host mappings and their locations. To give a real-world analogy, when a cell phone moves from one tower to another tower, the mobile number doesn't change as the cell tower control system maintains the location of the cell phone. For any calls, the cell tower system automatically sends the call to the cell tower the phone is connected to. The control plane node works in a similar fashion, maintaining the endpoint IDs and their locations. For redundancy, there can be multiple control plane nodes in a Cisco SD-Access fabric.

- **Fabric border node:** A device that speaks fabric and non-fabric to connect the external Layer 3 networks to the Cisco SD-Access fabric. There can be several borders in an SD-Access fabric depending on the connections to the external Layer 3 networks. One border might connect to the known networks outside the fabric, and another border can act as the default border for Internet connectivity. Fabric border nodes, depending on the connection to the external Layer 3 network, register known networks and/or the default network to the control plane nodes.

- **Fabric edge node:** A fabric device (e.g., Access or Distribution) that is the first hop for the users or endpoints connecting to the Cisco SD-Access fabric. The responsibilities of fabric edge nodes include authentication, authorizing the endpoints, and registering the endpoint ID (IPv4 or IPv6 address) with the control plane nodes. Cisco SD-Access uses an anycast Layer 3 gateway on the edge nodes so that all the endpoints see the same gateway regardless of the edge node they are connected into. An anycast L3 gateway is a common gateway (IP address and MAC address) used on every edge node to share the host IP subnet to provide host mobility and optimal forwarding.

- **Fabric WLAN controller (WLC):** Fabric-enabled Wireless LAN controller takes part in the control plane operations, such as registering the wireless clients to the control plane node, but does not participate in the data plane. Its role is to connect fabric access points (APs) and wireless endpoints to the Cisco SD-Access fabric. The wireless clients connect to the fabric APs, and the fabric-enabled WLC registers them to the control plane node. Wireless clients RLOC includes the AP the client is connected to and the local edge node the AP is connected to.

The fabric AP forms a CAPWAP tunnel to the WLC and a VXLAN tunnel to the edge node. Once the wireless client is associated over Control and Provisioning of Wireless Access Points (CAPWAP), client traffic uses the fabric through the AP-to-edge VXLAN tunnel. Consistent policy can be applied for wired and wireless clients with Cisco SD-Access because the data path is through the fabric for wired and wireless traffic.

The following flow explains how traffic traverses through a Campus Fabric for a wired client:

1. Client1 connects to Edge1 through a wired connection. Edge1 performs dynamic authentication, the user is assigned an IP address from a host pool (VLAN), and a Scalable Group Tag is pushed by Identity Services Engine.

2. Edge1 then registers the client's IP address MAC address and its location (Edge1 loopback) with the control plane nodes using LISP.

3. Client1 initiates traffic to Client2 on Edge2. Edge1 does a mapping lookup with the control plane node for the location of Client2. The control plane node provides the location (e.g., loopback of Edge2).

4. Edge1 encapsulates the user traffic in VXLAN, forming a dynamic VXLAN tunnel with Edge2. The encapsulated packet uses the underlay to route the traffic.

5. Edge2 receives the VXLAN packet, decapsulates the packet to see the SGT, and forwards the original packet to Client2 if the SGT policy is permit.

In summary, Cisco DNA Center provides the capability to manage a Cisco SD-Access campus fabric. Host mobility is powered by an anycast gateway, which is one of the biggest advantages of Campus Fabric because hosts are dynamic and roaming is inevitable in LANs. The roaming clients would see the same IP address and same IP gateway (anycast gateway) regardless of wired or wireless connection or location in the campus. Fabric wired and wireless clients use the same data path, ensuring consistent policy and user experience. Campus Fabric is agnostic of underlay topology as long as the underlay provides IP connectivity, giving an opportunity to simplify underlay networks for faster forwarding. Security policy is IP address and location independent because Cisco SD-Access brings in group-based policies. Cisco SD-Access is digitizing the network where IP addresses take the back seat and business intent is driving the network with Cisco DNA Center.

The next section provides an overview of the policy plane components of Cisco ISE and Cisco TrustSec.

Network Access Control

This section highlights the need for network access control (NAC) in enterprise networks. NAC ensures that any devices or endpoints connecting to the network via wired, wireless, or remote-access connections are validated and given the right level of access to connect to the corporate resources.

Why Network Access Control?

The demands of networks have changed. Along with the commodification of network access from traditional users, there has been a steep influx of nontraditional network demands. With BYOD users, IoT devices, and the explosion of machine-to-machine use cases requiring network access, the legacy methods of controlling access are too limited and cannot respond with the agility that is now required. In parallel to this, there exists a growing risk of exposing the network to bad actors without proper controls in place. Herein exists the classic struggle between security and connectivity. Users demand seamless integration into a secure environment, independent of geography and access medium.

As data networks become increasingly indispensable in day-to-day business operations, there is a higher possibility of unauthorized users or devices gaining access to controlled or confidential information. Some of the most frequent attacks come from within the network. BYOD users and roaming corporate devices often become infected away from the safety and security of a corporate environment. The traditional network access control places firewalls and intrusion detection or prevention systems at the egress of the infrastructure to detect and protect the network against malicious and anomalous behavior. However, these controls are insufficient when the traffic sent by the infected user does not traverse the firewall or IPS. These roaming infections are capable of exploiting a VLAN/subnet via an "East-West" proliferation. This means the firewall, IPS, and IDS would have no knowledge of this threat without spanning traffic or tapping a line to look at packet captures. With the growing demands of businesses, a network access solution is required to dynamically adapt to the transformations in the network without affecting user experience or compromising security. Network access control should start when the endpoint connects to the network. Providing visibility into user activity and the capability to periodically query the endpoint and take actions if deemed noncompliant is also critical. Regardless of how the endpoint is connecting to the network, whether via wired, wireless, or remotely using virtual private networks, network access control needs to be put in place.

Now, imagine a world where all switchports are configured identically, all wireless LANs defer responsibility for access control to a centralized location, and all VPN headends are authorized identically to local authorization from the perspective of roaming users. This world allows for authentication of a user to prove "who they are," appropriate authorization pushed dynamically to the access device according to the context of the moment, regardless of medium, and then finally a destination for all accounting of that user's session. With a single pane of glass, all policy can be orchestrated, from classic authorization with VLANs and ACLs to cutting-edge policies via downloadable ACLs and Scalable Group Tags.

The Cisco network access control solution, Identify Services Engine (ISE), is an industry-leading access control and policy enforcement platform. Cisco ISE secures the network at the moment an endpoint attaches and maintains granular visibility of endpoints, users, and applications. ISE ensures that the endpoint or device is authorized, secure, and compliant before permitting appropriate network connectivity. Not only that, ISE has the capability to share context with partner security and logging devices for enhanced functionality and context sharing. The following section goes into detail on the capabilities that Cisco ISE has to offer and various deployment models.

Introduction to Cisco Identity Services Engine

The previous section discussed the need for network access control in any networking infrastructure for secure user access, visibility, and business and security dynamics. Cisco ISE is a policy engine for controlling endpoint access and network device administration for all methods of access to a network. This includes wired, wireless, and remote VPN access. ISE enables an administrator to centrally manage access policies for wired, wireless, and VPN endpoints in the network.

Overview of Cisco Identity Services Engine

Cisco ISE works by building context about the endpoints that includes users and groups (who), type of device (what), access time (when), access location (where), access type (wired/wireless/VPN—how), threats, and vulnerabilities. Through sharing of enriched context with the technology partner integrations and the implementation of Cisco TrustSec policy for software-defined segmentation, Cisco ISE transforms the network from simply a conduit for data into a security enforcer that accelerates the time to detection and time to resolution of network threats. Figure 2-7 shows a summary of Cisco ISE centrally looking over the network, offering role-based access control, guest services, BYOD, and posture for workstations and mobile devices. The context created from attributes received from the network is shared with the partner ecosystem to enforce security policies and threat containment.

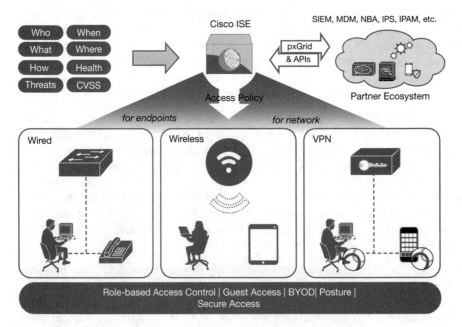

Figure 2-7   *Cisco Identity Services Engine High-level Overview*

Before digging deeper into the individual features of Cisco ISE, a high-level understanding of the building blocks and protocols ISE uses for network access would be beneficial.

Network access control comprises three main components:

- **Authentication:** Verifies whether the endpoint connecting to the network has valid credentials

- **Authorization:** Grants privileges the endpoint can have on a device or network

- **Accounting:** Tracks the services that endpoints are accessing and the amount of network resources they are consuming

These three fundamental ideals form what is commonly referred to as AAA (pronounced "triple A"). Cisco ISE is a AAA server providing authentication, authorization, and accounting services for users and devices connecting to the network. In this book, the terms *Cisco ISE* and *AAA server* often are used interchangeably because ISE *is* a AAA server.

There are two prominent protocols used by AAA servers to provide network access control: RADIUS (Remote Authentication Dial-In User Service) and TACACS+ (Terminal Access Controller Access-Control System Plus). Both protocols work on a client-server model. ISE supports both RADIUS and TACACS+ protocols.

Figure 2-8 illustrates a user connected to a switch. In this case, the switch is considered the network access device, and Cisco ISE is the AAA server. The network access device is also known as the AAA client. When the user is trying to connect to the network, the credentials provided by the user are sent to the AAA server.

Figure 2-8 *Network Access*

Table 2-1 highlights the differences between RADIUS and TACACS+.

Table 2-1 *Differences Between RADIUS and TACACS+ Protocols*

	RADIUS	**TACACS+**
Protocol and port used	UDP 1812, 1813 (new port) UDP 1645, 1645 (legacy port)	TCP 49
Encryption	Password-only encryption	Full packet encryption
Authentication and authorization	Combines authentication and authorization	Separates all three AAA packets; flexible
Primary use	Network access	Device administration
Command accounting	No	Yes

In Table 2-1, "Network access" refers to a user or endpoint trying to get access to the network as a means to a destination (reaching an internal database or Google.com), and "Device administration" is when an administrator or a network operator is trying to get access to the network device to view or make configuration changes on the device.

Key takeaways from Table 2-1 are that RADIUS uses UDP and is used for network access, and TACACS+ uses connection-based protocol TCP and is primarily used for device administration. Enterprise networks sometimes require accounting as granular as per command when administrators or network operators log in to the network devices to make changes on the devices. TACACS+ is the only protocol that can support command authorization and command accounting. Best practice is to use TACACS+ for device administration because of the command authorization and accounting capability for a granular audit trail.

Cisco ISE Features

This section covers some of the most common Cisco ISE features that are significant to securing campus networks and their role in software-defined segmentation. As discussed in the "Overview of Cisco Identity Services Engine" section, ISE is an intent-based networking policy engine providing a centralized security solution that automates context-aware access to network resources and shares contextual data.

The key features discussed in this section are listed here:

- Secure access

- Device administration

- Guest access

- Profiling

- Bring your own device (BYOD)

- Compliance

- Integrations with pxGrid

Secure Access

With growing security concerns, clients need to be authorized appropriately before they are provided access to corporate resources. IT security policies require users such as employees and contractors to be authenticated using their corporate-provided credentials before gaining access to the corporate resources. Older devices that require network access, such as IP phones, IP cameras, and access points, are sometimes not capable of doing authentication but should still be confirmed as corporate assets before being given access to the environment. Secure access capability on Cisco ISE ensures that any user or device connecting to the network is authenticated first and, upon successful authentication, the endpoint is granted the level of access to the corporate resources as per the security policies enforced by the organization. IT networks are moving toward two-factor authentication to alleviate issues with compromised user accounts by enforcing a second level of authentication using soft tokens or push notifications. ISE can be leveraged in these workflows to implement two-factor authentication.

Authentication and authorization on Cisco ISE can be performed against an internal database or an external database. External databases supported with ISE include Microsoft Active Directory, Lightweight Directory Access Protocol (LDAP) servers, RSA SecurID, Microsoft SQL Server, and Duo, among others. ISE offers various options for authorization, such as VLAN assignment, downloadable ACLs, redirection ACLs, and Scalable Group Tags to the endpoint. (The "Segmentation with Cisco TrustSec" section covers SGTs in detail.)

Figure 2-9 illustrates different scenarios of secure access based on the type of user and protocol used while connecting to the network device. Two users and two IoT devices are connecting to either a wired or a wireless network. One user is using 802.1X as the authentication method, and the other user is using MAC Authentication Bypass (MAB) as the authentication method. These are the two common types of secure access methods used in campus networks. The authentication methods shown in the illustration are discussed next at a high level.

IEEE 802.1X is an IEEE standard authentication framework providing an authentication mechanism for endpoints connecting into LAN networks. 802.1X consists of three main components: a supplicant, an authenticator, and an authentication server (Cisco ISE), as shown in Figure 2-10. A *supplicant* is software running on the endpoint that is capable of sending user credentials in an Extensible Authentication Protocol (EAP) (Layer 2) format. Most modern desktop operating systems and mobile operating systems have a built-in supplicant. Cisco also offers a supplicant software called AnyConnect Network Access Module (NAM), which is capable of providing advanced options for user authentication. The *authenticator* is the network device to which the user is connected, and its purpose is to encapsulate an EAP packet (Layer 2) in a RADIUS packet (Layer 3) to be sent to the authentication server. In LANs, authenticators usually are switches or wireless LAN controllers. Cisco ISE is the *authentication server* used here to illustrate the flow. RADIUS is the only protocol capable of encapsulating EAP packets and sending them to an authentication server, making it the desired protocol for network access, as discussed earlier in the context of Table 2-1. 802.1X allows passwords, secure tokens, or certificates to be used as credentials for authentication. With the focus on security embedded in campus networks, the demand for 802.1X support on endpoints has pressured manufacturers of recent IP phones, wireless access points, and some IoT devices to include 802.1X functionality.

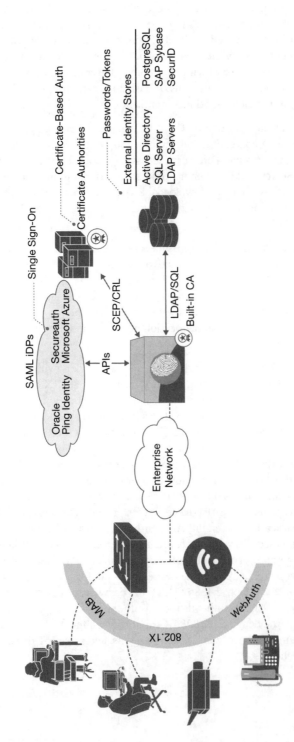

Figure 2-9   *Cisco ISE Secure Access*

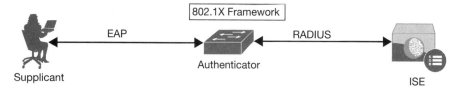

Figure 2-10 *802.1X Framework*

For users or endpoints that are not capable of running an 802.1X supplicant, such as older medical devices, legacy printers, legacy IP phones etc., MAC Authentication Bypass can be leveraged as an authentication mechanism for network access. With MAB, the endpoint MAC address would be used as the username and password for authentication purposes. Common use cases for MAB include users connecting on personal devices who do not have their supplicant enabled, guest users, printers, IoT devices, and so forth.

Even though 802.1X is the much-desired authentication mechanism, the challenge is the configuration of the supplicants, as corporate-owned devices are not the only ones requiring access. Cisco EasyConnect, as the name suggests, provides an easier way of implementing port-based authentication without using 802.1X for credentials but leveraging the user login when the user is logging in to the machine. With EasyConnect, the endpoint performs MAB upon entry of the network and Cisco ISE stitches together the MAB event to a separate username logon event from Active Directory to provide authorization based on the username, thereby avoiding the hassle of configuring 802.1X on the client.

In summary, Cisco ISE secure access provides network access to endpoints based on their authentication methods and authorizes based on the context of the moment to comply with security policies.

Device Administration

To maintain the network infrastructure, administrators often access the infrastructure devices for monitoring, configuration changes, software upgrades, or troubleshooting purposes. Differentiated access and accountability plays a vital role whenever infrastructure devices are being accessed. Unauthorized users should not be allowed to log in to the infrastructure devices, and any unauthorized changes could degrade the network or bring the network down. Device administration ensures that role-based access is enforced to the IT personnel accessing the infrastructure. Cisco ISE provides role-based access control for device administration using RADIUS and TACACS+. However, TACACS+ protocol primary use is device administration because it brings in the capability to perform command authorization to authorize every command before it's executed on the device. With Cisco ISE acting as the TACACS+ server for device administration, security policies can be enforced to push privilege level and limited command access through command authorization for administrators on network devices. Unlike RADIUS, TACACS+ offers command accounting to log the commands corresponding to the user, which can be helpful for auditing and compliance requirements.

Figure 2-11 provides an example of device administration using TACACS+ on Cisco ISE. Alice is an administrator who needs to have full access to the switch, and Bob is an IT helpdesk contact who needs read-only access to the switch. ISE policies are configured with full command access for Alice and read-only command access for Bob. Bob is presented with an error "Command authorization failed" when he tries to execute a command that is not permitted in the command authorization set. Though their privilege level is the same, Bob has a more restrictive set of commands that he may use when accessing the switch.

Figure 2-11   *Command Authorization Using ISE*

Guest Access

When guests or visitors outside the company would like to reach the Internet or broadly available services on the company network, IT policies often require validating the guest first prior to providing access. In practice, a "guest" is loosely defined as a noncorporate user on a noncorporate device. These users predominantly expect wireless access to the Internet and rarely more. Guest access provided by Cisco ISE allows enterprises the most flexibility for wireless (and wired) guest access, with several templated workflows for quick and easy deployment. A typical guest user in a network would experience the following flow, the packet flow for which is detailed in Figure 2-12:

1. The guest user connects to a wired port or wireless guest SSID. ISE learns the MAC address of the guest and pushes the user to the guest portal, hosted on ISE. The guest is restricted from going anywhere but this portal.

2. The guest is redirected to the guest portal to enter login details. ISE validates the user and initiates a Change of Authorization (CoA) to reauthorize the user, as the user is now a registered guest.

3. The guest is provided with Internet access.

A CoA is a request sent by ISE to the network device to reauthenticate the user. A CoA is commonly used in flows that involve a temporary access before providing full access. The power of CoAs should not be understated, as the AAA server is often privy to much more contextual information than the access device is because the AAA server constantly collects more information about the environment and posture of the endpoint. When ISE learns new information about an endpoint or learns that previous information about an endpoint has fundamentally changed, it sends the CoA in order to reauthorize with more appropriate privilege based on the additional context (e.g., guest registration, malware found, OS change).

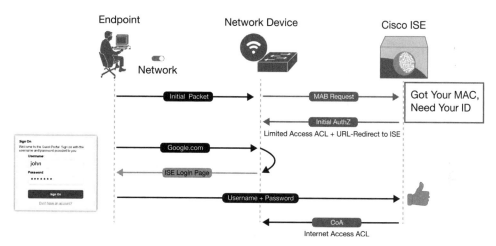

Figure 2-12   *Guest Access Packet Flow*

Guest access with Cisco ISE gives administrators the flexibility to create guest accounts, monitor guest activity, offer simple portals that are easily customizable for different languages, and add corporate logos without any web design background. If customers prefer to write their own in-house scripts, ISE guests can also be managed via the REST API.

Cisco ISE supports up to 1 million guest accounts. These guest accounts' credentials can be emailed, printed, or sent via SMS to the guest user. As shown in Figure 2-13, Cisco ISE supports three types of guest access:

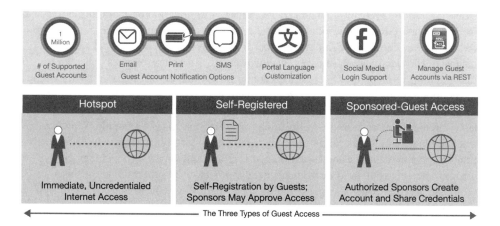

Figure 2-13   *Cisco ISE Guest Access Portals*

- **Hotspot Guest portal:** Guest users are redirected to the ISE on-box Hotspot Guest portal first and are provided Internet access by accepting an Acceptable Use Policy (AUP). No credentials are needed. This type of access is commonly used for a retail guest-user experience.

- **Self-Registered Guest portal:** Guest users are presented with a self-service page to register by providing required information. Guest account credentials are sent by email, print, or SMS for login to access the Internet. ISE supports social media login using Facebook credentials.

- **Sponsored-Guest portal:** Portal for sponsor users like lobby ambassadors to create guest accounts. The sponsor user creates a guest account and assigns the validity period of the account from the sponsor portal. Once created, the sponsor sends credentials to the guest user via email, print, or SMS. The guest can use those credentials to log in to the guest network.

As part of Cisco Software-Defined Access, Cisco DNA Center allows customers to configure Cisco ISE and network devices for guest access without ever leaving Cisco DNA Center, as all configurations are pushed across the External RESTful Services (ERS) API.

Profiling

Gone are the days of a network that simply allows printers, desktops, and phones to communicate. Modern networks see the number of types of devices increasing as quickly as the number of devices themselves. This section covers profiling services offered by Cisco ISE that corporate networks can benefit from to help them understand and provision new devices looking for network services. Context is the king in a shifting environment where network access is requested as frequently from a physical security officer as from a network admin. Classifying types of endpoints on the network helps businesses understand trends and aids in building a better segmentation strategy for future, similar endpoints. Effective authorization privilege can limit attack surfaces, prepare for future growth, and enforce security policies in case of any suspicious activity.

Cisco ISE profiling provides dynamic detection and classification of endpoints connected in the network. ISE uses the endpoint MAC address as the unique identifier received from the network device along with other attributes learned to create the internal endpoint database. The classification of endpoints involves matching the attributes collected for the endpoints to prebuilt or user-defined conditions, which in turn are used to determine the endpoint profile from an extensive profiling library. The Cisco ISE profiling library includes a granular level of device types, including mobile clients (iPads, Android tablets, Chromebooks, and so on), workstation operating systems (for example, Windows, macOS, Linux, and others), and numerous "headless" (no supplicant) systems such as printers, phones, cameras, and access points. The profiling library also includes IoT devices, encompassing even vertical-specific endpoints such as medical devices used in healthcare (such as X-ray machines), building automation systems to control HVAC systems, and manufacturing controllers and sensors.

Once classification is complete, endpoints or nonuser systems can be provided access to the network and authorization based on their endpoint profile. An IP phone can be put in a voice VLAN dynamically thanks to profiling, while an IP camera can be placed dynamically in the camera VLAN. For users, differentiated access can be enforced depending on the workstation they are connecting from. For example, a corporate user is provided full network access when connected from a corporate-owned machine and is provided guest-level access when connected from a personal device.

Profiling Probes

Cisco ISE profiling relies on data that is collected from the network. As ISE continues to collect profiling data, it attempts to classify endpoints into an endpoint profile that describes what the device is. An ISE probe is a component of profiling services that is used to collect attributes. The following Cisco ISE probes are available, each of which collects some unique attributes for an endpoint. The "best" probes to use always depend on the endpoints that are being profiled on a particular network.

- Active Directory (AD)

- AnyConnect Identity Extensions (ACIDex)

- DHCP SPAN

- Domain Name System (DNS)

- Dynamic Host Configuration Protocol (DHCP)

- Hypertext Transfer Protocol (HTTP)

- NetFlow

- Network Scan (NMAP)

- pxGrid

- SNMP Query

- Simple Network Management Protocol (SNMP) Trap

- RADIUS

Figure 2-14 depicts generally the role of probes in profiling. Based on the information collected from the probes, endpoints are profiled and updated in the ISE database. The following list highlights the most commonly used probes for endpoint profiling:

- **Active Directory probe:** Increases operating system fidelity through detailed info extracted via AD. ISE fetches AD attributes from Active Directory once the computer hostname is learned from the DHCP probe and DNS probe.

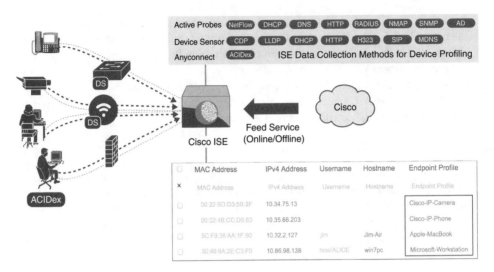

Figure 2-14 *Cisco ISE Profiling Probes*

- **ACIDex probe:** Profiling users connecting remotely, such as VPN users, is challenging for Cisco ISE when the clients have multiple NICs because RADIUS sends all the MAC addresses to ISE, making it difficult for ISE to profile. AnyConnect uses the *device-public-mac* attribute to signal to ISE which MAC address is used to establish the VPN connection. If *device-public-mac* is not supported by the AnyConnect version, then ISE uses the first value for *device-mac* to set the active MAC for the VPN connection. This probe is only applicable when the client is connecting using the AnyConnect VPN client.

- **DHCP probe:** The DHCP probe collects DHCP data to use in profiling policy. ISE needs to be configured as a DHCP server on the network device to receive the DHCP discovery packet to view the endpoint attributes. This probe is capable of IP-to-MAC address mapping of the endpoint.

- **DNS probe:** The DNS probe does a reverse DNS lookup for IP addresses learned by other means. Before a DNS lookup can be performed, one of the following probes must be started along with the DNS probe: DHCP, DHCP SPAN, HTTP, RADIUS, or SNMP for IP-to-MAC address binding.

- **HTTP probe:** For flows where sessions are redirected to a Cisco ISE portal, such as the Hotspot Guest portal, the HTTP request-header field contains a User-Agent attribute, which includes application, vendor, and OS information of the endpoint. Enabling HTTP probe on Cisco ISE uses the HTTP attributes to profile the endpoint.

- **SNMP probe:** SNMP probe consists of two probes: SNMP Trap and SNMP Query. SNMP Trap probe alerts ISE profiling services to the presence (connection or disconnection) of a network endpoint by configuring ISE as the SNMP server on the infrastructure device. When an SNMP link up/link down trap is sent to ISE, ISE triggers an SNMP Query to collect CDP, LLDP, and ARP data for the endpoint. The SNMP probe is not needed when the RADIUS probe is enabled because the RADIUS probe triggers an SNMP Query as well.

■ **RADIUS probe:** ISE can profile endpoints based on the RADIUS attributes collected from the RADIUS request/response messages from ISE RADIUS authentication service. This probe is capable of IP-to-MAC address mapping of the endpoint.

■ **Device-Sensor:** With the new device-sensor capability on switches and wireless LAN controllers, all information sent in probes RADIUS, DHCP, SNMP, HTTP (wireless only) can be gleaned to send in a RADIUS accounting packet. Device-sensor reduces configuration on the infrastructure device and consolidates attributes in one accounting packet. The RADIUS probe should be enabled on ISE to understand device-sensor attributes. Cisco DNA Center automates device-sensor configuration that is needed on infrastructure devices. Figure 2-15 shows all the information consolidated in a RADIUS accounting message collected through device-sensor. The RADIUS accounting message would contain the endpoint attribute information learned via CDP, LLDP, DHCP, and HTTP instead of sending in individual probes.

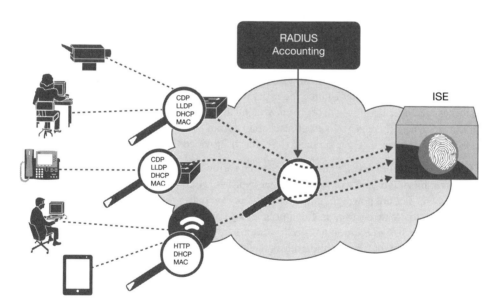

Figure 2-15 *Device-Sensor Capability*

Profiling Operation

The Cisco ISE profiling service uses the profiling probes to collect attributes for the endpoints and then matches them to profiling conditions that will be used in profiling policies. Figure 2-16 shows an example of a Cisco Provided endpoint profiling policy named Microsoft-Workstation containing four conditions. When the endpoint matches a condition in a profiling policy, a certainty factor (CF) or a weight associated with that condition is assigned to the endpoint for that profile. Although conditions may match in multiple profiles, the profile for which the endpoint has the highest cumulative CF, or Total Certainty Factor (TCF), is the one assigned to the endpoint.

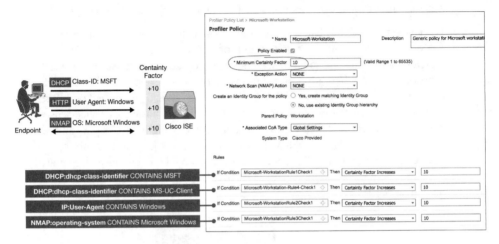

Figure 2-16   *Profiling Architecture*

Cisco ISE uses the profiling feed service to keep its profiling database up to date with the latest Organizationally Unique Identifier (OUI) information from the IEEE. Offline profiler feed updates are available for download and to import on ISE specially for environments where there is no Internet reachability from Cisco ISE. Profiling policies downloaded from the feed server are tagged as "Cisco Provided" policies.

The primary goal of profiling is to identify the various types of the endpoints in the network. Inevitably, some devices in the network won't be profiled and will be labeled as "unknown." For unknown endpoints without any prebuilt profiles, administrators have the option to create custom profiling policies and profiling conditions. The Cisco ISE web interface has an Endpoint Visibility dashboard to provide insight into the number of unknown endpoints. The dashboard lists the attributes learned for every endpoint MAC address, and the administrator can create custom profiling policies based on the common attributes learned for the unknown endpoints. The custom policies created are tagged "Administrator Created" policies.

Figure 2-17 shows an environment where Cisco ISE detected 18.93 percent unknown endpoints and profiled 80.7% of the total endpoints ISE discovered.

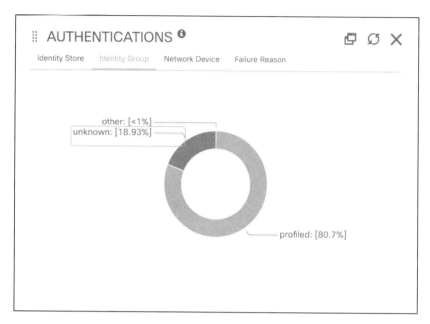

Figure 2-17 *Unknown Endpoints Detected by Cisco ISE*

Bring Your Own Device

Considering the number of personal devices allowed in corporate networks, managing and enforcing network access control in a nonintrusive way on these devices can be painful but is critical for the security of the network. Cisco Bring Your Own Device (BYOD) on ISE is applicable for wired and wireless use cases. Cisco ISE offers two versions of BYOD flow to securely allow the personal device into the network without affecting user experience and without requiring any administrator interference to enable NAC:

- **Simple BYOD:** Personal devices connecting to the corporate network are provided limited or Internet-only access. Guest access, discussed earlier, is an example of Simple BYOD. Another flavor of simple BYOD is creating a separate wireless SSID just for personal devices and authorizing users based on their credentials.

- **Full BYOD:** Does the corporate policy involve allowing only personal devices using 802.1X profiles and certificates/passwords similar to the corporate managed assets? If the answer is yes, full BYOD is the solution that places the BYOD device in an automated workflow to register the personal device, provision an 802.1X profile, and install certificates (optional) when the device is first connected to the network. An automated workflow requires minimal user education and less administrative overhead to enable network access on an unmanaged asset.

Figure 2-18 shows the one-time ISE BYOD workflow as a personal device connected to the network for the first time.

Figure 2-18   *Cisco Full BYOD Workflow*

When the BYOD user connects to the network the first time through either a wired or a wireless connection, the user's web browser is redirected to the Cisco ISE centrally managed BYOD portal page to start registering the device. This is followed by provisioning the 802.1X profiles to configure the supplicant on the device to comply with corporate policies. The next step typically installs a user certificate issued by either the Cisco ISE Internal Certificate Authority (ISE CA) or an external CA if the corporate policy involves connecting using certificates as credentials. At the end of the workflow, a BYOD user is provisioned with the certificates and 802.1X supplicant profile required by IT. The user is automatically connected using certificates with the 802.1X profile and given network access.

Compliance

Authenticating the user before providing access to the network is crucial for security. Networks need more than credentials to confirm the user is safe to be authorized to access the network, such as ensuring that the user's device has the latest antivirus/ antimalware updates, firewalls enabled, Windows security patches installed, disk encryption enabled, and so on. These endpoint operating criteria are deemed the "posture" of the client attempting to access the network. The Cisco ISE Compliance feature brings in the capability to perform posture checks on the endpoints, workstations, or mobile devices to confirm they are compliant with corporate security policies before granting network access.

Starting with workstation compliance, posture policies created on Cisco ISE are verified against an authenticated endpoint and, based on the result, the endpoint is marked as Complaint or Non-Compliant. Authorization policies can be configured on ISE that match on the posture state to provide full access to a Compliant endpoint or provide quarantine/remediation access to a Non-Compliant endpoint. For posture, the endpoint needs to have a posture agent, which could be either a permanent agent called "Cisco AnyConnect ISE Posture module" or a dissolvable agent pushed out by ISE during posture check. The posture flow is as follows:

1. **Authenticate User/Device:** The workstation connects to the network. The user is authenticated and the initial posture status is set to Unknown.

2. **Posture Assessment:** Based on the posture policies configured on Cisco ISE, posture assessment is performed for the endpoint. Posture checks may include Hotfix check, AV check, Pin lock, and USB device. The endpoint posture status on Cisco ISE is set to Compliant if all the posture checks are a success. The posture status is changed to Non-Compliant if the posture checks result in a failure.

3. **Authorization Change:** A change of authorization (CoA) happens where the endpoint is given access to the network if Compliant. The network access can be provided by placing it in a user VLAN, pushing a downloadable ACL (dACL), or assigning SGT.

4. **Quarantine/Limited Access or No Access:** If the endpoint posture status results in Non-Compliant, CoA is performed on ISE to place the user in Quarantine VLAN, restricted dACL, or Quarantine SGT. Some IT organizations would like to give the user access to remediation servers to update their AV or Windows updates. Some IT organizations might have policies to block access to a Non-Compliant. An access-reject is sent for such business requirements.

The following are various posture checks available on Cisco ISE Compliance. The endpoint workstation can be checked against the following conditions as part of a posture check:

- Antimalware Conditions

- Antispyware Conditions

- Antivirus Conditions

- Application Conditions

- Compound Conditions

- Disk Encryption Conditions

- File Conditions

- Patch Management Conditions

- Registry Conditions

- Service Conditions

- USB Conditions

The posture for mobile devices is similar to the posture for workstations except that there is no posture agent on the mobile device. Mobile devices connecting to the network through the full BYOD flow and corporate-owned mobile devices can be postured by Cisco ISE if the organization has a Cisco-supported Mobile Device Manager (MDM). ISE can leverage MDM information to enforce policy during network access. BYOD devices need to be registered with ISE, which in turn registers the device with the MDM. The MDM checks the compliance status of the mobile endpoint and returns the status to ISE to grant network access if the status is Compliant. The following MDM attributes can be used to create compliance policies for mobile devices:

- Device registration status

- Device compliance status

- Disk encryption status

- Pin lock status

- Jailbreak status

- Manufacturer

- Model

- IMEI

- Serial number

- OS version

- Phone number

Integrations with pxGrid

Cisco Identity Services Engine as discussed thus far creates a context for the endpoint based on who, what, where, when, how, and health status. This context is based on consolidating attributes received from various collection points in the network. It is very common in IT networks to use several security products to gain visibility to enforce security policies, each point product delivering a unique viewpoint to the mix. The contextual data created by ISE is beneficial if it can be shared with other security products running in the network to enrich their data. Conversely, ecosystem partners can share context with ISE to trigger a quarantine of users in case of any malicious activity.

Cisco Platform Exchange Grid (pxGrid) is an open, scalable, and IETF standards–driven platform that supports bidirectional, any-to-any partner platform integrations. Cisco pxGrid works on a publisher/subscriber model for Cisco ISE to publish contextual information to ecosystem partners (Cisco or non-Cisco) acting as subscribers. Ecosystem partners subscribe to topics (e.g., SessionDirectory, TrustSecMetaData, AdaptiveNetworkControl, etc.) relevant to them so that ISE publishes context related to only those topics. With the shared data, ecosystem partners could benefit from adding more context to an event to take further actions. Cisco DNA Center is a pxGrid subscriber that gains visibility into TrustSec data used for software-defined segmentation.

Cisco pxGrid has built an ecosystem of more than 100 partner integrations. Figure 2-19 depicts examples of context-sharing partners that currently benefit from information exchange using Cisco pxGrid. The list of all the ecosystem partners supporting pxGrid can be found at https://www.cisco.com/go/pxgrid for your reference. More partners are adopting to pxGrid because it is an RFC standard, and they are realizing the value of context sharing in a multivendor environment.

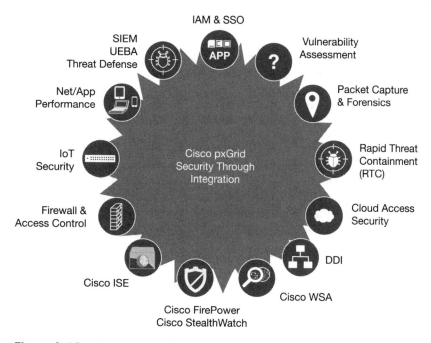

Figure 2-19 *Cisco pxGrid Ecosystem*

Cisco ISE introduced pxGrid 1.0, which is XMPP-based. The ecosystem partners download the SDK containing Java and C libraries. Cisco pxGrid 2.0 uses WebSocket and the REST API over STOMP (Simple Text Oriented Message Protocol) and was introduced with ISE version 2.4 to overcome SDK dependencies. Unlike pxGrid 1.0, where Cisco ISE can only publish contextual data, pxGrid 2.0 allows ISE to receive context from IoT asset vendors. With ISE pxGrid 2.0 accepting context from IoT asset vendors, ISE can use this information to profile each IoT device accurately.

Cisco pxGrid offers Cisco Rapid Threat Containment by invoking ISE to push quarantine action on a malicious user using Adaptive Network Control (ANC). If an IT environment has a firewall supporting pxGrid and ISE, pxGrid can be leveraged to share session information with the firewall so that the firewall can dynamically instruct ISE to mitigate a threat by rejecting the endpoint. This coordination of disparate security points in the network would not be possible without the context-sharing highway that pxGrid facilitates.

Cisco ISE Design Considerations

For any network access control implementation, a solid Cisco ISE design is necessary to ensure that the network is secure and the deployment is available in case of a failover scenario. Scale, sizing, high availability, network devices, and roaming events need to be considered in ISE design. This section details the components of Cisco ISE, design considerations, and various deployment models.

Cisco ISE Architecture

When an endpoint authenticates using Cisco ISE, ISE creates a session for the endpoint, and when the endpoint disconnects, ISE removes the session from the session database. ISE scale and sizing depend on the total concurrent sessions in the network. ISE can be installed on a physical appliance or as a virtual machine. ISE architecture consists of nodes, personas, and roles. A *node* is an ISE instance on an appliance or a VM. The *persona* of an ISE node depends on the services enabled on the ISE node. Following are the details of the four Cisco ISE personas and the services associated with them:

■ **Policy Services Node (PSN):** This node is a RADIUS and TACACS+ server making the policy decisions. These nodes provide ISE services: secure access, guest services, profiling, posture, BYOD, and device administration. PSNs directly communicate with network access devices (NADs) for authenticating the connected endpoints. PSNs directly communicate with external identity stores for user authentication. An ISE deployment must have at least one PSN and allow a maximum of 50 PSNs.

■ **Policy Administration Node (PAN):** This node provides a single pane of glass for ISE administration. It has a web interface to configure and view policies. The PAN is responsible for replication of configuration synchronization to the PSNs in the ISE deployment. An ISE deployment must have at least one primary PAN, and a secondary PAN could be added for redundancy. No more than two PANs are allowed in the deployment.

■ **Monitoring Node (MnT):** This node is a logging and reporting server. The node collects syslogs from all the ISE nodes and network access devices for logging and reporting. An ISE deployment must have at least one MnT, and a secondary MnT could be added for redundancy. No more than two MnTs are allowed in the deployment.

■ **pxGrid Controller (PXG):** This node facilitates sharing of context with ecosystem partners using pxGrid. An ISE deployment does not require a pxGrid node to function, but up to four pxGrid nodes can operate for scaled context sharing and redundancy.

In summary, a Cisco ISE deployment should have at least one PAN node, one MnT node, and one PSN node. ISE supports geographical separation between nodes as long as the round-trip time (RTT) between the nodes is less than 300 milliseconds.

Cisco ISE Deployment Options

Cisco ISE can be deployed in any of the following deployment models. The deployment models depend on a lot of factors, mainly the scale, redundancy requirements, and services in use.

- Standalone deployment

- Distributed deployment

- Dedicated distributed deployment

Standalone Deployment

In a standalone deployment, all the Cisco ISE personas (PAN, PSN, MnT, pxGrid) are running on one node. This can be turned into a basic two-node deployment with another node with all the personas enabled for redundancy. Scale numbers will remain the same for a standalone or two-node deployment. Figure 2-20 provides a visual of the ISE deployment in standalone versus two-node deployment models.

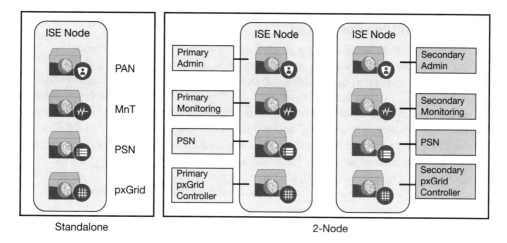

Figure 2-20 *Standalone and Two-Node Cisco ISE Deployments*

Distributed Deployment

In a distributed deployment, one or more personas are distributed on different nodes. There are two types of distributed deployments: hybrid and dedicated. In hybrid deployments, PAN and MnT personas are combined on two nodes—one being the primary node and the other being used for redundancy—and dedicated PSNs handle policy decisions. Because PSNs are the nodes performing policy decisions, this deployment model brings in not only additional scale with an increase in the concurrent sessions the deployment supports, but also better performance with logging, in comparison with a standalone deployment. Hybrid deployments allow a maximum of five PSNs in the deployment. Figure 2-21 provides a visual of ISE hybrid deployment.

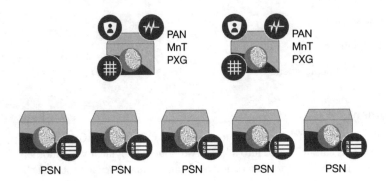

Figure 2-21   *Hybrid Distributed Deployment*

Dedicated Distributed Deployment

The dedicated distributed deployment model is the most commonly used model in large enterprise networks. Each persona has its own dedicated ISE node. This deployment model can support up to 2 million concurrent 802.1X/MAB endpoints, two Admin nodes, two MnT nodes, four pxGrid nodes, and fifty PSNs. Figure 2-22 shows a scenario of dedicated ISE deployment spread across multiple data centers. This architecture offers redundancy of Admin nodes, MnT nodes, and pxGrid nodes split across two data centers. The policy servers at the main campus are placed behind a load balancer to cater for campus endpoints. By placing the PSNs behind a load balancer, additional PSNs can be placed without making configuration changes to the network devices. Network devices communicate with the load balancer's virtual IP address (VIP), and in case of any PSN failure, the load balancer takes care of rerouting the authentication requests to the available PSNs.

Cisco DNA Center supports integration with any of the Cisco ISE deployment models. ISE is an integral part of software-defined campus networks. Before rolling out ISE, a clear understanding of the total number of endpoints in the network, concurrent sessions during peak hours, future growth rate, redundancy requirements within and across data centers, ISE features to be used, and link latency in the data center is critical to make a decision on the ISE deployment model to implement.

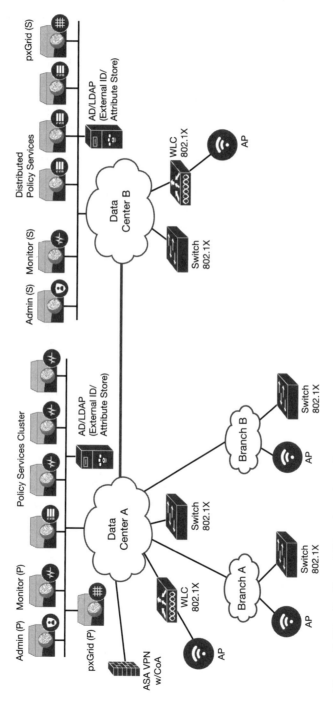

Figure 2-22 *Dedicated Distributed Deployment*

Segmentation with Cisco TrustSec

Over the past several years, businesses have been going through tremendous technology changes, requiring IT networks to keep up with the dynamics. Advancements in endpoints, smart devices, IoT devices, and BYOD have caused growing pains for network security. To name a few, additional complexity in the network, lack of administrative control, and expansion of the threat attack surface with the sophisticated endpoints have added to the IT burden of maintaining the environment. Effective network segmentation has become more important than ever, and it has to be able to scale and be topology independent to accommodate any topology changes that may incur in the future. The traditional way of segmenting the network includes placing the users or endpoints in their own VLANs, carving out DHCP pool(s), deploying ACLs on the devices to each of the enforcement points in the network, and finally pushing appropriate access control policy to the access edge devices. While these segmentation methods work, they also pose challenges in their own way. For example, in the event of company mergers and acquisitions, the network needs to be expanded by creating new VLANs, DHCP scopes. These new IP subnets need to be added in the user access-lists for access, but an increasing number of ACL entries may lead to ACL exhaustion on the devices apart from the additional administrative work to keep in line with the security requirements. Controlling access based on IP address is dependent on network topology, is not easily scalable, and causes additional operational expenses (OPEX) and the possibility of hitting TCAM limitations on the network devices themselves.

The Cisco TrustSec solution brings in centralized management, segmentation by logically grouping users and devices based on their role regardless of their location and IP subnet. Characteristics such as business function (like type of the user—Guest, Contractor, Employee) and the context derived through Cisco ISE services are used to group the user or device. These logical groupings, called Scalable Group Tags (SGTs), simplify network segmentation for access control. SGTs are independent of the IP address and provide a scalable, consistent segmentation solution by enforcing policies using the SGTs. Cisco TrustSec technology assigns an SGT to the user or device traffic at ingress, and the SGT traverses deeper into the network so that it can be used to enforce the access policy (on the firewall, for example). Enforcement based on SGTs can be done on Cisco routers, switches, access points, or firewalls. Cisco TrustSec is an open technology so that third-party vendors can implement it to securely communicate with Cisco devices in a network. The next section discusses Cisco TrustSec in action.

Cisco TrustSec Functions

These are the three main functions of TrustSec:

- Classification
- Propagation
- Enforcement

Classification

Classification is the ability to assign an SGT to the user or endpoint or a device that is connected to the network. SGTs can be assigned dynamically or statically. Dynamic SGT assignment is done by Cisco ISE based on the identity, profile, role, and overall context of the endpoint. A client connecting to the campus network using 802.1X, MAB, or web authentication is authenticated by ISE and is assigned an SGT per the policies defined on ISE. In Dynamic SGT assignment, ISE dynamically assigns the SGT for an authenticating endpoint. When endpoint authentication is not possible, static SGT classification is necessary. Static SGT assignments are usually applicable for static devices such as servers that do not do authentication. A static SGT can be mapped to a Layer 2 interface, VLAN, subnet, or Layer 3 switched virtual interface (SVI) instead of relying on assignment from ISE. Static IP-to-SGT mapping or subnet-to-SGT mapping can be created on ISE so that it can be pushed to the SGT-capable device instead of configuring the mapping on each device. The classification is propagated into the network for policy enforcement. Figure 2-23 summarizes the TrustSec classifications available.

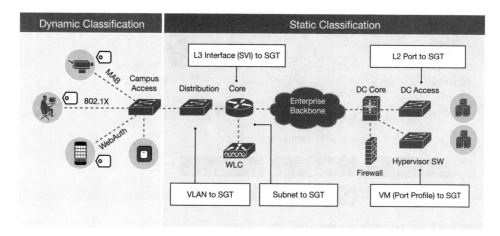

Figure 2-23 *Cisco TrustSec Classifications*

Propagation

Once the SGTs are assigned, they need to be propagated into the network, and the final goal of TrustSec is to enforce policies based on the source and destination SGTs. An SGT is a 16-bit value assigned either statically or dynamically to a user or device. Cisco TrustSec has two methods to propagate SGTs into the network infrastructure:

- Inline tagging
- SGT Exchange Protocol (SXP)

Inline tagging, as the name suggests, is the ability to include the SGT in the data packet to send it to the upstream SGT inline–capable device. When the next-hop device receives the SGT in the data packet, it can either enforce policies based on the SGT or forward the tag upstream. In Figure 2-24, a client connected to SW1 sends traffic to the server connected to SW2, and SW1 adds Employee SGT (value 10) in the Ethernet header before sending it to R1. Because R1 is not configured for enforcement, R1 propagates the SGT in the data packet to SW2. A number of inline-tagging propagation options are available: Ethernet, MACsec, VXLAN, IPsec, DMVPN, and GET VPN. In Cisco SD-Access networks, Cisco leverages a proprietary extension of VXLAN (VXLAN-GPO) so that SGTs are included in the VXLAN header. Because inline tagging is a data plane propagation, this allows large-scale deployments when compared to SXP, and it acts independently of any Layer 3 protocols.

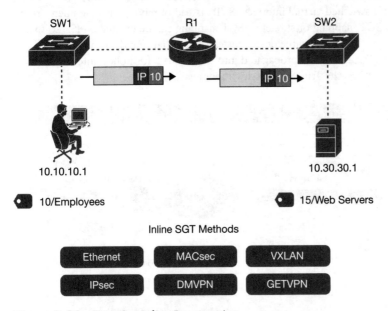

Figure 2-24   *TrustSec Inline Propagation*

In a perfect world, all devices in the campus infrastructure would be capable of inline tagging, but that's not the reality. Networks do have devices that do not understand SGTs or are not inline tagging capable. This leaves control plane propagation as the way to transport the SGT in such scenarios. SGT Exchange Protocol is a TCP-based peering protocol, port 64999, advertising IP-to-SGT mappings across network devices that do not have hardware support for Cisco TrustSec. SXP has a speaker and listener. The speaker sends the IP-to-SGT bindings to the listener over TCP and the listener adds them to the IP-to-SGT mapping database. Shown in Figure 2-25 is an example of SXP with the switches acting as the speakers sending IP-to-SGT mappings to the router, the SXP listener. Cisco ISE can be used as an SXP speaker/listener. ISE pxGrid can also be used for IP-to-SGT mappings for pxGrid clients such as Cisco Firepower, Cisco Web Security Appliance (WSA), and so forth.

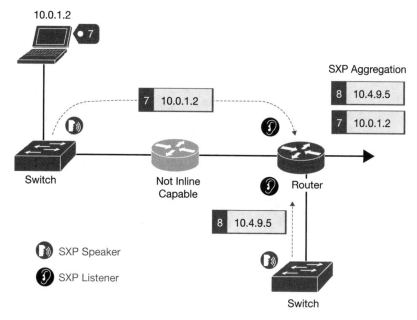

Figure 2-25   *SGT Exchange Protocol*

Enforcement

The primary purpose of SGT assignment and propagation is to use the SGT for enforcement. Enforcement uses source and destination SGTs, and enforcement policies are defined on ISE in the form of SGT ACLs (SGACLs). SGACLs are always based on a source tag and a destination tag. SGACLs on ISE are visualized as a spreadsheet, as shown in Figure 2-26. The highlighted box on the left shows that when traffic tagged Employee, SGT value 4, attempts to reach Contractors, SGT value 5, an SGACL named Anti_Malware is applied. This policy is applied at the egress of the enforcement device where the SGACL has been dynamically downloaded. Enforcement can be performed on infrastructure devices such as switches, routers, or firewalls.

Because of the central management of SGACL policies on Cisco ISE, they are available for all the enforcement devices in the network to be dynamically downloaded, and the policies can be applied consistently regardless of location or network topology. SGACLs, as shown in Figure 2-26, do not include IP addresses, making TrustSec IP version agnostic. Because these group-based policies are not tied to IP addresses, the policy can be applied anywhere, resulting in consistent policy throughout the enterprise. Because policies are tied to SGT instead of IP address, microsegmentation within a VLAN is achievable with Cisco TrustSec. By controlling access within SGTs, microsegmentation reduces the lateral movement of malware between users or servers within a security group, even within the same VLAN.

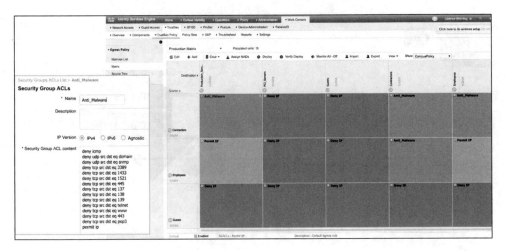

Figure 2-26   *ISE SGT Policy Matrix*

Cisco TrustSec is the key component in software-defined segmentation. All the functions of Cisco TrustSec are centrally managed through Cisco ISE, making the solution scalable and topology agnostic. Network Segmentation is simplified and error-prone through central management of Cisco TrustSec, thereby reducing operational expenses. Cisco TrustSec reduces tremendously the number of ACEs to maintain and removes a great deal of complexity by segmenting the network based on the business roles. In Cisco SD-Access environments where Cisco DNA Center is available, enforcement policies are created and managed from Cisco DNA Center. The upcoming chapters will discuss Cisco TrustSec implementation using Cisco DNA Center in detail.

Summary

Cisco SD-Access is a Cisco Campus Fabric managed by Cisco DNA Center. The need for automation, abstraction, and translating the business intent directly into network configuration is needed now more than ever. Cisco is leading in digitizing the modern networks while lowering operational overhead. This chapter provided insights into the control, data, and policy components of Cisco SD-Access. Every network needs security, but it is typically complicated to implement. Cisco TrustSec, through the use of Cisco ISE with Cisco DNA Center, greatly simplifies the journey of bringing together networking and security in campus networks.

Chapter 3

Introduction to Cisco DNA Center

This chapter covers the following topics:

- **Network Planning and Deployment Trends:** This section covers common network planning deployment processes, both past and present.

- **History of Automation Tools:** This section covers the need for network automation and some of the common ways automation is done today.

- **Cisco DNA Center Overview:** This section introduces Cisco DNA Center and some of the core concepts behind it.

- **Design and Visualization of the Network:** This section covers the various day zero tasks required to give a proper and scalable view of large networks.

- **Network Discovery and Inventory:** This section examines using Cisco DNA Center to intelligently discover and inventory existing networks and devices.

- **Device Configuration and Provisioning:** This section covers using Cisco DNA Center to configure and provision network devices in an automated way.

Network Planning and Deployment Trends

As discussed in the previous chapters, networks are not only constantly growing, but constantly evolving. Today's networks are required to provide services and connectivity to many different types of devices and users. Network architects and engineers have to adapt their processes to meet these new demands.

As networks started to grow in the late 1990s and early 2000s to adapt to new business requirements demanded by the growth of the Internet and connected networks, companies started to adopt a "cookie-cutter" approach to network design to allow for scale and easier repetition of deployments. Common architectures and models, such as Core – Distribution – Access, were adopted to suit this purpose. Organizations also started to standardize the technical details of their networks, including IP addressing, device naming conventions, and configurations.

Development of these designs and standards still involves a lot of manual planning and documentation, using spreadsheets and documents to keep track of standard architectures and topologies. Although using a cookie-cutter approach saves time when deploying multiple sites, the work involved to plan these sites is still cumbersome and prone to human error. A very common practice still in use today is to have a large spreadsheet to track IP address schemes and device configurations, with tabs representing each site or building in the network. Planning a new site involves creating a tab for the site, "reserving" IP subnets from a master tab, and detailing settings and services that are unique to the site. Over time, IP address managers (IPAMs) and design tools have been developed to assist with this process, but these tools are still disparate and do not provide a cohesive view of a network deployment plan. Cisco DNA Center aims to bring a lot of these design and planning functions together into one interface.

History of Automation Tools

Chapter 1, "Today's Networks and the Drivers for Change," summarizes the trends in the industry that are driving the need for increased automation of network deployments. Network automation, however, is not a new concept for network deployments and can mean different things to different people. The age-old (and very common) practice of copying a configuration from a text file or spreadsheet and pasting it into a network device is a form of automation. Although this type of automation doesn't necessarily mitigate the risk inherent in manually inputting device commands, it does make deployment of configurations a lot faster and more efficient. As the demand for even more automation grows, programmers have started to develop scripts that can generate device configurations based on a standard configuration in conjunction with custom variables that an IT operator can enter for each site or device. These automatically generated configurations can then be manually pasted directly into devices, further increasing the efficiency of deploying devices. This process is also vulnerable to risk, as users still must make sure that the custom settings for each device are input correctly and that the resulting commands in the raw configuration file are in the format expected by the device.

Over time, network automation has evolved with the demand, and tools have been created that aim to lower the risk of human error and ease deployments. Some of these newer generation tools, such as the following, are very popular today:

- Ansible

- Puppet

- Chef

- SaltStack

These tools provide a standard input format, such as Yet Another Markup Language (YAML), for the user to enter settings and custom attributes for a site or device. Each of these tools also includes publicly available modules for various vendors and platforms that use the inputted settings and connect to the network device to push the configuration. These tools and modules aim to abstract the configuration interface of the devices from the user to allow for more-efficient and lower-risk deployment, especially across multiple platforms that might each have different configuration interfaces or syntaxes. The largest benefit in efficiency that is realized with these tools is that they are run or deployed from a single server or workstation without the need to manually connect to each device to paste in the configurations.

All of these tools, however, are still text based and have a learning curve that requires some basic knowledge of scripting. Example 3-1 shows a very simple Ansible playbook in YAML format.

Example 3-1   *Ansible Playbook Example*

```
- name: VRF configuration
  hosts: csr
  connection: local
  gather_facts: no
  vars:
    vrf_name: ansible
    vrf_int: loopback111

  tasks:
  - name: Get Login credentials
    include_vars: /mnt/hgfs/vm_shared/ansible/access.yml

  - name: Define Provider
    set_fact:
      provider:
        #host: 192.168.50.105
        host: "{{ access['device_ip'] }}"
        username: "{{ access['username'] }}"
        password: "{{ access['password'] }}"

  - name: REMOVE VRF
    ios_config:
      provider: "{{ provider }}"
      authorize: yes
      lines:
        - no vrf definition {{ vrf_name }}
  #     - no rd 1:1
  #     - route-target export 1:1
  #     - route-target import 1:1
  #     - address-family ipv4
  #     - exit-address-family
      parents: ['vrf definition {{ vrf_name }}']
      match: exact
```

With the growing popularity of automation tools, some network vendors have also introduced GUIs for their platforms. These GUIs provide a unique layer of abstraction between the user and the raw configuration commands on the device. Although this abstraction lowers the risk of configuration errors, the GUIs come with a heavy cost in terms of efficiency. A user still has to access each individual device's GUI and step through various screens and tabs to perform very basic configuration tasks. Figure 3-1 shows the configuration GUI from a Cisco ISR 4331 router.

Figure 3-1   *GUI on Cisco ISR 4331 Router*

Cisco DNA Center aims to bring together the benefits of efficiency and lower risk by combining automation and abstraction in the form of a GUI and intent-based networking concepts to allow users to easily configure and deploy networks.

Cisco DNA Center Overview

In 2015, Cisco introduced the Application Policy Infrastructure Controller Enterprise Module (APIC-EM), representing Cisco's first foray into software-defined networking (SDN) for enterprise networks. APIC-EM provides users with a suite of SDN applications that enables them to deploy features and solutions to network devices using a single centralized GUI-based controller. Some of the core applications in APIC-EM are:

- **Cisco Network Plug and Play (PnP):** PnP allows users to quickly and easily onboard new devices to the network without needing to manually connect to the devices via a console cable, providing true zero-touch deployment (ZTP).

- **Cisco Intelligent WAN (IWAN):** IWAN provides true software-defined WAN capabilities featuring the ability to deploy WAN connectivity across an enterprise with features such as a secure overlay, intelligent routing based on business requirements, quality of service (QoS), and advanced visualization.

- **Cisco Network Visibility Application:** This application provides an automated way to discover devices in an existing network and map them to display a visual and interactive topology of the enterprise, allowing for troubleshooting and detailed device-level access.

- **EasyQoS:** EasyQoS enables network operators to create network QoS policies based on business intent and Cisco Validated Designs. Those policies are then pushed down to network devices automatically across a wide variety of platforms.

As the underlying technologies have evolved more around intent-based networking, Cisco recently (2018) released the next generation of SDN controller: Cisco DNA Center.

Cisco DNA Center is a network management controller for the enterprise that is based on the fundamentals of Cisco Digital Network Architecture (DNA) and intent-based networking (IBN), as described in Chapter 1. Cisco DNA Center provides a "single pane of glass" that enables businesses to deploy, manage, monitor, and troubleshoot their entire enterprise campus and branch networks from one centralized GUI (see Figure 3-2).

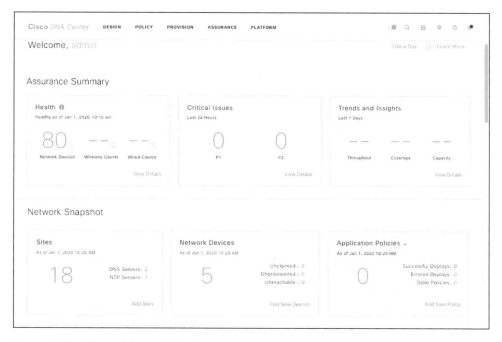

Figure 3-2 *Home Screen of Cisco DNA Center*

Like APIC-EM, Cisco DNA Center features a rich suite of tools and applications covering many IBN solutions. Newer and more powerful versions of some of the applications included in APIC-EM can be found in Cisco DNA Center, along with some new ones:

- **Cisco Software-Defined Access (SD-Access):** Provides a policy-based fabric with full automation and secure segmentation. This simplifies and scales operations while providing complete visibility and delivering new services quickly. It is covered in Chapter 1 and is the main topic of this book.

- **Provisioning:** This tool allows customers to define and push standard network settings and features to their network devices without needing to learn specific device configuration syntax for each platform.

- **Cisco DNA Assurance:** Assurance is a network monitoring and analytics tool that correlates network management data and provides insights into trends, issues, and activities occurring on the network. Assurance is covered in Chapter 9, "Cisco DNA Assurance."

- **Software Image Management (SWIM):** SWIM allows users to select standard versions of network device operating systems and to automatically download, stage, and upgrade the devices in a safe and secure way.

Note   Screenshots in this book were taken with Cisco DNA Center 1.3 and may differ slightly from the currently available version.

The rest of this chapter focuses on some of the fundamental tools and applications in Cisco DNA Center.

Design and Visualization of the Network

The Cisco DNA Center GUI is designed to show network operators a geographical representation of their network on a map. They can then drill down into this representation to view the network at a more granular level, as described in this section.

Site Design and Layout

Companies, like the networks that enable them, come in all different shapes and sizes and span many types of geographic areas. Some companies are global and are segmented by continent or country, while other companies are national or local, and might be segmented by region or city. A network management and monitoring tool must have the flexibility to allow users to define exactly how their network is laid out and displayed in the tool. Cisco DNA Center provides the Design tool for this purpose.

The Design tool is where many of the "day zero" tasks are performed, starting with defining the layout and visualization of the network in the Network Hierarchy section (**Design > Network Hierarchy**). This section enables users to define their network hierarchy in a custom way based on how the company is laid out, using the hierarchical elements areas, buildings, and floors.

This section uses an international company as an example. Suppose that ACME is a global company with locations in most countries around the world. In the Cisco DNA Center Design tool, an operator could define within the default Global site areas for each of the continental regions in which ACME has locations:

- AMERICAS

- APAC

- EMEAR

Within each continental area, the network operator can define areas for each country with an ACME location:

- AMERICAS

  - Brazil

  - Canada

  - United States

- APAC

  - Japan

  - Singapore

- EMEAR

  - Germany

  - United Kingdom

Taking it one step further, ACME has many offices in many cities in the United States, so the network operator could define more granular subareas based on these cities:

- AMERICAS

  - Brazil

  - Canada

  - United States

    - Richardson

    - RTP

    - San Jose

After designating a city, the next most specific element in the Design tool is a building. Whereas areas and subareas in Cisco DNA Center are broad geographical locations that do not have physical addresses, a building must represent an existing physical location. When defining a building in the Design tool, an actual address or latitude/longitude pair is required. When the network operator enters this information, the map on the screen automatically zooms in to where the building is located. Figure 3-3 shows the input window for a building.

Figure 3-3   *Building Input Window*

At the Cisco Systems headquarters in San Jose, California, the campus has many buildings that are numbered and lettered as per the Cisco corporate naming standard. Here is what the hierarchy might look like for Cisco in San Jose with two buildings defined in Cisco DNA Center:

- AMERICAS
  - Brazil
  - Canada
  - United States
    - Richardson
    - RTP
    - San Jose
      - SJC-01
      - SJC-13

The last and most granular element in the Design tool is a floor. At the floor level of the Network Hierarchy section, the network operator can import JPEG or AutoCAD drawings of the floors, or wireless heatmaps from Cisco Prime Infrastructure or Cisco Connected Mobile Experiences (CMX). This gives the operator an accurate visualization of each floor of the network along with wireless coverage. Figure 3-4 shows the input window for a floor along with an imported floor map.

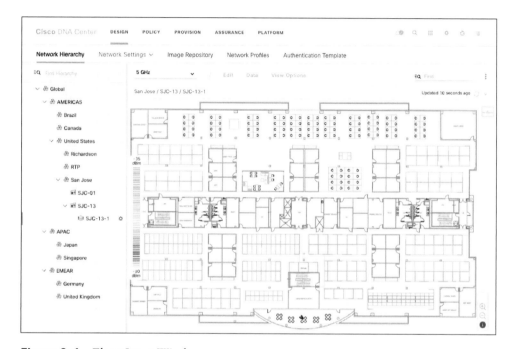

Figure 3-4 *Floor Input Window*

Wrapping up the San Jose example, the final network hierarchy would look like this:

- AMERICAS
    - Brazil
    - Canada
    - United States
        - Richardson
        - RTP
        - San Jose
            - SJC-01
                - SJC-01-1

- SJC-13
  - SJC-13-1
  - SJC-13-2

Figure 3-5 shows the final network hierarchy in Cisco DNA Center.

Figure 3-5   *Final Network Hierarchy*

Having an accurate representation of a company's geographical hierarchy allows for more specific standards or configuration parameters for each area to be used if required. If, for example, a specific version of Cisco IOS XE is required for a particular country or region that is different than the Global standard, the user could specify this version as the "Golden Image" for that particular country and every element underneath it. The concept of defining standard device software images will be covered in Chapter 8, "Advanced Cisco DNA Center." Figure 3-6 describes the concept of inheritance with the network hierarchy. Child areas, buildings, and floors inherit the settings and standards of the parent area.

Figure 3-6   *Inherited Settings Dialog Box*

Network Settings

After creating the network hierarchy in the Design tool, the network operator can move to **Design > Network Settings** to define standard configuration settings for the network. Among the settings available to define in the Network Settings section, shown in Figure 3-7, are the following:

- Authentication, authorization, and accounting (AAA) servers for both network devices and clients

- Dynamic Host Configuration Protocol (DHCP) servers

- Domain Name System (DNS) servers

- Network Time Protocol (NTP) servers

- Syslog servers

- Banner or message of the day

- Command-line interface (CLI) credentials

- Simple Network Management Protocol (SNMP) credentials

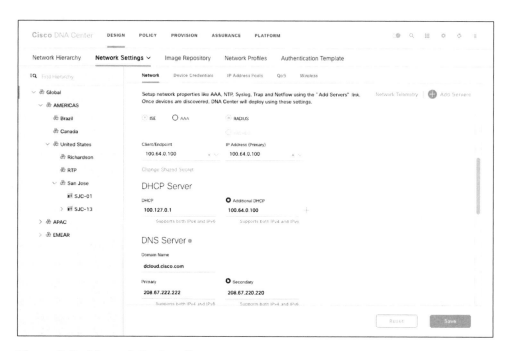

Figure 3-7 *Network Settings Screen*

Wireless Deployments

Deploying a wireless network today can be a cumbersome, multistep process, with the majority of the configuration work performed in the Cisco Wireless LAN Controller (WLC) GUI for a specific building or site. A manual deployment involves logging in to each WLC to manually set wireless parameters on an ad hoc basis and having to create access point (AP) groups to keep everything together. The Cisco DNA Center Design tool can help streamline this process while making it more efficient and reliable.

With Cisco DNA Center, standard wireless network settings such as service set identifiers (SSIDs), access point (AP) radio frequency (RF) profiles, security controls, and guest portals can be defined in the Design tool. These settings are then added to network profiles (**Design > Network Profiles**), which provide a modular way to deploy wireless configurations that might have multiple components (an enterprise SSID and a guest SSID, for example). The final step is to assign network profiles to the sites defined in the previous section. When a WLC is later provisioned to a site in the Provision tool, discussed later in this chapter, Cisco DNA Center automatically pushes the configuration components from the network profile that is also assigned to the site. Figure 3-8 shows the configuration screen for common wireless settings and parameters, and Figures 3-9 and 3-10 show an example of assigning and editing network profiles in the Network Profiles section.

Figure 3-8 *Wireless Settings in Cisco DNA Center*

Figure 3-9   *Network Profile Site Selection*

Figure 3-10   *Network Profile Summary Screen*

One benefit to wireless deployments with Cisco DNA Center is that it provides a central controller to store an entire enterprise's wireless settings and profiles, while still harnessing the power of the hierarchical site design to support a flexible, distributed, and custom deployment. SSIDs, security policies for both enterprise and guest wireless, and RF profiles can be defined globally and still customized for regions or areas, if needed.

Defining these wireless settings and profiles can be a day-zero task or can be done at any point thereafter, which would significantly save time for a wireless deployment in a new building. Prior to the building opening, the wireless settings could be staged, and once the WLCs and APs were onboarded in Cisco DNA Center and assigned to the new site, they would be automatically configured with the SSIDs and other parameters.

Network Discovery and Inventory

Cisco DNA Center is primarily a network controller and orchestration tool, and as such it requires visibility to the network and devices that it orchestrates. This section covers the methods that can be used to provide this visibility to Cisco DNA Center via discovery of existing network devices and the tracking of the devices in the Cisco DNA Center inventory.

Discovery Tool

To take advantage of Cisco DNA Center, devices must be added to its inventory. New, not yet configured devices can be automatically configured and added to Cisco DNA Center through the PnP tool using zero-touch provisioning (ZTP), which is discussed in Chapter 8. Existing devices can be added to the inventory manually by using the GUI or by importing a comma-separated values (CSV) file; however, the fastest way to add existing devices is to use the Discovery tool, which you can access by clicking the Tools icon (the three-by-three grid of squares) at the top right of the Cisco DNA Center home screen.

The Discovery Dashboard shows statistics on past discoveries, already discovered devices, and other information about Discovery activity. Figure 3-11 shows the Discovery Dashboard.

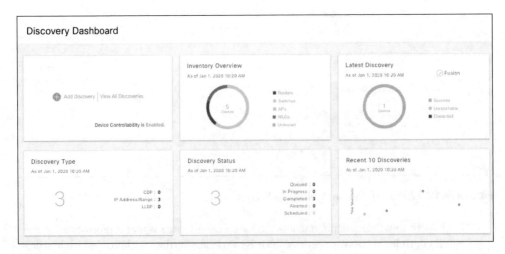

Figure 3-11 *Discovery Dashboard in Cisco DNA Center*

The automated discovery process can use three different methods to find devices:

■ Cisco Discovery Protocol (CDP)

■ Link Layer Discovery Protocol (LLDP)

■ IP address range

Using CDP or LLDP to do a discovery can possibly produce unpredictable results if not limited in scope, as even non-Cisco devices that are not supported by Cisco DNA Center may be discovered. Performing a discovery by IP address range allows the greatest control over the scope of the discovery. Provide a starting IP address and ending IP address, and Cisco DNA Center attempts to reach devices on every IP address in the given range. Figure 3-12 shows a typical discovery job configuration using IP address range.

Figure 3-12 *Discovery Job Configuration*

In order for Cisco DNA Center to properly discover and add each device to its inventory, it needs to be provided with credentials to be used for device access. At a minimum, CLI (SSH/Telnet) and SNMPv2 Read Only credentials must be provided for the discovery job to run. Multiple credentials can be added to Cisco DNA Center, and a user can select credentials to use for a given discovery job. Figure 3-13 shows an example of adding credentials to a discovery job.

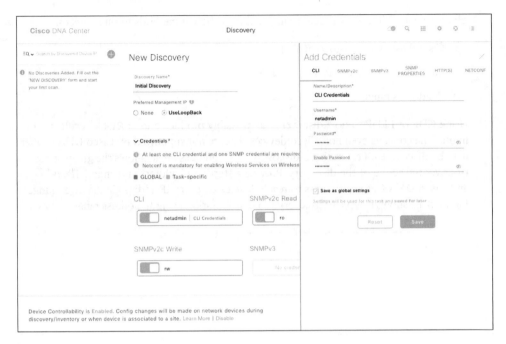

Figure 3-13 *Discovery Credentials Input Screen*

By default, Cisco DNA Center has the Device Controllability feature enabled. Device Controllability pushes some basic configuration commands to newly discovered devices to assist with data collection and device tracking. This configuration varies between platforms, but two common scenarios are a WLC that receives Streaming Telemetry settings for wireless network assurance and a Catalyst 9000 Series Switch that has IP Device Tracking (IPDT) configured on each of its ports. Cisco DNA Center also configures Cisco TrustSec (CTS) credentials on each device that it discovers if this feature is enabled.

You can disable Device Controllability prior to running a discovery, which prevents any configuration from being pushed. Figure 3-14 shows a description of Device Controllability.

Figure 3-15 shows results of a successful discovery job completion.

Inventory

After a device is discovered, it is displayed in the Inventory tool, which you can access via the Provision link on the Cisco DNA Center home screen. When a device is in Inventory, Cisco DNA Center performs a full "sync" on the device every 6 hours (360 minutes) by default. This sync process connects to the device and gathers data via **show** commands and SNMP, so that Cisco DNA Center has an accurate view of the state of the device and its configuration. Cisco DNA Center also connects to network devices on a more frequent basis to collect data and statistics for Cisco DNA Assurance, which is covered further in Chapter 9.

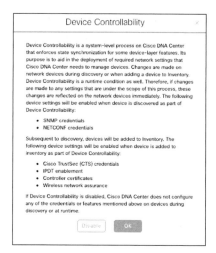

Figure 3-14 *Device Controllability in Cisco DNA Center*

Figure 3-15 *Discovery Job Results*

Cisco DNA Center automatically attempts to determine the device's role in the network after it is discovered. The predefined roles that are available are CORE, DISTRIBUTION, BORDER, and ACCESS. These roles can be used to designate standard device images using the SWIM tool; they also determine the layout of the Topology view, which is discussed in Chapter 8. These roles can be changed by the user at any time.

The Inventory tool displays a centralized list of all the network devices that Cisco DNA Center is aware of. The view of this list can be narrowed down by site, custom filter, or device type. The Inventory list provides basic but useful information about each device, including

- Host name

- IP address

- Site

- Reachability status

- Software version

- Platform

- Serial number

Figure 3-16 shows an example of the information that is displayed in the Inventory tool.

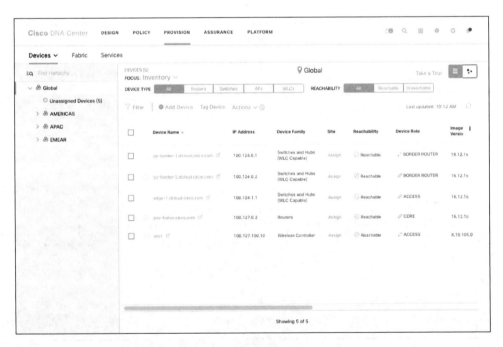

Figure 3-16 *Inventory Display in Cisco DNA Center*

In the past, network device inventory details were traditionally kept in large spreadsheets and would need to be updated manually as devices were replaced, relocated, or upgraded. More recently, numerous tools are available to keep track of network device inventories.

Cisco DNA Center brings together the intelligence and flexibility of the discovery and inventory tools to provide current information in an automatically updated list of devices and their statuses.

Device Configuration and Provisioning

As discussed in Chapter 1 and the previous sections, making device-by-device manual network changes not only is inefficient but comes with risk. A network operator must connect via console port, SSH, or Telnet to each device and enter multiple configuration commands or paste generated configuration sections one at a time. A typical enterprise also has network change windows to contend with, which means scheduling operators to perform these changes off-hours or during weekends. In some cases, many changes must be pushed to the network, and these change windows might not allow enough time for all devices to be configured properly if done manually. Further, it's very easy for a network operator to inadvertently log in to the incorrect device before pushing a configuration or make a typo in a command or entry that might not be discovered until a later network outage. These types of outages can cause disruptions to lines of business and cost companies money and resources in both lost business and time spent troubleshooting.

Cisco DNA Center solves these issues by providing the Provision tool for an operator to easily and quickly push configuration changes to multiple devices simultaneously. Changes can be pushed immediately or even scheduled in advance to take place during a change window.

Selection of devices for provisioning changes is very easy and flexible. Devices can be selected at any level of the network hierarchy, by device type, or even by using a custom filter or tag.

The Provision tool makes changes based on settings that are provided in the Network Settings section of the Design tool, including standard network parameters or wireless profiles. The Provision tool can also perform software upgrades with the SWIM tool discussed in Chapter 8.

Provisioning a device in Cisco DNA Center is accomplished with just a few clicks and is composed of the following tasks:

- Assign a device to a site in the network hierarchy.

- Select any customized templates and variables, which are covered in Chapter 8.

- Review the summary of changes that will be pushed.

- Select whether to push the changes immediately or to schedule the push for a later time.

Figures 3-17, 3-18, and 3-19 show these phases of the provisioning workflow.

Figure 3-17   *Provision Process: Assigning Devices to Sites*

Figure 3-18   *Provision Process: Summary Display*

Following a successful configuration change pushed by the Provision tool, Cisco DNA Center either displays a message confirming a successful change or informs the user if there were any problems.

Figure 3-19   *Provision Process: Provision Schedule Input*

Summary

This chapter provided a high-level overview of Cisco DNA Center and its features and the evolution in automation tools and practices that preceded it. This chapter described many of the more powerful Cisco DNA Center applications, along with the associated benefits such as efficiency and lower risk through automation and the capability to visualize the entire network in a hierarchical fashion. This chapter also covered the day-zero tasks and the subsequent workflows that can be used to discover devices and provision them with a configuration.

Summary

Chapter 4

Cisco Software-Defined Access Fundamentals

This chapter covers the following Cisco Software-Defined Access topics:

- **Network Topologies:** This section covers the various physical network topologies that are supported in a Cisco SD-Access network.

- **Cisco Software-Defined Access Underlay:** This section discusses the role of the underlay in Cisco SD-Access and describes the manual and automated configuration options.

- **Wireless LAN Controllers and Access Points in Cisco Software-Defined Access:** This section covers Cisco Wireless LAN Controller placement and wireless operation in a Cisco SD-Access network.

- **Shared Services:** This section covers Cisco SD-Access connectivity to services that are shared with the rest of the network, such as DHCP (Dynamic Host Configuration Protocol), DNS (Domain Name System), and NTP (Network Time Protocol).

- **Transits Networks:** This section covers the transit options in Cisco SD-Access for connectivity to the outside world.

- **Fabric Creation:** This section covers the design and creation of a Cisco SD-Access fabric.

- **Fabric Device Roles:** This section discusses the device roles in a Cisco SD-Access network.

- **Host Onboarding:** This section covers the authentication and IP pool options for onboarding hosts to a Cisco SD-Access fabric and demonstrates how to override these settings on a per-interface basis.

Network Topologies

Unlike their data center counterparts, campus network topologies come in a variety of different shapes and sizes. Although many campus topologies are based on the traditional three-layer model of core, distribution, and access, the building layout and cabling considerations typically mandate customization of how devices are cabled to each other and customization of the physical layout of the entire network. Some campus networks use a star configuration with a collapsed core, with all access switches connected into a large core switch. Other networks, such as those in tall buildings, daisy-chain access switches together, leading to a distribution switch or core switch.

Figure 4-1 shows a typical network topology based on the traditional three-layer model of core, distribution, and access.

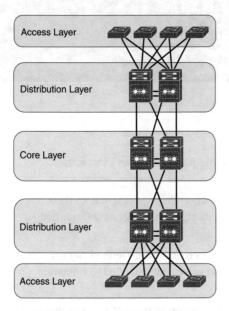

Figure 4-1   *Three-Layer Network Topology*

Because its fabric is an overlay-based solution, Cisco Software-Defined Access is topology agnostic, meaning it can run with any type of physical topology so long as there is Layer 3 IP reachability between fabric nodes. This includes daisy-chaining topologies where fabric edge nodes are connected to other fabric edge nodes that provide connectivity upstream toward fabric borders and control planes. In other topologies where the fabric edge nodes are many physical hops away from fabric border and control plane nodes, there may be any number of intermediate nodes in between that provide the Layer 3 reachability. Intermediate nodes are discussed later in this chapter.

Cisco Software-Defined Access Underlay

As discussed in Chapter 2, "Introduction to Cisco Software-Defined Access," the underlay in a Cisco SD-Access fabric should provide fast, robust, and efficient reachability between all fabric nodes in the network. The underlay configuration should also be very simple and static, with the focus being on resiliency and speed, as its role is very critical to fabric stability. The underlay should also provide for efficient load balancing across redundant links between the devices. There are two ways to configure a Cisco SD-Access underlay: manually or using LAN Automation.

Manual Underlay

As discussed, the role of the underlay is to route packets between fabric nodes as quickly and efficiently as possible. The underlay should be built completely with Layer 3 links to avoid potential Layer 2 limitations such as loops and spanning-tree blocked ports. This is typically accomplished using a routing protocol, such as Open Shortest Path First (OSPF), Intermediate System to Intermediate System (IS-IS), or Enhanced Interior Gateway Routing Protocol (EIGRP), and multiple physical links between devices in the underlay for redundancy and increased bandwidth. The links between devices should be configured as point-to-point interfaces (with /30 or /31 subnet masks), and the routing protocol should use a load-balancing mechanism such as equal-cost multipath (ECMP) for optimal bandwidth usage.

It is also important to advertise each fabric node's /32 loopback interface address explicitly in the routing protocol without summarization, as these interface addresses are used as a destination field in each fabric packet's header, and in some cases, reachability can occur only with a specific /32 route. Fabric encapsulation is discussed in detail in Chapter 6, "Cisco Software-Defined Access Operation and Troubleshooting."

Other routing protocol features such as aggressive timers and Bidirectional Forwarding Detection (BFD) can be used to decrease failover and convergence times.

In Example 4-1, IS-IS is configured as the routing protocol, and BFD is enabled on the interfaces to other devices.

Example 4-1   *Excerpt from Sample Manual Underlay Configuration*

```
interface Loopback0
 description Fabric Underlay RID - do not change
 ip address 100.124.0.1 255.255.255.255
 ip router isis
!


interface GigabitEthernet1/0/13
 description To Border-2 te1/0/13
 no switchport
 ip address 100.125.0.33 255.255.255.252
 ip router isis
 bfd interval 300 min_rx 300 multiplier 3
 no bfd echo


!


interface GigabitEthernet1/0/21
 description To edge1 te1/0/23
 no switchport
```

```
ip address 100.125.0.1 255.255.255.252
ip router isis
bfd interval 300 min_rx 300 multiplier 3
no bfd echo

router isis
 net 49.0000.0011.0111.0010.00
 is-type level-2-only
 router-id Loopback0
 domain-password cisco
 metric-style transition
 log-adjacency-changes
 bfd all-interfaces
```

Automated Underlay: LAN Automation

Cisco DNA Center provides an automated workflow called LAN Automation that enables companies to build their Cisco SD-Access underlay in greenfield environments. LAN Automation enables a company to connect a new out-of-the-box switch and have it automatically onboarded and configured to be part of the company's Cisco SD-Access underlay. LAN Automation also automatically upgrades the software on the switch to match the company's "Golden Image" version if required. No manual configuration is necessary via console or Secure Shell (SSH) on the switch when using LAN Automation. After onboarding is complete, the switch can be fully managed and configured from Cisco DNA Center and assigned to a fabric role. This feature greatly shortens the time, effort, and risk when deploying new switches in a Cisco SD-Access network.

LAN Automation requires an existing configured device in the fabric to be used as a seed (along with an optional peer) device as the basis for device discovery and automatic configuration. The seed device does not have to be part of the fabric already or have a complex configuration on it. It only needs to be fully reachable by Cisco DNA Center and already discovered and in the Cisco DNA Center Inventory. LAN Automation then utilizes the Cisco PnP (Plug and Play) Agent, which is enabled by default on most Cisco devices, to facilitate the process for each new device.

Figure 4-2 shows a LAN Automation topology with one seed device and three new switches to be onboarded.

LAN Automation requires the following fields (other than the optional field) to be completed before starting the process:

- **Primary Device:** An existing device in the network (and in Cisco DNA Center) to use as the LAN Automation seed device.

- **Peer Device (optional):** A second existing device that can be used to get a more accurate view of the network topology.

- **Primary Device Ports:** The interface(s) on the primary device that the new devices are connected to. Multiple interfaces can be selected to use for the device discovery process.

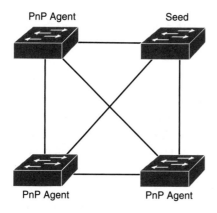

PnP Agent   Seed

PnP Agent   PnP Agent

Figure 4-2 *Sample LAN Automation Topology*

- **Discovered Device Site:** The site that newly discovered devices are assigned to after discovery.

- **IP Pool:** An IP pool that has been configured in the Design tool of Cisco DNA Center (introduced in Chapter 3, "Introduction to Cisco DNA Center"). This pool will be subnetted and the addresses will be assigned to the appropriate uplink and downlink physical interfaces as /31 subnets as well as /32 loopback interfaces on each new device. The IP pool configured here must have at least 126 addresses available (a /25 network mask).

Figure 4-3 shows the LAN Automation screen with the preceding settings filled in.

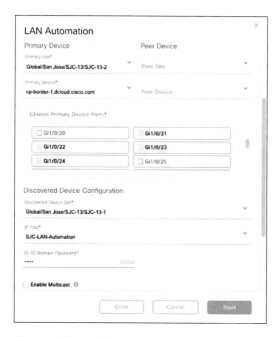

Figure 4-3 *LAN Automation Options Screen*

Note   As of Cisco DNA Center version 1.3, LAN Automation discovers devices up to two layers deep below the seed device.

The LAN Automation process consists of two phases. The first phase begins when the user inputs the required information on the LAN Automation screen and clicks Start. During the first phase, a temporary configuration is applied to the seed device to facilitate the PnP process and then the initial discovery of new devices in the network begins. The length of time that this process takes depends on the network speed and number of new devices to be discovered and configured, but you should expect it to take a minimum of ten minutes to discover and initially configure all new devices.

Figure 4-4 shows the first phase of LAN Automation with three devices discovered and in a Completed state. The process remains in this state until it is stopped.

Figure 4-4   *LAN Automation Status During Phase One*

Note   Because Cisco DNA Center does not know the exact number of devices that will be discovered, the first phase of LAN Automation runs indefinitely until you click Stop in the LAN Automation Status dialog box, which you should do after the number of expected network devices are discovered. This action automatically starts phase two of the LAN Automation process.

During phase two, a final configuration based on the site's network settings is applied to the new devices, including a software upgrade and reload, if required. The temporary configuration applied in phase one is also removed from the seed device. Again, the length of this process depends on the number of newly discovered devices but typically takes a minimum of ten minutes to complete. Once this phase is complete, the LAN Automation process automatically ends and all newly discovered devices are placed in the Cisco DNA Center Inventory and fully configured to be part of the Cisco SD-Access underlay.

Figure 4-5 shows a fully completed LAN Automation Status screen with three devices discovered and fully onboarded. Note that the status shows as Completed.

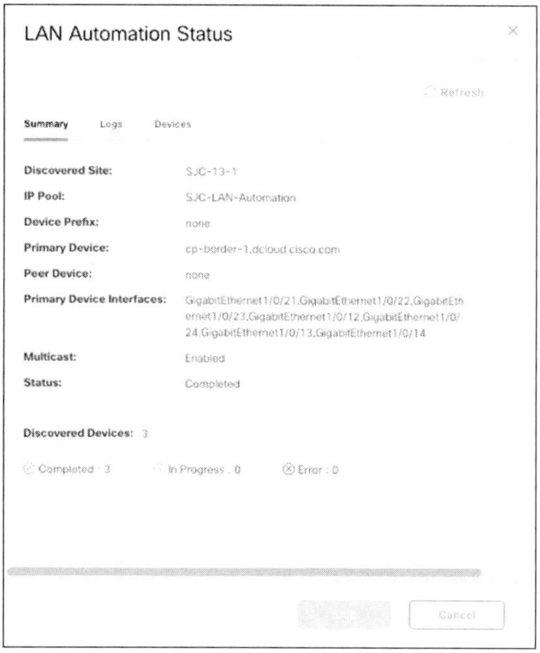

Figure 4-5 *LAN Automation Status Completed Screen*

Example 4-2 is a configuration excerpt following a successful LAN Automation process showing the configuration that is pushed to the newly onboarded switches.

Example 4-2 *Excerpt from Sample LAN Automation Configuration*

```
interface Loopback0
 description Fabric Node Router ID
 ip address 100.124.128.141 255.255.255.255
 ip pim sparse-mode
 ip router isis
 clns mtu 1400
!
```

```
interface GigabitEthernet1/0/21
 description Fabric Physical Link
 no switchport
 dampening
 ip address 100.124.128.148 255.255.255.254
 ip pim sparse-mode
 ip router isis
 ip lisp source-locator Loopback0
 load-interval 30
 bfd interval 100 min_rx 100 multiplier 3
 no bfd echo
 clns mtu 1400
 isis network point-to-point
!
interface GigabitEthernet1/0/22
 description Fabric Physical Link
 no switchport
 dampening
 ip address 100.124.128.146 255.255.255.254
 ip pim sparse-mode
 ip router isis
 ip lisp source-locator Loopback0
 load-interval 30
 bfd interval 100 min_rx 100 multiplier 3
 no bfd echo
 clns mtu 1400
 isis network point-to-point
!
router isis
 net 49.0000.1001.2412.8141.00
 domain-password cisco
 metric-style wide
 log-adjacency-changes
 nsf ietf
 bfd all-interfaces
```

Figure 4-6 shows the Cisco DNA Center Inventory tool with the newly discovered and onboarded devices assigned to the site.

Figure 4-6 *Cisco DNA Center Inventory Following LAN Automation*

Wireless LAN Controllers and Access Points in Cisco Software-Defined Access

The Cisco Wireless LAN Controller (WLC) plays a special role in a Cisco SD-Access network, as it physically lives outside of the fabric underlay yet still provides control channel capabilities to fabric-enabled access points (APs) and service set identifiers (SSIDs).

> **Note** The exception to this is the Cisco Catalyst 9800 Embedded Wireless feature that is available for the Cisco Catalyst 9300, 9400, and 9500 Series Switch platforms. This feature supports only fabric-enabled SSIDs and runs on switches inside the fabric.

Fabric-enabled access points connect to fabric edge switches and use the underlay to establish a Control and Provisioning of Wireless Access Points (CAPWAP) tunnel with the WLC. This tunnel carries control channel information, including wireless host reachability information, from the APs to the WLC, which is in turn advertised to the fabric control plane node in the fabric. AP connectivity in Cisco SD-Access is discussed further in Chapter 5, "Cisco Identity Services Engine with Cisco DNA Center."

Figure 4-7 shows a typical Cisco SD-Access topology with WLC placement outside of the fabric and wireless access points connecting to fabric edge nodes.

Data plane (or endpoint) traffic is sent directly from the AP to the fabric edge switch so that traffic stays local to the fabric, where it is subject to the same policy and flow as applied to wired endpoint traffic. This also increases the efficiency and performance of wired-to-wireless communication, because wireless traffic is no longer centralized at the WLC as it is in traditional wireless environments.

Fabric access points and WLCs can also run in hybrid configurations, supporting both fabric-enabled SSIDs and traditional centralized SSIDs on the same hardware. This setup is useful for migration scenarios where legacy SSIDs are still required for a set of clients. Provisioning of non-fabric SSIDs in Cisco DNA Center is discussed in Chapter 3.

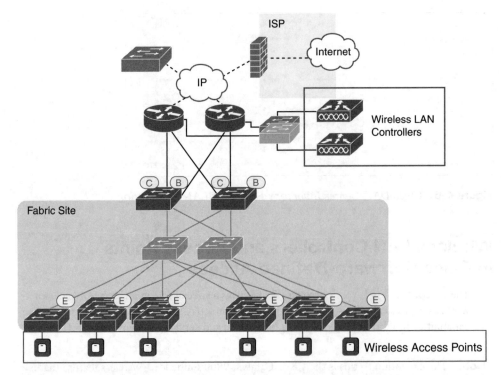

Figure 4-7 *Cisco SD-Access Topology with Wireless Infrastructure*

Shared Services

Shared services in a Cisco SD-Access environment are any services that are common to the enterprise and typically live outside of the Cisco SD-Access fabric but still need to communicate with hosts in the fabric on all virtual networks (VNs). Some common examples of shared services are

- **Dynamic Host Configuration Protocol (DHCP):** Provides IP addresses and other settings to hosts on a network using a centralized database

- **Domain Name System (DNS):** Provides name-resolution services to hosts in a network

- **Network Time Protocol (NTP):** Provides accurate time information for hosts and network devices to synchronize their system clocks

Figure 4-8 is an example of shared services placement in a typical enterprise. These services are in the data center and outside of the Cisco SD-Access fabric.

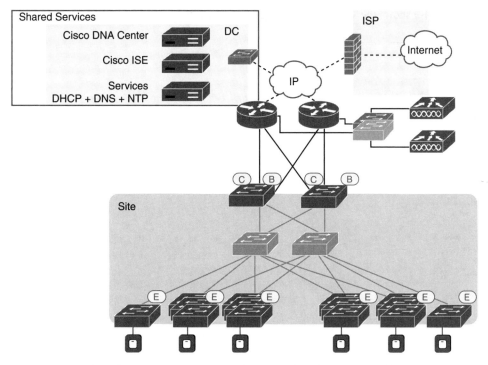

Figure 4-8 *Shared Services in a Cisco Software-Defined Access Topology*

Shared services typically need to be reachable from all networks, including the underlay, so an intermediate device or connection point is required outside the fabric to facilitate these connections. Cisco SD-Access uses the concept of a *fusion router* for this purpose, which lives outside of the fabric and is connected directly to the border node(s). The fusion router is discussed later in this chapter.

Transit Networks

Transit (or peer) networks in Cisco SD-Access define the type of networks that exist outside of the fabric and that are connected to the fabric border node(s). The actual network medium could be a WAN in the case of a branch, or a data center LAN connection in the case of a large campus. Regardless of the medium, there are two types of transits that can be defined with Cisco SD-Access: IP-Based and SD-Access.

IP-Based Transit

IP-Based transits provide traditional IP connectivity from the outside world to the fabric and vice versa. To maintain macro-segmentation outside of the fabric, the connections should use VRF-lite for traffic separation. Traffic is typically routed from the border to the transit next-hop router using external Border Gateway Protocol (eBGP), but any routing protocol can be used so long as it is VRF-aware, as next-hop peers are needed across each of the VNs/VRFs as well as the underlay.

Figure 4-9 shows the Transit/Peer Network configuration screen for an IP-Based transit.

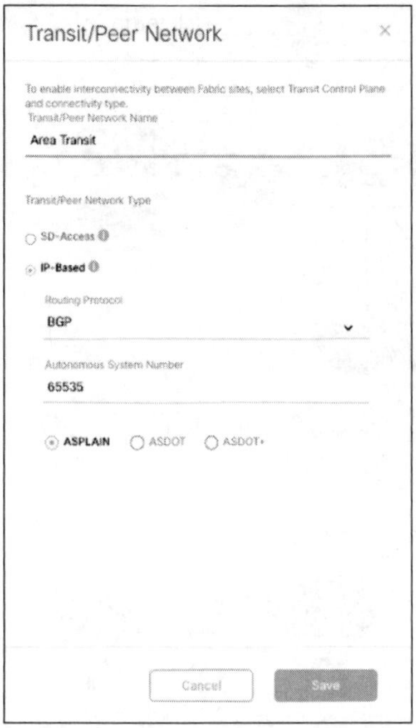

Figure 4-9   *IP-Based Transit Creation Screen*

An important consideration for IP-based transits is that the SGTs (Scalable Group Tags) are removed from packets exiting the border, which impacts micro-segmentation policies. Options for extending policies outside of the fabric using Cisco TrustSec SGT Exchange Protocol (SXP) are covered in Chapter 7, "Advanced Cisco Software-Defined Access Topics."

SD-Access Transit

SD-Access transits are a special type of transit unique to Cisco SD-Access and provide a way for companies to extend their connections between separate fabric sites while maintaining both macro- and micro-segmentation end to end. This type of transit is used with the Cisco Software-Defined Access for Distributed Campus feature, which is discussed in Chapter 7.

The actual configuration for both of these transits is done on the fabric borders and can be completed either manually or by using border automation, discussed later in this chapter.

Fabric Creation

Fabric creation in Cisco DNA Center is a very simple process and initially requires only three parameters: fabric name, fabric location, and a selection of which VN(s) to make part of the fabric.

Fabric Location

You need to give careful consideration to overall fabric design and the selection of the fabric location, as these decisions determine the scope and size of the Cisco SD-Access fabric and which devices are available for it based on the device locations chosen during provisioning. In general, a building would be one fabric, which would include all building access switches, endpoints, users, and wireless access points. However, a campus with high-speed connectivity between buildings could also be defined as a single fabric, depending on the scale, device/user counts, and building survivability requirements.

For example, a university with six buildings and high-speed links between each building could be defined as a single fabric as long as the number of devices is within the supported scale. However, if some of the buildings have dedicated external high-speed links to a data center or to the Internet that must remain available during an outage, then those buildings should be defined as separate fabric locations. This consideration is necessary because fabric node roles, such as the control plane and border, are shared within a single fabric and are required for proper operation of the fabric. If connectivity is lost to any of these devices, the fabric operation degrades. In this example, a better alternative would be to define each building as a fabric site and then provide end-to-end fabric connectivity between them using the Cisco Software-Defined Access for Distributed Campus feature, mentioned previously and discussed further in Chapter 7.

Figure 4-10 shows the Add Fabric configuration screen with the San Jose area selected as the US West fabric location. Any devices that are assigned to the San Jose area and its child areas, buildings, or floors can be part of this fabric.

Figure 4-10 *Add Fabric Location Configuration Screen*

Fabric VNs

Figure 4-11 shows the Add Fabric VN selection screen with two virtual networks selected. New VNs can be added after the fabric is created, but a fabric must start with a minimum of one VN.

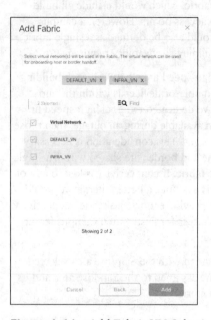

Figure 4-11 *Add Fabric VN Selection Screen*

> **Note**   Virtual network (VN) creation and concepts are discussed in Chapter 5.

Fabric Device Roles

There are four device roles in a Cisco SD-Access fabric:

- **Control plane node:** Provides endpoint reachability and host tracking information to the other fabric nodes
- **Border node:** Provides connectivity in and out of the fabric
- **Fabric edge node:** Provides physical connectivity to endpoints and access points
- **Intermediate node (optional):** Provides basic Layer 3 connectivity between other fabric nodes

This section describes these device roles in detail along with the automation, design considerations, and connectivity options for the Cisco SD-Access fabric.

Figure 4-12 shows a typical high-level Cisco SD-Access architecture with the various device roles.

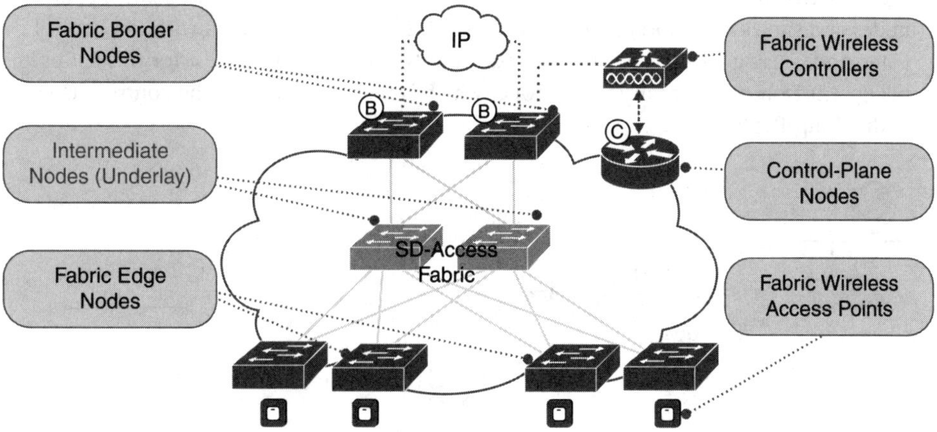

Figure 4-12   *Cisco SD-Access Device Roles*

Control Plane

The control plane node in a Cisco SD-Access fabric is an endpoint registration and database system providing reachability information to other fabric nodes for all endpoints in the fabric. It essentially the brain of the fabric. The control plane node also tracks endpoint movement to allow for host mobility required in wireless networks. All fabric nodes communicate with the control plane node, both to register new endpoints as they are onboarded and to request endpoint reachability information to facilitate traffic between nodes.

For high availability and redundancy, multiple control plane nodes are supported in a Cisco SD-Access fabric. The maximum number of control planes depends on the types of endpoints in the fabric. For a wired-only implementation, up to six control planes can be used per fabric. Wireless-only environments and mixed wireless and wired environments support a maximum of two control planes.

As discussed in Chapter 2, Location Identifier Separation Protocol (LISP) is the control plane protocol for Cisco SD-Access. Although the LISP configuration is abstracted by Cisco DNA Center automation, from a technical perspective, the control plane acts as a LISP Map-Server (MS) and Map-Resolver (MR).

When an endpoint connects to a fabric edge node and authenticates to the network, the fabric edge sends a LISP Map-Register message to all control plane nodes containing the MAC address and IP address of the endpoint. The control plane(s) then creates an entry for the endpoint in its LISP mapping database, which associates this information with the fabric edge. When an endpoint needs to reach another endpoint in the fabric, its connected fabric edge sends to a control plane node a LISP Map-Request message asking for the location of the destination endpoint. The control plane replies with a LISP Map-Reply message containing the location of the destination endpoint's connected fabric edge.

Figure 4-13 illustrates the communication flow between fabric edge and control plane nodes and shows an endpoint with IP address 10.2.0.1 being registered with the control plane nodes using a Map-Register message, followed by a Map-Request for this endpoint being sent from another fabric edge node, which is then answered by the control plane with a Map-Reply.

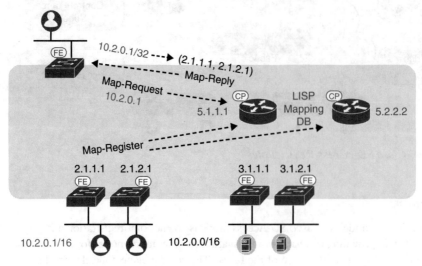

Figure 4-13 *Control Plane and Fabric Edge Communication Example*

> **Note**   The technical and complete traffic flow details of Cisco SD-Access along with examples are discussed in Chapter 6.

Fabric Borders

The fabric border node in a Cisco SD-Access network is responsible for routing traffic in and out of a fabric. Any traffic that needs to exit the fabric toward the Internet, a data center, or another fabric must pass through a fabric border. Three types of fabric borders can be configured in Cisco SD-Access:

- **Rest of company border (or internal border):** A border that routes traffic from the fabric destined for networks inside of a company or enterprise, such as a data center or a different site. The internal border has these routes in its routing table and registers them explicitly with the control plane.

- **Outside world border (or external border):** A border that routes traffic from the fabric destined for any unknown addresses, including the Internet. It also is the gateway of last resort. The external border does not register any routes with the control plane, but instead functions as a LISP Proxy Egress Tunnel Router (PETR).

- **Anywhere border (or internal and external border):** A border that combines the functionality and purpose of both the internal border and the external border types. For internal destinations, it registers routes with the control plane, similar to how an internal border does. For external destinations, it functions as a LISP PETR.

Details of LISP operation on a border are discussed in Chapter 6.

Proper border selection is crucial for successful operation of a fabric, and you must give careful consideration when designing the fabric and selecting the border types. That said, most Cisco SD-Access implementations require only external borders, as they have only one path in and out of the fabric. Other, more complex networks with multiple egress paths may need a combination of border types to ensure efficient traffic flows.

Figure 4-14 is an example of a Cisco SD-Access fabric in a large campus with a connection to the data center and internal WAN and a different connection to the Internet. This fabric has internal borders for the data center/WAN connection and external borders for the Internet connection.

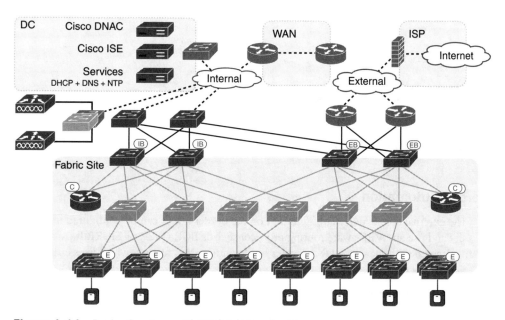

Figure 4-14 *Large Campus with Multiple Border Types*

In Cisco DNA Center version 1.3 and higher, the border configuration workflow reflects a different terminology for border types than the ones defined in the previous list, and instead presents the options Default to All Virtual Networks and Do Not Import External.

Table 4-1 shows the appropriate configuration options for the border types in Cisco DNA Center.

Table 4-1   *Border Type Selection*

	Default to All Virtual Networks	**Do Not Import External Routes**
Internal Border	—	—
External Border	✓	✓
Anywhere Border	✓	—

Figure 4-15 shows the border configuration dialog box with the check boxes enabled for an external border. It also shows some of the options required for border automation, which is discussed next.

Figure 4-15   *Border Configuration Dialog Box in Cisco DNA Center*

Border Automation

The external connectivity configuration on the border nodes can be configured manually and use any VRF-aware routing protocol such as BGP, OSPF, or EIGRP. It can also be automated with the Cisco DNA Center border automation feature, which uses eBGP as the routing protocol.

The following parameters are required for the border automation workflow:

- **Local Autonomous Number:** The BGP autonomous system (AS) number to configure on the borders.

- **IP Pool:** An IP pool that has been reserved in the Design tool of Cisco DNA Center. This pool will be subnetted into /30 subnets and the addresses will be assigned to switch virtual interfaces (SVIs) on the border that are created during the automation.

- **Transit/Peer Network:** The transit network, which can be either an IP-based transit or SD-Access transit (as discussed earlier in this chapter).

- **External Interface:** The physical interface on the border device that provides connectivity to the transit. This interface will be configured as an Ethernet trunk by Cisco DNA Center.

- **Virtual Network (VN):** The VN or virtual routing and forwarding (VRF) instance that border automation should be configured for. For each VN selected, an SVI will be created and an eBGP peering statement will be configured that points to the next hop outside the border.

Multiple external interfaces and VNs can be selected during border automation, allowing for flexible connection options on or across borders. Figure 4-16 shows the border automation configuration dialog box with external interface and VN selection options. You can add additional VNs to border automation later, after they are created.

Figure 4-16 *Border Automation Configuration Dialog Box in Cisco DNA Center*

As of this writing, border automation is supported only on the border devices themselves, and automation is not done on the next-hop external device, which means that network operators need to configure the corresponding addresses and eBGP peering statements manually. This is because the next-hop device could be any type of routing or switching platform, provided that it supports VRFs and BGP. This is discussed further in the "Fusion Router" section later in this chapter.

INFRA_VN is a special VN in Cisco SD-Access that exists in the global routing table (GRT) and does not correspond to a VRF on the fabric devices, providing connectivity access to wireless access points. This topic is discussed further in Chapter 7.

Border and Control Plane Collocation

The border and control plane functions in Cisco SD-Access can be run on any supported platform listed on the Cisco SD-Access Product Compatibility matrix. Although these functions can exist on separate devices, most implementations run them on the same device in a collocated configuration, typically as a pair for redundancy and high availability.

Figure 4-17 shows the border configuration dialog box for device cp-border-1 being configured as both a border node and a control plane.

Figure 4-17 *Border Configuration Dialog Box Options for a Collocated Border Node/Control Plane Configuration*

Running the border node and control plane in a collocated architecture simplifies the network design along with the configuration and troubleshooting. In larger network environments with many endpoints or different border types, running the functions on dedicated devices is recommended for scale purposes.

Figure 4-18 shows a typical Cisco SD-Access topology with a collocated border node and control plane configuration.

Fabric Edge Nodes

Fabric edge nodes provide access-layer connectivity to endpoints, such as desktop computers, wired laptops, IoT devices, and telephones. Fabric edge nodes also provide connectivity to wireless APs, which in turn provide access to wireless endpoints. Another type of device that connects to a fabric edge node are specific Cisco switches that provide SD-Access Extension for IoT functionality (discussed in Chapter 7).

Figure 4-19 shows a typical Cisco SD-Access topology highlighting the fabric edge nodes.

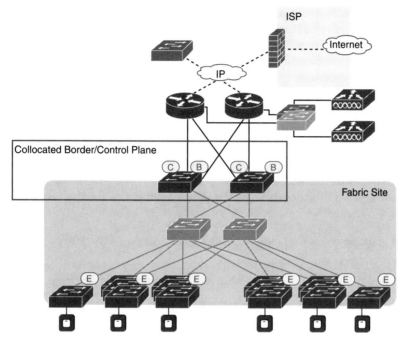

Figure 4-18   *Cisco SD-Access Topology with Collocated Border and Control Plane*

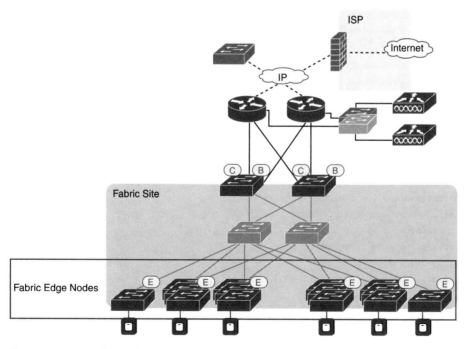

Figure 4-19   *Fabric Edge Nodes in a Cisco SD-Access Topology*

In traditional Layer 3 routed-access networks, IP subnets are dedicated to each of the access-layer switches. As a result, each switch functions as the default gateway for any endpoints that are connected to it. These requirements not only result in a lot of wasted IP address space, but also make host mobility and policy more complex because IP endpoint addresses change depending on to which switch the endpoint is connected. This traditional approach also presents a scale issue, especially if multiple VLANs exist on each access-layer switch.

Although Cisco SD-Access is also a Layer 3 routed-access solution, this limitation is removed, as the fabric edge switches use anycast for the default gateway configuration and IP pools can be used across the entire fabric for both wired and wireless endpoints. Anycast is a technology that allows multiple network devices to share the same IP address without causing conflicts or issues on the network. Among the benefits of using anycast gateways in Cisco SD-Access are the following:

- IP subnets spanning across the fabric, allowing for efficient use of IP address space

- Predictable and stable host mobility, for both wired and wireless, as hosts no longer need to change IP addresses or subnets when moving to a different fabric edge node

- Consistent configurations, as all SVIs on fabric edge nodes are configured the same way

- Efficient traffic flow, as the default gateway for every endpoint is always the connected switch

Example 4-3 shows a sample of an SVI configuration that would be pushed to every fabric edge node in the fabric. All fabric SVIs on all fabric edge nodes would then have an identical MAC and IP configuration because of anycast, allowing for client roaming and mobility.

Example 4-3 *Sample SVI Configuration on a Fabric Edge Node*

```
interface Vlan1021
 description Configured from Cisco DNA-Center
 mac-address 0000.0c9f.f45c
 vrf forwarding Campus
 ip address 100.100.0.1 255.255.0.0
 ip helper-address 100.127.0.1
 ip helper-address 100.64.0.100
 no ip redirects
 ip route-cache same-interface
 no lisp mobility liveness test
 lisp mobility 100_100_0_0-Campus-IPV4
end
```

Intermediate Nodes

Intermediate nodes are unique in Cisco SD-Access in the sense that although they physically exist in the fabric and are logically in the underlay, they are not part of the fabric overlay and are not configured in Cisco DNA Center as part of the fabric workflow.

The determination of whether intermediate nodes are required depends on the physical topology of the network. If the existing network has a distribution layer to aggregate many access-layer switches together due to interface considerations in the core, then the devices in the distribution layer would potentially become intermediate nodes in the Cisco SD-Access fabric. Another factor is the cabling layout of the building and how devices connect into the core. In some buildings, there might be multiple physical hops between access-layer switches and the core. These extra hops would be configured as intermediate nodes in a Cisco SD-Access fabric.

Figure 4-20 shows a typical Cisco SD-Access topology highlighting the intermediate nodes.

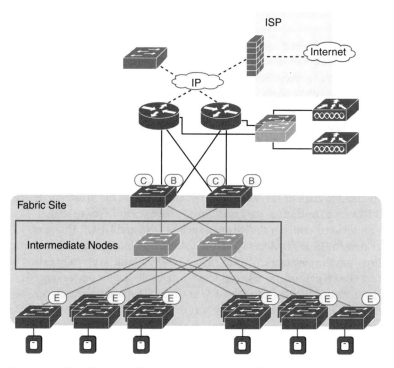

Figure 4-20   *Intermediate Nodes in a Cisco SD-Access Topology*

The function of an intermediate node is very simple: to route Layer 3 packets between other fabric nodes (edge, control plane, and border). From a logical perspective, an intermediate node has IP addressing only in the underlay's routing domain, and only takes part in the underlay routing protocol (IS-IS, if LAN Automation was used to build the underlay). Intermediate nodes have no knowledge of fabric overlay IP addressing or any of the other protocols, such as LISP and VXLAN, that enable the fabric.

Any platform that supports IP routing can be used for an intermediate node, even non-Cisco devices, as long as they meet the interface and cabling requirements and support the underlay routing protocol.

External Connectivity

As discussed earlier in this chapter, no single recommended or required solution exists for external connectivity outside of the fabric in Cisco SD-Access. A company could connect the border nodes directly into its existing network core or distribution switches or to a WAN device in the case of a branch network. The upstream devices only need to support the routing protocol that is running on the borders along with VRF-lite to maintain macro-segmentation out of the fabric.

Fusion Router

Although they were initially created for use with Multiprotocol Label Switching (MPLS) L3VPNs, today virtual routing and forwarding (VRF) instances are used by many large enterprises, government agencies, and other regulated industries in their existing networks for traffic separation. VRFs provide security in the form of macro-segmentation, as endpoints in one VRF cannot communicate with endpoints in another VRF without passing through an intermediate device. This is because each VRF has its own unique routing table and routing protocol. In Cisco SD-Access, VNs are used to create this separation, but they are technically configured as VRFs on the underlying fabric devices.

For companies with existing VRFs in their networks, the hand-off from each of the fabric VNs should directly map to each of the VRFs already configured on the upstream device. If these existing VRFs are in operation, they may already have reachability to shared services resources, discussed earlier in this chapter, such as DNS and DHCP. However, customers who are new to Cisco SD-Access and VRFs require an intermediate device to provide reachability from the new fabric VNs to shared services, which typically exist in the global routing table (GRT) of the existing network. This device (or devices) needs to "fuse" the newly created VN/VRFs into the GRT. In Cisco SD-Access, this device is called a *fusion router*. Although it is not actually part of the fabric, a fusion router is required in order to provide connectivity between the endpoints in the fabric and the shared services in the existing network.

> **Note**   A feature will be released for Cisco SD-Access in the future that will eliminate this functional requirement, but it is not available as of this writing.

Figure 4-21 illustrates the placement of a fusion device in a Cisco SD-Access network. The border nodes hand off the IoT and Employee VNs to the fusion device, which then leaks shared services routes and traffic from the global routing table into the VRFs.

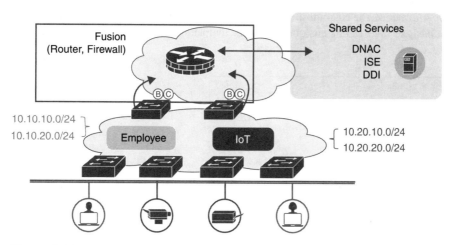

Figure 4-21 *Fusion Device in a Cisco SD-Access Topology*

The fusion router does not need to be a dedicated device and can be the existing upstream switch or router, as long as it is capable of VRF-lite and route leaking between VRFs and the GRT.

Host Onboarding

After you create the Cisco SD-Access fabric and define the fabric device roles, you need to set a few more basic parameters for the fabric to operate. You find these settings in the "Host Onboarding" section of Cisco DNA Center.

Authentication Templates

Authentication templates define the global host authentication policy that is set on all fabric edge nodes in a fabric. After a template is selected and an IP pool is assigned to a VN, the global authentication template cannot be changed. You can choose one of the following four authentication templates, depending on the security policy of the network and network authentication mechanisms in place:

- **Closed Authentication:** This is the most secure authentication template and requires an 802.1X RADIUS server implementation using a product such as Cisco Identity Services Engine (ISE) to handle network authentication.

- **Open Authentication:** Similar to Closed Authentication, this authentication supports 802.1X, but it can also allow network access even without authentication.

- **Easy Connect:** This authentication template relies on Active Directory (AD) authentication instead of 802.1X.

- **No Authentication:** With this authentication template, no authentication is required for network access.

Figure 4-22 shows the customization dialog box for the Closed Authentication template. Some basic settings can be customized for the templates in the Design tool of Cisco DNA Center.

Figure 4-22   *Customization Dialog Box for the Closed Authentication Template*

More details on authentication templates are provided in Chapter 5.

VN to IP Pool Mapping

Assigning IP pool(s) to VNs in a fabric is the final step required to make the fabric operational. This step finalizes the configuration on the border, control plane, and fabric edge nodes, including

- Creation of the appropriate VLANs and SVIs on all fabric edge nodes

- Configuration of the anycast default gateway on all fabric edge nodes

- Creation of loopback interfaces on appropriate border nodes for each selected IP pool

- Configuration of eBGP on appropriate border nodes to advertise the new IP pools to the outside world

- LISP configurations for each IP pool on all fabric nodes to facilitate communication

Example 4-4 shows a sample of the configuration pushed to a collocated border and control plane node in a Cisco SD-Access network after an IP pool is assigned to a VN. In this case, the IP pool 100.101.0.0/16 has been assigned to the Campus VN. As a result, a loopback interface has been created in the Campus VRF, BGP network and aggregate-address statements have been added, and LISP commands have been configured to facilitate communication in the overlay.

Example 4-4 *Sample Configuration Pushed to Border/Control Plane Node*

```
interface Loopback1023
 description Loopback Border
 vrf forwarding Campus
 ip address 100.101.0.1 255.255.255.255


!
router bgp 65534
 address-family ipv4 vrf Campus
  aggregate-address 100.101.0.0 255.255.0.0 summary-only
  network 100.101.0.1 mask 255.255.255.255
!
router lisp
 ipv4 source-locator Loopback0
 service ipv4
  etr map-server 100.124.0.1 key 10c70a
  etr map-server 100.124.128.140 key 10c70a
  etr map-server 100.124.0.1 proxy-reply
  etr map-server 100.124.128.140 proxy-reply
 service ethernet
  etr map-server 100.124.0.1 key 10c70a
  etr map-server 100.124.128.140 key 10c70a
  etr map-server 100.124.0.1 proxy-reply
  etr map-server 100.124.128.140 proxy-reply
 instance-id 4097
  service ipv4
   route-export site-registrations
   distance site-registrations 250
   map-cache site-registration
 site site_uci
  authentication-key 10c70a
  eid-record instance-id 4099 100.101.0.0/16  accept-more-specifics
  eid-record instance-id 8191 any-mac
```

The following information is required to map an IP pool to a virtual network:

- **Virtual Network:** If the VN was not assigned during the creation of the fabric, it can be added during this process.

- **IP:** Select an IP pool that was defined in the Design tool of Cisco DNA Center. This is the subnet that endpoints will be placed in.

- **Traffic:** Select between Data and Voice.

■ **Groups (optional):** If you prefer a static SGT assignment for this pool, select it here; however, note that using Cisco ISE for dynamic SGT assignments is recommended.

■ **Wireless Pool:** If this pool will be used for both wired and wireless endpoints, check this check box.

Figure 4-23 shows the IP pool to VN assignment dialog box where the IP pool SJC-Campus-Users is being assigned to the Campus VN for data traffic.

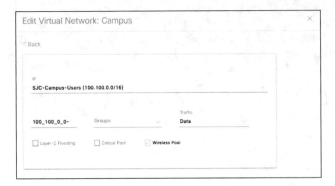

Figure 4-23 *IP Pool to VN Assignment Dialog Box*

SSID to IP Pool Mapping

If the fabric will contain wireless endpoints, you must assign an IP pool to each SSID in the fabric. Making this assignment enables the SSID on the Wireless LAN Controller and makes it active in the network and on the fabric.

Figure 4-24 shows the IP pool 100.100.0.0 being assigned to the SDA-Campus wireless SSID.

Figure 4-24 *IP Pool to Wireless SSID Assignment*

This setting is mandatory for a fabric SSID to become active, but the actual IP pool that is offered to an endpoint can be overridden by Cisco ISE during authentication. This override is discussed further in Chapter 5.

Switchport Override

Cisco DNA Center provides the capability to override the following global Host Onboarding settings on fabric edge node interfaces to allow for exceptions or customized devices in the Cisco SD-Access fabric. These changes can be made on individual ports or on a range of ports.

- **Connected Device Type:** This can be set to User Devices, Access Point (AP), or Server.

- **Address Pool:** This setting can force an IP pool assignment to an interface rather than depending on Cisco ISE to make a dynamic assignment.

- **Group:** This setting forces an SGT to be assigned to endpoints on the interface rather than depending on Cisco ISE to make a dynamic assignment.

- **Authentication Template:** This setting overrides the global authentication template selected (as described earlier in this chapter).

Figure 4-25 shows a switchport override example where a range of interfaces is assigned a static IP pool and SGTs and the Authentication Template field is set to Easy Connect.

Figure 4-25 *Switchport Override in Host Onboarding*

Summary

This chapter covered configuration concepts and fundamentals of Cisco Software-Defined Access, from fabric creation to host onboarding. In addition, it discussed some design considerations for different types of environments, network sizes, and topologies. The function that each type of device role plays in the fabric was covered along with design and selection criteria for these roles.

References in This Chapter

Cisco DNA Center—Compatibility Information: https://www.cisco.com/c/en/us/support/cloud-systems-management/dna-center/products-device-support-tables-list.html

Cisco Software-Defined Access—Solution Design Guide: https://www.cisco.com/c/en/us/td/docs/solutions/CVD/Campus/sda-sdg-2019oct.html

Cisco SD-Access Product Compatibility: https://www.cisco.com https://www.cisco.com/c/en/us/solutions/enterprise-networks/software-defined-access/compatibility-matrix.html

Cisco Software-Defined Access Solution Overview: https://www.cisco.com/c/en/us/solutions/collateral/enterprise-networks/software-defined-access/solution-overview-c22-739012.html

Chapter 5

Cisco Identity Services Engine with Cisco DNA Center

This chapter covers the following topics:

- **Policy Management in Cisco DNA Center with Cisco ISE:** This section covers the integration between Cisco ISE and Cisco DNA Center, showing the value of centralized management at a policy level.

- **Group-Based Access Control:** This section covers the new group-based access control feature on DNA Center and its benefits to the Cisco TrustSec policy plane in a Cisco SD-Access fabric.

- **Segmentation with Third-Party RADIUS Server:** This section unveils the option of using a third-party RADIUS server while still benefiting from segmentation through integration with Cisco ISE.

- **Secure Host Onboarding in Enterprise Networks:** This section covers the various secure host onboarding modes available for enterprise networks. Understanding of various 802.1x modes is helpful in evaluating the mode applicable for the IT business needs.

- **802.1X Phased Deployment:** This section continues the focus on the goal of moving toward secure network access using a recommended phased approach to implement network access control in enterprise networks.

- **Host Onboarding with Cisco DNA Center:** This section goes into detail on host onboarding clients in Cisco SD-Access fabric in a simplified approach using Cisco DNA Center.

- **Security in Cisco Software-Defined Access Network:** This section provides an overview of macro- and micro-segmentation methods available in a secure campus fabric. Differences between virtual networks and scalable groups are highlighted.

- **Policy Set Overview in Cisco ISE:** This section provides a high-level overview of the policy set model on Cisco ISE.

- **Segmentation Policy Construction in Cisco SD-Access:** This section details various use cases of segmentation in Campus Fabric and the steps to configure them from Cisco DNA Center and Cisco ISE.

- **Segmentation Outside the Fabric:** This section covers protocols to maintain segmentation when traffic leaves the Cisco SD-Access fabric.

Policy Management in Cisco DNA Center with Cisco ISE

Chapter 2, "Introduction to Cisco Software-Defined Access," details the building blocks of Cisco Software-Defined Access and describes the role of Cisco Identity Services Engine (ISE) as an essential component for the policy plane in creating a fabric. Cisco DNA Center enables network and security administrators to create policies that reflect the organization's business intent for a particular aspect of the network, such as network access. For example, healthcare networks need secure segmentation and profiling, as healthcare records are just as valuable to attackers as credit card numbers or online passwords. In the wake of recent cyberattacks, hospitals are required to have wired and wireless networks that not only comply with the Health Insurance Portability and Accountability Act (HIPAA) but also can provide complete and constant visibility into the hospitals' network traffic to protect sensitive medical devices (such as servers for electronic medical records, vital signs monitors, and nurse workstations) so that a malicious device cannot compromise the networks. A patient's mobile device, when compromised by malware, can change network communication behavior to propagate and infect other endpoints. It is considered abnormal behavior when a patient's mobile device communicates with any medical device. Cisco SD-Access powered by Cisco DNA Center addresses the need for complete isolation between patient devices and medical facility devices by using macro-segmentation and putting devices into different overlay networks, enabling the isolation.

Cisco SD-Access takes this need for segmentation beyond simple network separation by profiling devices and users as they come on to the network and applying micro-segmentation within an overlay network. Flexible policy creation provides the ability to have SGTs based on the user role, control communication within a group or to enable communication among groups only as needed to implement the intent of the policies of an organization. Cisco SD-Access automation and segmentation benefits are applicable to organizations in other sectors beyond healthcare, such as education, where access needs to be controlled between student devices and faculty networks. Similarly, isolation for point-of-sale machines supporting Payment Card Industry (PCI) compliance is a business requirement in the retail sector. The manufacturing vertical requires isolation for machine-to-machine traffic in manufacturing floors. In enterprise environments where mergers and acquisitions result in overlapping address spaces, separation of different internal organizations and their respective IoT devices is a growing business intent.

Cisco DNA Center integration with Cisco ISE is the first step toward micro-segmentation in a Cisco SD-Access fabric. The next section provides the details on the integration and the steps involved.

Integration of Cisco DNA Center and ISE

Cisco DNA Center integrates securely with Cisco ISE over Secure Sockets Layer (SSL), Cisco Platform Exchange Grid (pxGrid), and External RESTful Services (ERS) API calls. To understand more about the integration and best practices, understanding the certificates in Cisco DNA Center and Cisco ISE is crucial.

Certificates in Cisco DNA Center

Cisco DNA Center, by default, uses self-signed certificates for HTTPS communications and to manage the network devices. Figure 5-1 shows the default self-signed certificate installed in Cisco DNA Center by default during the installation. This default certificate, issued by Cisco Systems and valid for 1 year, has a key size of 2048 bits and SHA-256 RSA encryption.

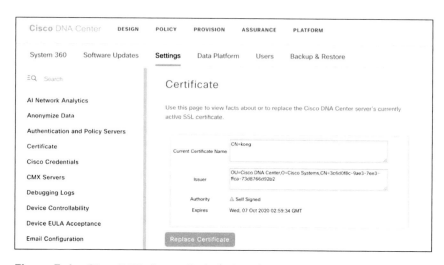

Figure 5-1 *Cisco DNA Center Default Certificate Settings*

Figure 5-2 provides additional details about the Cisco DNA Center self-signed certificate. The common name of the certificate is kong.

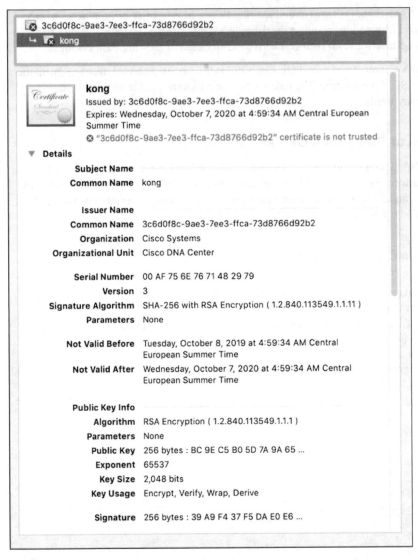

Figure 5-2 *Cisco DNA Center Default Self-Signed Certificate Details*

Note   All the Cisco DNA Center screen captures shown in this chapter use version 1.3.x, which is the latest version at the time of writing.

Cisco recommends using certificates from well-known third-party certificate authorities (CAs) in Cisco DNA Center to avoid trust issues during integration and to avoid certificate warnings. Cisco DNA Center uses the Public Key Infrastructure (PKI) Certificate

Management feature to import, store, and manage X.509 certificates from well-known CAs. The imported certificate becomes an identity certificate for Cisco DNA Center, which presents this certificate to its clients for authentication. The clients are the northbound API applications and southbound network devices.

Cisco DNA Center supports the following import files (in either PEM or PKCS file format):

- X.509 certificate (certificate issued by the third-party certificate authority)

- Private key (*only* RSA keys are supported; recommendation is to use a 2048-bit key size or larger)

The first step is to obtain a valid X.509 certificate and private key from a well-known CA. Replace the self-signed certificate with the new certificate and private key. After the import, the security functionality based on the X.509 certificate and private key is automatically activated. Cisco DNA Center presents this new certificate to any device or application that requests it. Northbound API applications and southbound network devices can use these credentials to establish a trust relationship with Cisco DNA Center. Cisco DNA Center supports only one X.509 imported certificate and private key at a time. If a second certificate and private key are imported, the new pair overwrites the existing pair.

Certificate requests and private keys can also be generated using Open SSL or using an API platform in Cisco DNA Center. Log in to the Secure Shell (SSH) of Cisco DNA Center on port 2222 to access the command-line interface (CLI) for the Open SSL method of generating a certificate request. For more details on the certificate request step-by-step process, refer to the *Cisco DNA Center User Guide* for the release you are using.

Note   Install the third-party certificate in Cisco DNA Center or the DNA Center cluster before any deployment implementation and integration with Cisco ISE. Replacing the certificate in Cisco DNA Center causes network disruption because the services are restarted. Proceed with caution to make the changes.

Certificates on Cisco Identity Services Engine

Cisco ISE, as discussed in the previous chapters, provides network access control for corporate users using 802.1X, MAB, and guest services. Cisco ISE supports various certificates for different purposes. Cisco ISE has a built-in Certificate Authority (ISE Internal CA) feature to act as a certificate authority to issue certificates. ISE, by default, uses the certificate issued by the Cisco ISE Internal CA for pxGrid and uses self-signed certificates for admin, EAP, and portal services. Figure 5-3 shows the Certificates section on a newly installed ISE node. The highlighted pxGrid certificate is used during the integration with Cisco DNA Center.

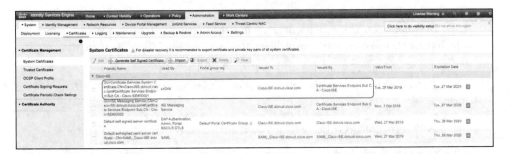

Figure 5-3 *Cisco ISE System Certificates*

Note   Cisco recommends using third-party certificates in Cisco ISE specifically for client services such as EAP and portal usage. Replacing the Admin certificate in Cisco ISE results in a restart of the services, which may or may not cause network disruption, depending on the ISE role (PAN, PSN, or MnT, introduced in Chapter 2).

Cisco ISE and Cisco DNA Center Integration Process

To integrate Cisco ISE with Cisco DNA Center, you first must ensure that several prerequisites are met, as described in this section.

Make sure Cisco ISE is running the minimum version supported for Cisco SD-Access integrations. Refer to the Cisco SD-Access Compatibility Matrix at https://www.cisco.com/c/en/us/solutions/enterprise-networks/software-defined-access/compatibility-matrix.html.

You need to enable pxGrid on at least one ISE node in the ISE deployment. An ISE deployment can have a maximum of four pxGrid nodes. You can assign a pxGrid persona to an existing ISE node acting as a PAN, MnT, or PSN node, but the recommended practice is to use a dedicated pxGrid node to avoid any pxGrid issues caused by other services running on the same node. Figure 5-4 shows how to configure an ISE node to act as a pxGrid node for a standalone ISE installation.

Figure 5-5 shows the Cisco ISE Deployment screen with pxGrid service enabled on the standalone ISE deployment.

After the pxGrid persona is enabled in a deployment, the pxGrid services should go to Connected status in the pxGrid Services tab of the ISE web interface. If there are multiple pxGrid nodes, the status should show as Connected for all the nodes. Figure 5-6 indicates the Connected status in a standalone ISE deployment. Cisco pxGrid services use the certificate issued by the Cisco ISE Internal CA for the services, but you can replace it with a third-party CA certificate.

Cisco DNA Center uses ERS API calls to read and write the policy configuration in ISE. As a prerequisite, External RESTful Services (ERS) needs to be enabled on ISE. In a distributed deployment, ERS read/write needs to be enabled on the PAN, as this node is used to configure and maintain the configuration database. Other nodes need an ERS read-only permission, as shown in Figure 5-7.

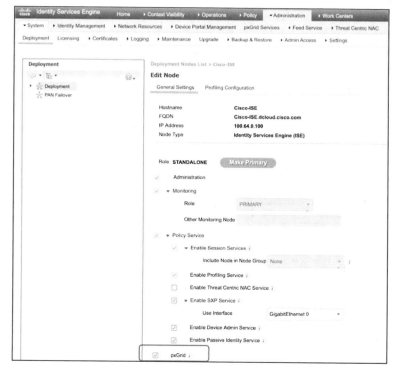

Figure 5-4 *Cisco ISE pxGrid Persona Enablement*

Figure 5-5 *Cisco ISE pxGrid Persona in a Deployment*

Figure 5-6 *Cisco ISE pxGrid Services in a Connected State*

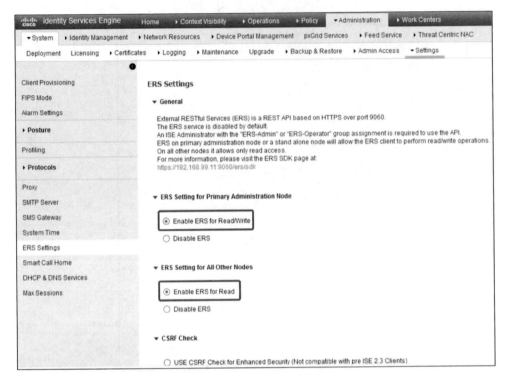

Figure 5-7 *Enabling ERS Settings in Cisco ISE*

Make sure the CLI and web interface username and password in Cisco ISE are set to the same credentials. Cisco DNA Center uses the same credentials to log in to the CLI and web interface of ISE as of Cisco DNA Center version 1.3.x. Also make sure Cisco DNA Center and Cisco ISE have communication open on TCP ports 22, 443, 5222, 8910, and 9060.

From the web UI of Cisco DNA Center, ISE is added as an "Authentication and Policy Server." Navigate to **System > Settings > Authentication and Policy Servers > Add.** In the Add AAA/ISE Server dialog box, the following details are required for ISE integration:

- **Server IP Address:** IP address of the ISE PAN in the deployment. Must be Interface Gig0 IP Address on ISE; NAT is not supported between Primary ISE admin and Cisco DNA Center.

- **Shared Secret:** Shared secret between the network devices and ISE policy servers.

- **Username:** Same username to log in to ISE using SSH and GUI. The user account should be a superadmin user.

- **Password:** Same password for the username for login to ISE SSH and web UI.

- **FQDN:** Fully qualified domain name associated with Interface Gig0 in the ISE primary administration node.

- **Subscriber Name:** Used to identify the Cisco DNA Center client name in ISE.

- **SSH Key:** (Optional) SSH key, which can be created "offline" and provided to ISE or Cisco DNA Center.

- **Virtual IP Address(es):** (Optional) Virtual IP address(es) if the ISE policy nodes are behind a load balancer.

The following optional settings are configured in the Advanced Settings section:

- **Protocol:** Enable RADIUS and/or TACACS depending on whether ISE deployment is used for RADIUS and/or TACACS. RADIUS is enabled by default on the ISE integration page.

- **Authentication Port:** Port used for RADIUS authentication. Default is 1812.

- **Accounting Port:** Port used for RADIUS accounting. Default is 1813.

- **Port:** Port used for TACACS. Default is 49.

Figure 5-8 shows an example of Cisco ISE integration in a lab deployment.

Figure 5-8 *Addition of Cisco ISE as AAA Server in Cisco DNA Center*

In Cisco ISE, Cisco DNA Center is added as a pxGrid subscriber automatically if ISE pxGrid settings are configured to automatically accept pxGrid connections. Otherwise, the ISE administrator needs to manually accept the pxGrid connection from Cisco DNA Center. Figure 5-9 shows the communication flow between Cisco ISE and Cisco DNA Center when ISE is added.

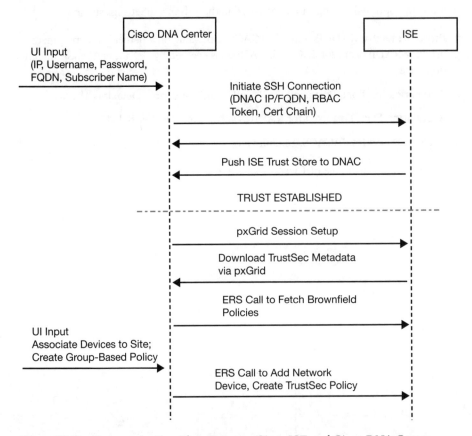

Figure 5-9   *Communication Flow Between Cisco ISE and Cisco DNA Center*

The following list summarizes the messages between Cisco DNA Center and Cisco ISE as depicted in Figure 5-9:

- Cisco DNA Center logs in to ISE from the credentials provided using SSH.

- Identity certificates are exchanged dynamically over an SSH session established from Cisco DNA Center to ISE. After the SSH session has been established, Cisco DNA Center invokes the CLI configuration on ISE using the command **application configure ise**, option **[19]** Establish Trust with controller, to begin the certificate exchange.

- Cisco DNA Center invokes an ERS API call to ISE to download the pxGrid certificates from ISE.

- The pxGrid connection request is sent to ISE securely from Cisco DNA Center. After successful connection, ISE pushes all the Cisco TrustSec information, such as Scalable Group Tags (SGTs), to Cisco DNA Center. Cisco pxGrid version 2.0 is used from Cisco DNA Center version 1.3.x onward.

- An ERS call also happens from Cisco DNA Center to ISE to download any existing scalable group tag access control lists (SGACLs).

To verify successful integration between Cisco ISE and Cisco DNA Center, make sure the ISE status is ACTIVE and System 360 shows the ISE nodes as Available in Cisco DNA Center. In ISE, Cisco DNA Center should be listed as a pxGrid client and its status should be Online. Figure 5-10 shows an example of successful integration between ISE and Cisco DNA Center.

Figure 5-10 *Verification of Cisco ISE and Cisco DNA Center Integration*

After you have verified the success of the integration, Cisco DNA Center should be able to read the SGTs and SGACLs that are configured in ISE. The Policy page of Cisco DNA Center shows the SGTs learned from ISE after the integration is done. However, the Policy page also displays the error message shown in Figure 5-11, reproduced next for easier reading. This is related to the group-based access control feature introduced in Cisco DNA Center version 1.3.1, which is discussed in detail in the next section.

> In order to begin using Group Based Access Control, Cisco DNA Center must migrate policy data from the Cisco Identity Services Engine (ISE):

> Any policy features in ISE that currently [are] not supported in Cisco DNA Center will not be migrated, you will have a chance to review the migration rule after [you] click on "Start migration"

> Any policy information in Cisco DNA Center that does not already exist in ISE will be copied to ISE to ensure the 2 sources are in sync

Once the data migration is initiated, you cannot use Group Based Access Control in Cisco DNA Center until the operation is complete. Start migration.

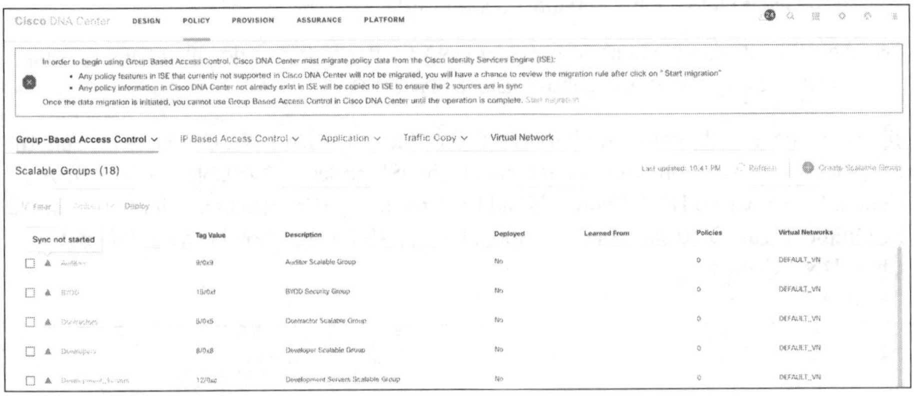

Figure 5-11   *Group-Based Access Control on Cisco DNA Center Prior to Policy Migration*

Group-Based Access Control

When Cisco DNA Center version 1.3.0 or a prior version is integrated with Cisco ISE, SGTs present in ISE can be viewed and managed in Cisco DNA Center. However, if ISE has any prior SGACLs that were present before the integration, Cisco DNA Center can't read those policies. In addition, SGTs and SGACLs can be managed from ISE and Cisco DNA Center after the integration. This results in conflicts due to the management of policy in two places: Cisco DNA Center and Cisco ISE. Group-based access control, introduced in Cisco DNA Center version 1.3.1, alleviates these issues and brings in the following benefits:

- Prevents conflicts of policy by making the Cisco ISE TrustSec UI portion read-only after Cisco DNA Center integration is done

- Improves the user experience to create and manage SGTs and SGACLs from Cisco DNA Center

- Provides a policy matrix view in Cisco DNA Center similar to the matrix view in Cisco ISE

- Adds granular access control and segmentation functions to Cisco DNA Center

- Improves scale in the number of SGTs, SGACLs, and access contracts supported in Cisco DNA Center

- Supports a third-party AAA server with Cisco ISE as the TrustSec policy enforcer

After the integration of Cisco ISE with Cisco DNA Center, group-based access control checks for a minimum required version of ISE and displays the error message shown in Figure 5-12 if ISE is not running the required version.

Figure 5-12 *Error with Group-Based Access Control Without Supported ISE Version*

If ISE is running the supported version, the Cisco DNA Center Policy page shows the message noted in the previous section (and shown in Figure 5-11) with the option to Start Migration to enable group-based access control. Customers who are not using Cisco SD-Access do not see this option and do not have to worry about policy migration as of version 1.3.x. This is subject to change in future Cisco DNA Center versions. As described next, take caution before starting the migration, as ISE policies might be affected during migration.

Clicking the Start Migration link results in the following actions:

■ A warning message to make a backup of Cisco ISE and Cisco DNA Center, as the migration might result in policy changes.

■ **SGTs:** Cisco ISE security groups are compared to scalable groups in Cisco DNA Center, with the following possible outcomes:

   ■ If the name and SGT value are the same on Cisco DNA Center and ISE, no action is performed, as the information in Cisco DNA Center is consistent with Cisco ISE.

   ■ If a Cisco ISE security group SGT value does not exist in Cisco DNA Center, a new scalable group is created in Cisco DNA Center.

   ■ If a Cisco ISE security group SGT value exists in Cisco DNA Center but the names do not match, the name of the Cisco ISE security group replaces the name of that scalable group in Cisco DNA Center.

   ■ If the Cisco ISE security group name is the same but the SGT value is different, the security group from Cisco ISE is migrated. It retains the name and tag value, and the Cisco DNA Center scalable group is renamed and a suffix of "_DNA" is added.

■ **Contracts:** The SGACLs in Cisco ISE referenced by policies are called *access contracts* in Cisco DNA Center. The SGACLs and contracts are compared, with the following possible outcomes:

   ■ If the SGACL and access contract have the same name and content, no further action is required, as the information in Cisco DNA Center is consistent with the information in Cisco ISE.

- If the SGACL and access contract have the same name but the content is different, the SGACL content from Cisco ISE is migrated. The previous contract content in Cisco DNA Center is discarded.

- If the SGACL name does not exist in Cisco DNA Center, a new access contract with that name is created and the SGACL content from Cisco ISE is migrated.

■ **Policies:** A policy is uniquely identified by a source group and destination group pair. All Cisco ISE TrustSec Egress Policy Matrix policies are compared to the policies in Cisco DNA Center, with the following possible outcomes:

- If a policy for a source group and destination group pair references the same SGACL/access contract name in Cisco ISE, no changes are made.

- If a policy for a source group and destination group pair references a different SGACL/access contract name in Cisco ISE, the Cisco ISE access contract name is referenced in the policy. This overwrites the previous access contract reference in Cisco DNA Center.

- The Cisco ISE default policy is checked and migrated to Cisco DNA Center.

■ If the migration does not result in any error messages, a success message is displayed, as shown in Figure 5-13, and the policy matrix in ISE is changed to read-only. Cisco DNA Center is now the policy management platform to make any Trustsec policy changes.

Note The administrator has the option to manage the group-based access control in ISE instead of in Cisco DNA Center. If this option is enabled, the Cisco DNA Center group-based access control UI becomes inactive.

Figure 5-13 *Successful Migration to Group-Based Access Control*

Cisco DNA Center group-based access control is used to create segmentation policies based on the business intent. These segmentation policies are then pushed to Cisco ISE, which will eventually enforce them on the network devices. A typical segmentation policy created from Cisco DNA Center involves these steps:

Step 1. Groups are created based on the applications/services and the groups that need to access them in Cisco DNA Center. These groups are also referred to as scalable groups.

Step 2. Access contracts are created in Cisco DNA Center using group-based access control to permit or deny certain types of traffic based on the business intent.

Figure 5-14 shows an example of an access contract created in Cisco DNA Center to allow HTTP(s), Internet Control Message Protocol (ICMP), and File Transfer Protocol (FTP) traffic. The default action is configured as Deny. An access contract can be used by multiple policies.

Create Access Contract

Name*
Permit_http_icmp_Ftp

Description
Permit_http_icmp_Ftp

CONTRACT CONTENT (5)

#	Action*	Application	Transport Protocol	Source / Destination	Port	Logging	Action
1	Permit	ftp-agent	UDP/TCP	Destination	574/574		+ ✕
2	Permit	ftp	TCP	Destination	21,21000		+ ✕
3	Permit	https	UDP/TCP	Destination	443/443		+ ✕
4	Permit	http	TCP	Destination	80		+ ✕
5	Permit	Advanced	ICMP	...	...		+ ✕

Default Action   Deny   Logging

Figure 5-14   *Access Contract from Cisco DNA Center*

Step 3.   A policy is applied for every source group and destination group. The policy consists of a source scalable group, a destination scalable group, and an access contract with the permissions between the source group and destination group. Policy is applied on the enforcement point. Figure 5-15 shows an access contract called Anti-Malware applied between source group Contractors and destination group Guests.

Figure 5-15   *Policy Matrix from Group-Based Access Control*

Figure 5-16 depicts the following simplified flow of the policy function offered by Cisco DNA Center and all the security pieces coming together through ISE integration:

- Cisco DNA Center group-based access control is used to create groups and policies between the groups through access contracts. The policies are maintained in a policy matrix.

- The policy management in Cisco DNA Center pushes these groups, access contracts, and SGACLs to ISE.

- When a client connected to the fabric connects to the network, the client is authenticated and authorized by ISE. As part of authorization, an SGT is assigned to the client.

- ISE pushes the policy to the fabric edge that needs to be applied to the client (also known as an SGACL).

- Cisco DNA Center as part of fabric configuration makes all the fabric edges as the SGACL enforcement points. The fabric edge enforces the SGACL for client traffic at the egress point.

- (Optional) Through pxGrid or SXP, ISE integrates with various security solutions to send the SGT information of the client to provide more context for the different security solutions. In Figure 5-16, Cisco ISE is sharing the SGT context to security solutions such as Cisco ASA and Cisco Cognitive Threat Analytics.

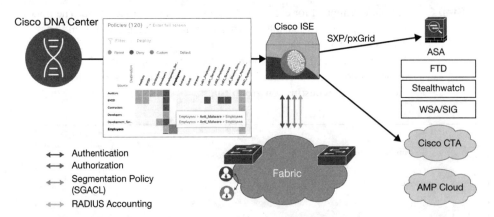

Figure 5-16 *Policy Push from Cisco ISE to Other Security Devices Through Cisco DNA Center*

Segmentation with Third-Party RADIUS Server

The previous section highlighted that IT administrators can leverage Cisco DNA Center with Cisco ISE to enforce security policies using scalable groups and policies between them. However, in the broad networking world, many enterprise network designs exist that have a non-Cisco RADIUS server doing network access control. For such designs, one can still reap the benefits of Cisco SD-Access and the advanced segmentation capabilities of Cisco DNA Center as of version 1.3.1.0. Cisco DNA Center is used to create and maintain the Cisco SD-Access fabric. Cisco DNA Center also integrates with ISE for segmentation policies. Figure 5-17 provides the connection flow for a third-party RADIUS server with Cisco DNA Center.

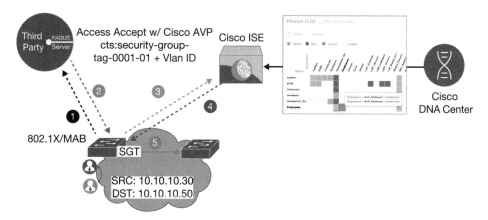

Figure 5-17   *Third-Party RADIUS Server Connection Flow*

The connection flow in a third-party RADIUS server is described in the following steps:

Step 1.   A client connects to the fabric edge using 802.1X or MAC Authentication Bypass (MAB). The fabric edge authenticates with the third-party RADIUS server.

Step 2.   The third-party RADIUS server authenticates and authorizes the client. In the response, it sends a RADIUS Access-Accept, client VLAN ID, and the SGT for the client in an attribute Cisco-Attribute Value pair (AVP). Cisco AVP is a Cisco-specific attribute that all Cisco devices understand.

Step 3.   The fabric edge initiates a policy request if the policy associated with the newly connected SGT doesn't exist.

Step 4.   ISE pushes the policies associated with the newly connected SGT.

Step 5.   The fabric edge enforces the policy for the client traffic. The policy is applied at the egress of the fabric edge for the client SGT.

As mentioned in the flow, ISE is a required component for segmentation in Cisco SD-Access for policy download even with an existing third-party RADIUS server.

Note   As of Cisco DNA version 1.3.2, some of the flow steps are not directly configurable options, and day N configuration templates need to be leveraged to configure network devices to use a third-party RADIUS server for authentication and Cisco ISE for policy download.

Secure Host Onboarding in Enterprise Networks

Host onboarding, as the name suggests, is the process of onboarding the clients in a network, which could include workstations, users, BYOD devices, IoT devices, IP phones, cameras, network devices such as access points, and so on. This section focuses on the security aspects of onboarding the hosts in the network in a flexible way with minimal disruption to the network or the clients. A high-level overview of the different host onboarding techniques is provided in the subsequent sections to help you understand its value in a software-defined campus network and the approach toward the Cisco Zero Trust model.

Endpoint Host Modes in 802.1X

As per the new industry buzzword, *zero trust network*, Cisco Zero Trust is a security model based on the principle of maintaining strict access controls and not trusting anyone by default, even those already inside the network perimeter. Network access control is a security requirement in any IT networks, as detailed in Chapter 2, and Cisco ISE plays a key role in making sure the endpoint connecting into the network is authenticated and given proper authorization based on the endpoint and its role. This is implemented using 802.1X, which is a port-based authentication that restricts unauthorized clients from connecting to a LAN through publicly accessible ports. An authentication server validates each client (supplicant) connected to a network access device (authenticator) port before making available any services offered by the switch or the LAN. An 802.1X-enabled port goes to an authorized state after being successfully authorized by the authentication server. If the authentication server is unable to authorize the client, the port goes to an unauthorized state.

The 802.1X port's host mode determines whether more than one client can be authenticated on the port and how authentication is enforced by the switch. An 802.1X port can be configured to use any of the four host modes described in the following sections.

Single-Host Mode

In a single-host mode, only one MAC address is allowed on the switchport. The switch authenticates the port and places it in an authorized state. Detection of a second MAC address on the port results in a security violation, as shown in Figure 5-18. Single-host mode is mainly used in environments that have a strict restriction of connecting only one client per port.

Multi-Host Mode

In multi-host mode, the first MAC address attached is authenticated. Subsequent hosts that are attached to the port bypass authentication and piggyback on the first MAC address's authentication, as shown in Figure 5-19. Multi-host mode on the port, along with port security, can be used to manage network access for all the MAC addresses on a port.

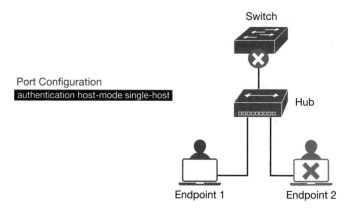

Figure 5-18 *Single-Host Mode*

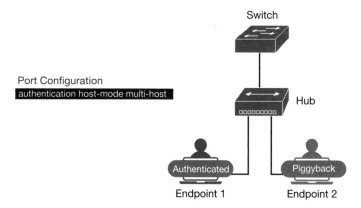

Figure 5-19 *Multi-Host Mode*

Multi-Domain Mode

Multi-domain mode refers to two domains: data and voice. In multi-domain mode, also known as multi-domain authentication (MDA), an IP phone and a host connected behind the phone are authenticated independently. Even though they are connected to the same port, the IP phone is placed in the voice VLAN and the host is placed in the data VLAN as per the policies pushed by the authentication server. Any second MAC address detected on the data or voice domain results in a security violation. Figure 5-20 shows MDA in action.

Multi-Auth Mode

In multi-auth mode, one client is allowed on the voice domain and multiple authenticated clients are allowed on the data VLAN. Cisco DNA Center by default provisions multi-auth mode on all the 802.1X-enabled ports. Multi-auth mode is the most commonly used host mode, as it ensures that every client is authenticated before connecting into the network, as depicted in Figure 5-21.

Note   In multi-auth mode, only one VLAN needs to be enabled for all the hosts connected to the port. You cannot have two data hosts connected with different data VLANs assigned by the authentication server.

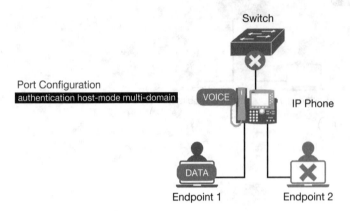

Figure 5-20   *Multi-Domain Mode*

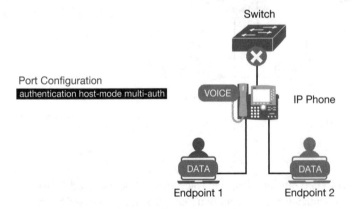

Figure 5-21   *Multi-Auth Mode*

802.1X Phased Deployment

This book focuses on Cisco SD-Access. Previous chapters have noted that 802.1X is the most secure way of connecting an endpoint into the network. The end goal of an IT administrator is to have the network use 802.1X for every client connecting to the network. However, moving toward this end goal should be done in a phased approach.

Why a Phased Approach?

If a network currently does not have port authentication, any client connected to the port is given some level of access depending on the port configuration, such as the VLAN configured on the port. However, the goal is to move toward a secure network, which means enabling port authentication. If 802.1X port authentication is enabled on all the ports overnight, the expectation is that every client coming into the network should have a successful 802.1X authentication. As indicated in the flowchart shown in Figure 5-22, when an endpoint is connected to the 802.1X-enabled port, if the authentication fails, the client is in an unauthorized state, which is the goal here.

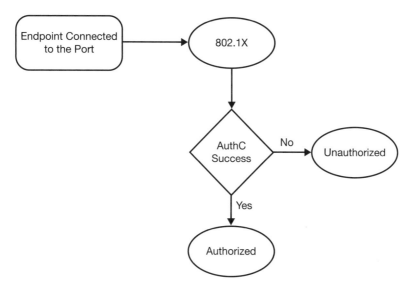

Figure 5-22   *802.1X-Enabled Port Flow Chart*

The network administrator would be happy to switch over to port authentication within a day, but 802.1X, as discussed in Chapter 2, involves client configuration, authentication server configuration, and network device configuration. For example, Bob, an employee of ACME, tried to connect to the port where 802.1X is implemented. Bob's laptop supplicant was not enabled, and Bob is now not able to connect after enabling 802.1X. This generates a service ticket to the operations team, who is now bombarded with 802.1X issues. A phased approach is necessary when a solution involving multiple components is involved. The phased approach initially needs to be placed in a monitor or audit mode to gain visibility into the environment that's being handled, and after continuous monitoring, the solution can be moved toward an enforcement mode.

The 802.1X deployment model recommendation is to follow a phased approach. There are two phases in this approach.

Phase I: Monitor Mode (Visibility Mode)

The 802.1X deployment model recommendation is to start with monitor mode. In monitor mode, the port status is open authentication, in which traffic is allowed irrespective of the authentication status, unlike the standard 802.1X status, where traffic is allowed only when authentication is successful. Figure 5-23 depicts traffic on the network port placed in open authentication as part of monitor mode. Before authentication and after authentication, all traffic is permitted. Even when the user fails authentication, the user is able to access the file servers and the rest of the resources available on the network. Monitor mode does not have an effect on the end user's access, which makes it seamless, and the administrator can gain visibility into the endpoint authentication status without disrupting the endpoint access.

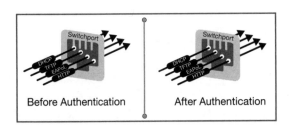
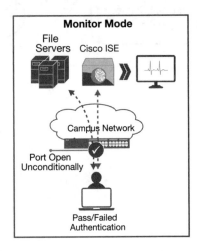

Figure 5-23 *Port Behavior with Open Authentication*

The commands to enable monitor mode on the port are shown in Example 5-1.

Example 5-1 *802.1X Open Authentication Port Configuration*

```
interface GigabitEthernet1/0/1
switchport access vlan 100
switchport mode access
switchport voice vlan 101
authentication host-mode multi-auth
authentication open          ----------------> enables Monitor mode
authentication port-control auto
mab                          ----------------> enables MAB
dot1x pae authenticator ----------------> enables 802.1X
```

Starting with monitor mode has multiple benefits. This mode provides visibility into the types of devices connecting to the network. It also lists users who successfully authenticate (that is, present valid credentials) and users who fail authentication (that is, present invalid credentials). Network administrators can see all this information in ISE authentication reports and summary reports of passed and failed authentications. Network administrators use this phase to gain visibility, evaluate remaining risk, and prepare for network access control by working on the failure reasons reported by ISE for the users who failed authentication.

One of the failure reasons could be that the supplicant is not configured correctly. The administrator can work with the endpoint management team to configure the supplicant correctly, installing the appropriate certificates or credentials. This is a continuous learning phase, as the changes made by the administrator based on the observations should result in increasing the overall authentication success percentage in the network. Network administrators typically spend a much longer time in phase I than in phase II to make sure the effects of 802.1X enablement are minimal to the end clients.

Phase II: Low-Impact Mode

Phase II has two modes: low-impact mode and closed mode. Some customers opt for low-impact mode as the end goal, whereas customers in sectors such as federal government or banking typically opt to move toward closed mode. Which mode to be finally placed in completely depends on the enterprise security and business requirements. Compared to monitor mode, low-impact mode incrementally increases the security level of the network by configuring an ingress port ACL on top of monitor mode at the port level. In low-impact mode, security is added to the framework that was built on monitor mode by applying an ACL to the switchport, allowing very limited network access prior to authentication. After users or devices have successfully authenticated, they are granted full network access, as shown in Figure 5-24.

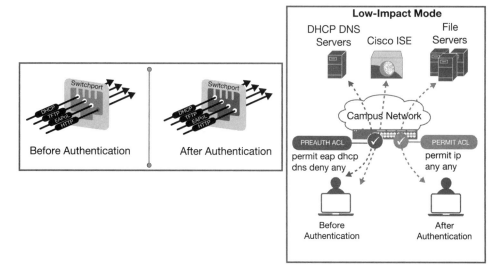

Figure 5-24   *Port Behavior with Low-Impact Mode*

The ACL is configured statically on the access port and provides basic connectivity for guests, contractors, and unauthenticated hosts while selectively limiting access, thereby introducing a higher level of security. The level of access given to the endpoints can be differentiated based on successful authentication and authorization by pushing a downloadable ACL (dACL). dACLs are configured in ISE depending on the corporate security and business intent. dACLs overwrite the ACL configured statically on the switchport.

Example 5-2 shows a port in low-impact mode.

Example 5-2   *802.1X Low-Impact Mode Port Configuration*

```
interface GigabitEthernet1/4
 switchport access vlan 60
 switchport mode access
 switchport voice vlan 61
 ip access-group PRE-AUTH in ----------> pre-auth access control list (Low Impact
   Mode)
 authentication open
 authentication port-control auto
 mab
 dot1x pae authenticator
```

An example of how this feature may be used is to enable any device attaching to the network to use Dynamic Host Configuration Protocol (DHCP), Domain Name System (DNS), and Active Directory and perhaps get to the Internet while blocking the device's access to internal resources. When a device connected to that same switchport passes authentication, a dACL is applied by ISE that permits all traffic. This mode continues to use open authentication on the switchports while providing strong levels of security for non-authenticated devices. However, because a limited set of traffic always flows regardless of the authentication state of a device, this mode becomes ideal for today's enterprises by allowing "regular" IT operational activities to occur, such as reimaging workstations with Preboot Execution Environment (PXE) solutions.

The purpose of the statically configured ACL in low-impact mode is to allow critical traffic to flow prior to authentication. It may be necessary to open additional traffic depending on the environment, such as to allow access to remediation systems. After users or devices successfully authenticate, they are granted full network access with a dACL that permits all traffic. This is a critical component of this phase of TrustSec deployment.

Phase II: Closed Mode

Closed mode is one of the end goals as part of the phased deployment model of 802.1X. In a properly prepared network, closed mode provides total control over switch-level network access. This type of deployment is recommended only for environments in which administrators are experienced with 802.1X deployments and have considered all the nuances that go along with it. This mode can also be described as "deploy with caution" mode.

In closed mode, the switchport does not allow any traffic except EAP over LAN (EAPoL) until a successful authentication takes place. Traffic such as DHCP, HTTP, and DNS is not permitted while authentication is in progress, as shown in Figure 5-25.

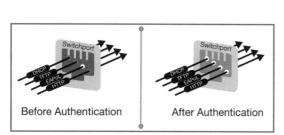

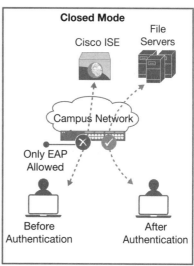

Figure 5-25   *Port Behavior with Closed Mode*

Closed mode can be useful for VLAN-based enforcement because the client does not get an IP address until it has been successfully authenticated. Closed mode is perfect for Cisco SD-Access deployments because no default VLAN is assigned at the port level. To add more granular access control, you can configure Cisco ISE to do dynamic VLAN assignment and push SGTs to restrict or permit traffic between different groups. By isolating traffic from different classes of users into separate VLANs and SGTs, closed mode provides the foundation for virtualized network services. Devices that cannot authenticate or fail to authenticate retain the same level of access that they had before authentication. In other words, they have no access to the network, because in closed mode, denying access is more desirable than providing limited or guest access.

Example 5-3 shows the 802.1X port configured in closed mode. Removing "authentication open" from monitor mode puts the port in closed mode. As you can see, no pre-authentication ACL is applied at the port level.

Example 5-3   *802.1X Closed Mode Authentication Port Configuration*

```
int GigabitEthernet1/4
   switchport access vlan 60
   switchport mode access
   switchport voice vlan 61
   no authentication open -------------> enables Closed Mode.
   authentication periodic
   authentication timer reauthenticate server
   authentication port-control auto
   mab
   dot1x pae authenticator
```

Deploying closed mode with VLAN assignment can have a significant impact on network architecture. Understanding these potential impacts is essential to a successful deployment of this mode. Therefore, the deployment of closed mode requires strategic planning and a variety of considerations. The beauty of using closed mode in a Cisco SD-Access world is that all the fabric edge nodes have the same VLAN database, they all support dynamic VLAN assignment, and Cisco DNA Center automates the configuration needed for the 802.1X phased approach.

Host Onboarding with Cisco DNA Center

An 802.1X phased approach is the best way to make sure the transition toward secure network access control is seamless to the end clients and to the administrator. However, a phased approach requires additional work by the network administrator whenever configuration changes need to be performed on the network devices to move from phase I to phase II or to make changes based on the monitor mode observations. Phased deployment, as mentioned in the previous section, involves changing the port-level configuration on the network devices, such as switches. It is time consuming and error prone to make the changes manually on all the network devices. In the Cisco SD-Access world, the Cisco DNA Center web GUI is equipped with flexible options to enable the 802.1X mode (and change the mode if needed) and provides granular control to modify the default templates.

Chapter 4, "Cisco Software-Defined Access Fundamentals," provides a glimpse of the authentication templates. This section provides under-the-hood details of various authentication options available in Cisco DNA Center. When a campus fabric is created, the fabric edge ports need to be configured with port-level authentication. Cisco DNA Center has various authentication templates available to choose from during the fabric host onboarding configuration, as shown in Figure 5-26 and described in the following sections.

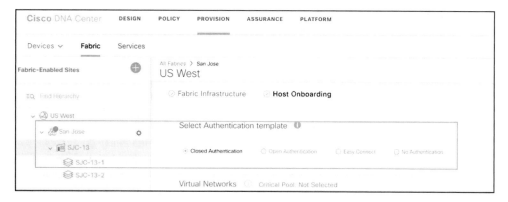

Figure 5-26 *Authentication Templates in Fabric Host Onboarding*

No Authentication Template

With the No Authentication template selected, the fabric edge ports are not configured to do a port authentication. Example 5-4 shows the port interface configuration when No authentication template is applied. Notice that no authentication commands or authentication templates are applied on the switchport.

Example 5-4 *"No Authentication" Template Port Configuration*

```
edge-1# sh run int gi1/0/3
interface GigabitEthernet1/0/3
 switchport access vlan 1021
 switchport mode access
 device-tracking attach-policy IPDT_MAX_10
 load-interval 30
 access-session inherit disable interface-template-sticky
 access-session inherit disable autoconf
 no macro auto processing
 spanning-tree portfast
end
```

When a client is connected to the port GigabitEthernet 1/0/3, the client is placed in VLAN 1021. A "No authentication" template option is not recommended, because the end clients are not validated before connecting to the network. Use caution when enabling this template at a global level or a port level, as it could introduce security risk. No authentication template should be applied for troubleshooting or when dealing with clients who do not support 802.1X and have static IP configuration.

Note the "device-tracking attach-policy IPDT_MAX_10" applied to the interface, as shown in Example 5-5.

Example 5-5   *Device-Tracking Policy Pushed by Cisco DNA Center*

```
edge-1# sh run | sec IPDT_MAX_10
device-tracking policy IPDT_MAX_10
 limit address-count 10
 no protocol udp
 tracking enable
```

IP Device Tracking (IPDT) keeps track of the connected hosts and their IP addresses. This host-to-IP address mapping is used to populate the dACLs applied by ISE, limits the number of hosts authenticating on the interface, and is used to detect IP address conflicts. IP Device Tracking is enabled on the Layer 2 switchports during the initial device discovery in Cisco DNA Center.

Open Authentication Template

Open authentication, as discussed in the previous section, always allows the traffic in either a passed or failed authentication. With the Open Authentication template selected, the fabric edge ports are configured in monitor mode. Example 5-6 shows the fabric edge with the Open Authentication template in place.

Example 5-6   *"Open Authentication" Template Port Configuration*

```
edge-1# sh run int gi1/0/4
interface GigabitEthernet1/0/4
 switchport mode access
 device-tracking attach-policy IPDT_MAX_10
 dot1x timeout tx-period 7
 dot1x max-reauth-req 3
 source template DefaultWiredDot1xOpenAuth
 spanning-tree portfast
end
```

A template named DefaultWiredDot1xOpenAuth is applied on the host-facing ports. As part of the Cisco TrustSec deployments, Cisco moved toward the new version of Identity Based Networking Services 2.0 (IBNS 2.0).

Figure 5-27 provides an overview of IBNS 2.0 and the various components involved. IBNS 2.0 makes use of class map, policy map, attaching the policy in a template and using this template in the interface configuration similar to the Quality of Service (QoS) policy configurations. As shown in Figure 5-27, a policy map contains the actions to be performed when an event is triggered. The template consists of the policy map as well as the service template with the attributes that need to be applied. The template is applied at an interface level. This approach helps to reduce the number of lines needed because the template is globally configured, making configuration easy to modify via the template instead of making changes on every interface.

Note   Cisco DNA Center from version 1.2.x forward provisions the authentication templates in the IBNS 2.0 style.

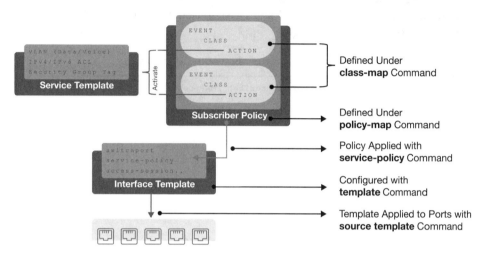

Figure 5-27   *IBNS 2.0 (New-Style 802.1X) Overview*

The **show template interface source user** *template name* command shows the configuration in the specified template. As shown in Example 5-7, a policy map with the name PMAP_DefaultWiredDot1xOpenAuth_1X_MAB is referenced in the template.

Example 5-7   *802.1X Open Authentication Template in IBNS 2.0*

```
edge-1# show template interface source user DefaultWiredDot1xOpenAuth
Template Name        : DefaultWiredDot1xOpenAuth
Template Definition :
 dot1x pae authenticator
 switchport access vlan 2047
 switchport mode access
 switchport voice vlan 2046
 mab
 access-session port-control auto
 authentication periodic
 authentication timer reauthenticate server
 service-policy type control subscriber PMAP_DefaultWiredDot1xOpenAuth_1X_MAB
!
end
```

Example 5-8 shows the output of **show policy-map type control subscriber PMAP_DefaultWiredDot1xOpenAuth_1X_MAB,** which includes the complete policy map with the events, the class maps, and the service templates.

For example, in the highlighted section of the output where the event is authentication-failure, if the authentication-failure is because the AAA server is down (class – AAA_SVR_DOWN_UNAUTHD_HOST) and the client has not been authenticated yet, the action is to activate DefaultCriticalAuthVlan_SRV_TEMPLATE, which places the unauthenticated client in the Critical VLAN. Take some time to view the policy map and the template outputs in Example 5-8.

Example 5-8   *802.1X Open Authentication Policy Map Configuration*

```
edge-1# show policy-map type control subscriber PMAP_DefaultWiredDot1xOpenAuth_
  1X_MAB
PMAP_DefaultWiredDot1xOpenAuth_1X_MAB
  event session-started match-all
    10 class always do-until-failure
      10 authenticate using dot1x retries 2 retry-time 0 priority 10
  event authentication-failure match-first
    5 class DOT1X_FAILED do-until-failure
      10 terminate dot1x
      20 authenticate using mab priority 20
    10 class AAA_SVR_DOWN_UNAUTHD_HOST do-until-failure
      10 activate service-template DefaultCriticalAuthVlan_SRV_TEMPLATE
      20 activate service-template DefaultCriticalVoice_SRV_TEMPLATE
      30 authorize
      40 pause reauthentication
    20 class AAA_SVR_DOWN_AUTHD_HOST do-until-failure
      10 pause reauthentication
      20 authorize
    30 class DOT1X_NO_RESP do-until-failure
      10 terminate dot1x
      20 authenticate using mab priority 20
    40 class MAB_FAILED do-until-failure
      10 terminate mab
      20 authentication-restart 60
    60 class always do-until-failure
      10 terminate dot1x
      20 terminate mab
      30 authentication-restart 60
  event aaa-available match-all
    10 class IN_CRITICAL_AUTH do-until-failure
      10 clear-session
    20 class NOT_IN_CRITICAL_AUTH do-until-failure
      10 resume reauthentication
```

Closed Authentication

Closed authentication is one of the end goals in Phase II. In closed authentication, traffic is permitted only if the authentication is successful. Prior to authentication, only EAPOL

traffic is allowed. With the Closed Authentication template selected for Cisco
DNA Center host onboarding, the fabric edge ports are configured in closed mode.
Example 5-9 shows the fabric edge port configuration provisioned by Cisco DNA Center.

Example 5-9 *"Closed Authentication" Template Port Configuration*

```
edge-1# sh run int gi1/0/6
Building configuration...

Current configuration : 225 bytes
!
interface GigabitEthernet1/0/6
 switchport mode access
 device-tracking attach-policy IPDT_MAX_10
 dot1x timeout tx-period 7
 dot1x max-reauth-req 3
 source template DefaultWiredDot1xClosedAuth
 spanning-tree portfast
end
```

The commands **show policy-map type control subscriber PMAP_DefaultWiredDot1x
ClosedAuth_1X_MAB** and **show template interface source DefaultWiredDot1x
ClosedAuth** can be used to view the configurations of the policy map and the template,
respectively.

Easy Connect

Easy Connect is an authentication template, also known as low-impact mode, that
applies an ACL to a port in open authentication. The ACL acts as an additional security mechanism to make sure that only certain traffic is allowed if the client fails
authentication. Example 5-10 shows sample output of a switchport with the Easy
Connect template provisioned by Cisco DNA Center. An inbound ACL named
IPV4_PRE_AUTH_ACL is applied on the interface, and the source template in use is
DefaultWiredDot1xLowImpactAuth in Easy Connect. The preauthorization ACL is only
allowing DHCP and DNS traffic.

Example 5-10 *Easy Connect Template Port Configuration*

```
edge-1# sh run int gi1/0/3
interface GigabitEthernet1/0/3
 switchport access vlan 1021
 switchport mode access
 device-tracking attach-policy IPDT_MAX_10
 ip access-group IPV4_PRE_AUTH_ACL in
 load-interval 30
```

```
ipv6 traffic-filter IPV6_PRE_AUTH_ACL in
access-session inherit disable interface-template-sticky
access-session inherit disable autoconf
dot1x timeout tx-period 7
dot1x max-reauth-req 3
no macro auto processing
```

If you need to change the pre-auth ACL or the authentication template parameters, you can modify them from Cisco DNA Center, the options for which are shown in Figure 5-28 and described in the list that follows.

Figure 5-28 *Authentication Template Edit from Cisco DNA Center*

- **Deployment Mode:** Displays Open for open authentication and Easy Connect; displays Closed for closed authentication.

- **First Authentication Order:** Selecting the 802.1X radio button causes 802.1X to be executed before failing over to MAB.

- **802.1X to MAB Fallback:** In this example, maximum retries is set to 3, and 802.1X timeout is set to 21 seconds.

- **Wake on LAN:** Option to enable Wake on LAN if that feature needs to be enabled.

- **Number of Hosts:** Choose a Single host or Unlimited hosts.

- **Pre-Auth Access Control (Low Impact Mode):** This ACL option is available only for low-impact mode (Easy Connect). You can modify the standard ACL from the Select Authentication Template section shown previously in Figure 5-26.

It is rather difficult to remember all the commands needed to configure class maps, policy maps, service templates, and source templates to enable port authentication. With Cisco DNA Center, you can easily deploy these templates with a click of the button. Irrespective of the fabric edge device operating system (Cisco IOS or Cisco IOS-XE), Cisco DNA Center pushes the equivalent configuration to all the fabric edges.

There may be a use case where the global authentication template is not applicable at a floor level. For example, suppose a retail customer with all the devices in the fabric has implemented the Easy Connect authentication template (low impact mode) globally. However, a new floor is being added to the fabric, and the customer wants to start with the Open Authentication template instead. Can the global authentication template be overridden at a site level? The answer is yes. You can override the global authentication template at a specific site level in Cisco DNA Center by navigating to **Provision > Fabric > Fabric Enabled Sites**, choosing the specific site, and clicking the Host Onboarding tab. Figure 5-29 shows the template as Easy Connect at the San Jose site level. Figure 5-30 shows the template as Open Authentication at the SJC-13 building level.

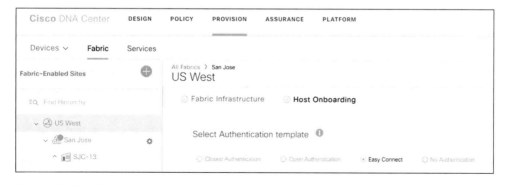

Figure 5-29 *Easy Connect at San Jose Site Level*

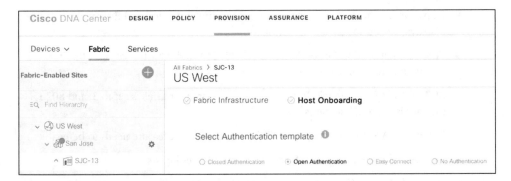

Figure 5-30   *Open Authentication at SJC-13 Site Level*

Security in Cisco Software-Defined Access Network

Campus fabric orchestrated by Cisco DNA Center, as discussed in detail in Chapter 4, has several components, such as border nodes, control nodes, and edge nodes. A fabric should not only provide network connectivity but also ensure that the users, devices, resources, and applications are segmented properly. This section discusses in detail various security mechanisms ingrained in Cisco SD-Access. The following are the two main ways of ensuring security is incorporated in the Cisco SD-Access fabric through segmentation:

■ Macro-segmentation using virtual networks

■ Micro-segmentation using scalable groups

Macro-Segmentation in Cisco SD-Access

Cisco SD-Access implements macro-segmentation using virtual networks. As introduced in Chapter 4, a virtual network (VN) in Cisco SD-Access fabric is a virtual routing and forwarding (VRF) instance in the traditional network. Virtual networks (or VRFs) maintain a separate routing and switching instance for the devices, interfaces, and subnets within it. In an enterprise network that has users such as employees or contractors who need to communicate with each other, those users are placed in the same VN. That VN may be called "Campus," for example. Usually guests do not communicate with any other users in the network and can be placed in a separate virtual network.

In essence, a virtual network consists of similar entities where there is a possibility of communication between these entities, meaning the endpoints that usually talk to each other constantly are placed in the same virtual network. Similar to VRFs, traffic between the VNs is not permitted within a Cisco SD-Access fabric. In a shared services network, discussed in Chapter 4, scenarios arise where campus users in the Campus VN need to communicate with shared services in the Shared Services VN for services such as DHCP,

DNS, Active Directory, and so forth. The network administrator needs to leverage route leaking to allow traffic between VNs. For inter-VN communications, such as access to shared services from the Campus VN, traffic needs to leave the SD-Access fabric, and the route leaking is performed outside the fabric. Virtual networks are first-level segmentation and ensure *zero communication* between forwarding domains.

Once the traffic leaves the fabric from a VN, the VN either can be handed off to a VRF in the traditional world to keep the macro-segmentation throughout or can be fused to the global routing table through a fusion router (covered in Chapter 4).

Cisco DNA Center provisions the configuration for the user-defined VNs. Figure 5-31 shows an example of two VNs, Building Management and Campus Users, where traffic is not permitted between the VNs. Within each specific VN, the endpoints are able to communicate with each other. To restrict communication between users in the same VN, micro-segmentation needs to be put in place, as described next.

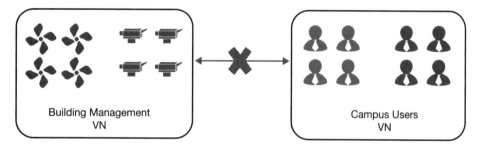

Figure 5-31   *Traffic Between VNs Is Blocked by Default*

Micro-Segmentation in Cisco SD-Access

Cisco SD-Access uses Scalable Group Tags for micro-segmentation. SGTs ensure that you can logically segment the network based on role instead of segmenting it based on physical topology or IP address. Using SGTs provides the ability to segment the network into either lines of business or functional blocks. Using SGTs brings in a second-level segmentation and ensures role-based access control between two groups within a VN. With SGTs, policies can be created to permit or restrict traffic for clients in the same VN.

SGTs are discussed in greater detail in Chapter 2 as part of the coverage of Cisco TrustSec building blocks. SGT values can be propagated either inline in a header such as VXLAN or pxGrid or using protocols such as SXP, which uses TCP. By default, traffic between SGTs is permitted. Business intent can be translated into policies through ACLs between SGTs. Figure 5-32 shows the use of SGTs within a VN. The Building Management VN has SGTs for IP cameras and building fans. As shown, building fans should be able to communicate with each other but shouldn't be able to communicate with IP cameras. IP cameras shouldn't be able to communicate with either fans or other IP cameras in the Building Management VN.

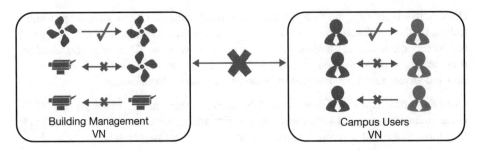

Figure 5-32 *Micro-Segmentation Within VN*

SGTs are assigned to a connecting endpoint based on their role, and the enforcement devices (for example, edge nodes) dynamically download the SGACLs associated for that SGT. Within the Campus fabric overlay, edge nodes and border nodes use SGACLs downloaded from ISE to make enforcement decisions based on the SGTs.

Policy Set Overview in Cisco ISE

Cisco ISE is a policy-based engine providing flexibility in configuration to achieve the security requirements for different type of customers. From Cisco ISE version 2.3 onward, ISE uses policy sets to logically group authentication and authorization policies within the same set. Multiple policy sets can be configured based on parameters such as device location, type of access, device type, and so on. A fresh installation of Cisco ISE has one policy set defined, called the default policy set. The default policy set contains predefined default authentication, authorization, and exception policy rules.

Policy sets are configured with conditions and results in order to choose the network access services on the policy set level, the identity sources on the authentication policy level, and network permissions on the authorization policy levels. Cisco ISE is all about customization, and one or more conditions can be configured using any of the attributes from the Cisco ISE–supported dictionaries for a variety of different vendors. Cisco ISE allows you to create custom conditions as individual policy elements that can be reused.

Figure 5-33 shows a sample policy set created in ISE. Every policy set has a condition defined, and if the condition is matched, the policy set is selected. The network access service to be used per policy set to communicate with the network devices is defined at the top level of that policy set. Network access services include

- **Allowed protocols:** The protocols configured to handle the initial request and protocol negotiation

- **A proxy service:** Sends requests to an external RADIUS server for processing

Figure 5-33 *Policy Sets in Cisco ISE*

Policy sets are configured hierarchically. The policy set evaluation stops when a policy set condition is matched. Within the policy set, authentication and authorization rules are configured. When a policy set is matched, rules of the set are applied in this order:

1. Authentication policy rules

2. Local policy exceptions

3. Global policy exceptions

4. Authorization policy rules

The common principle for a policy in ISE is that when the policy condition is matched, the action provided in the result is enforced. An example of a policy is shown in Figure 5-34. In a below policy, the condition is based on the dictionary attributes. For an IP phone policy, if the IP phone condition (Endpoint Identity Group = IP Phones) is matched, then the result is to push a voice VLAN for that incoming authentication request.

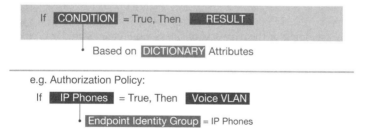

Figure 5-34 *Policy Logic in Cisco ISE*

Figure 5-35 shows an example of authentication and authorization policies configured in a policy set. In ISE, the first matched rule always applies. In authentication policy, an authentication method (Wired_802.1X OR Wireless_802.1X) is the condition. When the condition is met, the action is to do an identity lookup against the identity store configured. If the authentication from the identity lookup fails, there are more actions to perform. A successful authentication result moves the request to validate against authorization rules from top to bottom.

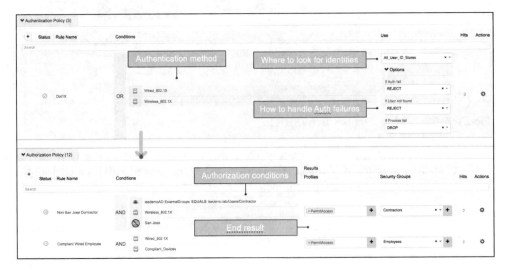

Figure 5-35   *Authentication and Authorization Policies in Cisco ISE*

Similar to authentication policy, authorization policies have authorization conditions and results. An authorization result is an authorization profile, which usually contains attributes that are pushed as part of the RADIUS response, such as VLAN, dACL, SGT, Airespace-ACL, guest redirection URL, and so forth.

Segmentation Policy Construction in Cisco SD-Access

You need a thorough understanding of the network, business requirements, and security requirements before proceeding with implementing segmentation policies. To understand the flow, this section continues with our example company ACME that is interested in implementing Cisco SD-Access. As part of business growth, ACME has a new building coming online in San Jose, California, that is going to be part of the campus fabric using Cisco DNA Center.

Following the guidelines introduced in Chapter 4, ACME has already built a fabric at the San Jose site level based on the topology shown in Figure 5-36.

ACME has six edge nodes, two border/control plane nodes co-located, and one Cisco wireless LAN controller. Cisco ISE, Cisco DNA Center, and DDI (DNS, DHCP, IP Address Management) are in the data center. No micro- or macro-segmentation has been implemented yet. Cisco ISE is already integrated with Cisco DNA Center. The following section examines ACME's business intent, segmentation requirements, and leverage of Cisco DNA Center and ISE to apply business intent to the network.

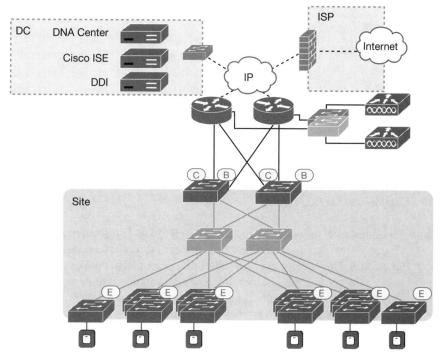

Figure 5-36 *ACME Fabric Topology*

Corporate Network Access Use Case

ACME in San Jose has campus users that include employees, accounting teams, and HR teams who need to be connected to the network. As part of the security strategy, all the campus users should connect using 802.1X.

Within the network, accounting users should not be able to communicate with other accounting users. Accounting users should also have access to the HR file server using FTP, but no other traffic should be permitted. Based on the requirements, a VN named Campus needs to be created with three main groups: Employees, accounting, and hr. To implement this use case, ACME needs to complete the following steps.

Step 1.   In Cisco DNA Center, create scalable groups named Employees, acct, and hr. Because ISE is already integrated, the groups created in Cisco DNA Center are automatically replicated to ISE.

Step 2.   Create a virtual network named Campus and allow the SGTs created in Step 1 to be part of the VN. This step results in the workflow of automatically extracting VNs based on SGTs when creating the policies in ISE. Figure 5-37 shows the Campus VN created in Cisco DNA Center and the SGTs that will be used within the VN.

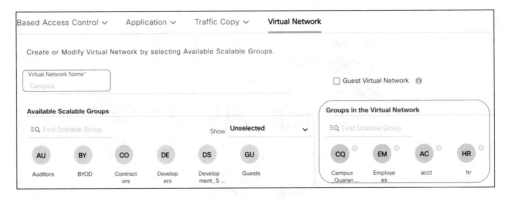

Figure 5-37   *Campus VN for ACME*

Step 3.   For Campus VN users, create and reserve an IP pool. As discussed in Chapter 4, the IP pool should be reserved at the fabric site level (San Jose for ACME). This IP pool can be a subset of a larger global pool or can be individually configured. The idea of micro-segmentation is to move away from the IP address dependency and use the SGTs to control network access. A larger IP pool such as /16 is recommended if the plan is to apply security policies based on SGTs. Figure 5-38 shows the IP pool created for the Campus VN for ACME at the San Jose level.

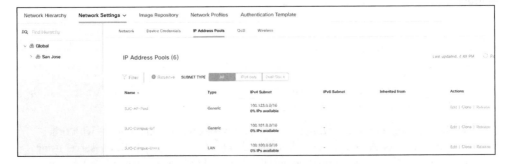

Figure 5-38   *IP Pool Reservation for Campus VN Users*

Note   If border automation is used to automate the handoff between the border nodes and the non-fabric network, the Campus VN needs to be allowed as part of the border automation.

Step 4.   Map the Campus IP pool to the Campus VN in fabric host onboarding. In Figure 5-39, the IP pool SJC-Campus-Users created in Step 3 is associated with the Campus VN. Note the authentication policy named

100_100_0_0-Campus for the IP pool. You can have multiple IP pool associations to one VN. In the example to follow, there are two Campus pools: Campus Users and Campus-IoT pool. ISE is the decision maker in pushing the pool the client will be placed in.

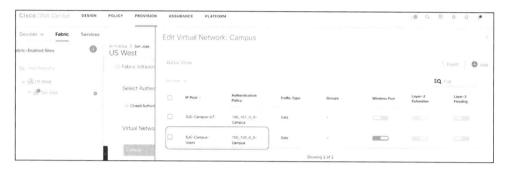

Figure 5-39 *Campus VN to Campus IP Pool Mapping*

When a VN-IP pool mapping is done, it results in a switch virtual interface (SVI) creation on all the fabric edge nodes with an anycast gateway. ACME topology consists of six fabric edge nodes resulting in the SVI creation for Campus IP pool on the nodes. This step also ensures that the SVI is part of the LISP instance on edge and border nodes. Example 5-11 shows the configuration pushed on the edge nodes and border nodes as a result of Step 4. The VLAN is created with the name 100_100_0_0-Campus, which can be customized if needed. The configuration on all the edge nodes would be the same, as Cisco SD-Access leverages anycast. Example 5-11 is an excerpt of the configuration pushed by Cisco DNA Center on edge nodes. An overlay VLAN 1021 is created in the Campus VN. The VLAN address is the anycast gateway address so that the users see the same default gateway in case the user moves from one edge to another. The VLAN is part of the LISP so that the client endpoint identifier (EID) information is sent to the LISP control plane when a client is placed in the overlay VLAN.

Example 5-11 *Edge Node Configuration Automated by Cisco DNA Center*

```
edge-1#
vlan 1021
 name 100_100_0_0-Campus  -◇ VLAN name is the mix of IP pool and VN


interface Vlan1021
 description Configured from Cisco DNA-Center
 mac-address 0000.0c9f.f45c
 vrf forwarding Campus
 ip address 100.100.0.1 255.255.0.0  ----> Anycast Gateway
```

```
ip helper-address 100.127.0.1
ip helper-address 100.64.0.100
no ip redirects
ip route-cache same-interface
no lisp mobility liveness test
lisp mobility 100_100_0_0-Campus-IPV4 ----->LISP command for EID mappings
end
```

Step 5.   Configure ISE policies so that the ACME employees are authenticated successfully using 802.1X. If the user is part of the accounting group, the user should be placed in the Campus Users VLAN and assigned the acct SGT. Similarly, an HR user should be placed in the Campus Users VLAN and assigned the hr SGT. Figure 5-40 shows a snippet of the policies ACME has configured. For ease of configuration, the internal database is used. In enterprise networks, ISE policies are usually configured to match on an external database like Active Directory membership or LDAP group. A single policy set is created for wired and wireless 802.1X users, under which authentication and authorization policies are configured.

Figure 5-40   *Policy Set for ACME 802.1X Users*

The authentication policy configured checks the internal database for 802.1X authentications. The Active Directory database is the most common database used in enterprise networks. Figure 5-41 shows the authentication rule configured for ACME 802.1X users.

Figure 5-41   *AuthC Policy for ACME 802.1X Users*

After the user is successfully authenticated, the user needs to be placed in the Campus Users VLAN (Campus IP pool) and assigned an SGT based on the user role. In ISE, the authorization profile consists of the attributes that need to be pushed to the end client. The authorization profile is used as a result in authorization rules. Figure 5-42 shows the authorization profile for an accounting user. The authorization profile CAMPUS_ACCT_USER_AUTHZ is pushing the acct SGT and Campus Users VLAN name. With ISE-DNAC integration, when an SGT is selected in the authorization profile, it shows the VN(s) the SGT is associated with and the IP pools mapped to that VN. Using the drop-down options, the SGT, VN, and IP pools are configured to avoid manual typos with the IP pool names (VLAN names). The authorization profile is pushing the SGT and the VLAN. A similar authorization profile is created for an HR user, with the SGT as hr.

Figure 5-42   *AuthZ Profile for ACME 802.1X Accounting User*

An authorization rule is created to match on the identity group of the user. If the user is part of the ACCT identity group, the accounting AuthZ profile created earlier is pushed. Similarly, an authorization rule for the HR identity group is configured as shown in Figure 5-43.

Figure 5-43   *AuthZ Rules for ACME 802.1X Users*

Step 6. Conduct user testing. Begin by attempting to connect an accounting user to the Edge-1 switchport using 802.1X authentication. In Cisco ISE, choose **Operations > RADIUS > Live Logs** to view the authentications coming to ISE and the policies matched for the users, as shown in Figure 5-44. On the edge switch, the **show authentication sessions interface** *interface number* **details** command shows the user authentication information.

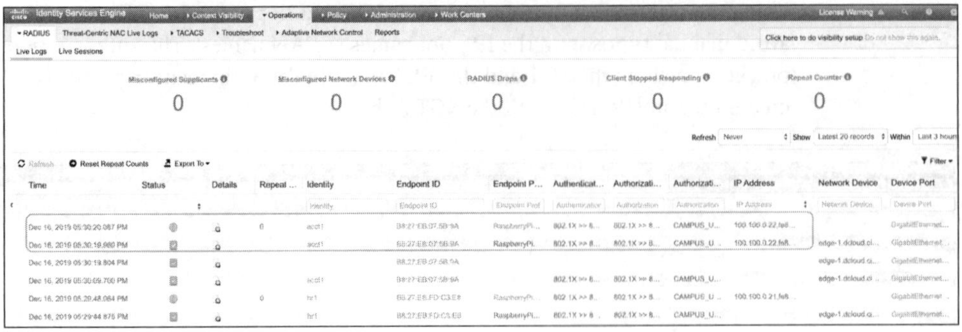

Figure 5-44 *RADIUS Live Logs in Cisco ISE*

Example 5-12 shows user authentication session details from the edge device. The acct1 user is connected on interface GigabitEthernet 1/0/36, is placed in Campus Users VLAN 1021, is provided an SGT of 17 (acct), has the Closed Authentication template applied, and has the status of Authorized.

Example 5-12 *acct1 User Connected Using 802.1X*

```
edge-1# show authentication sessions int gi1/0/36 details
            Interface:  GigabitEthernet1/0/36
              IIF-ID:  0x1D0836E7
         MAC Address:  b827.eb07.5b9a
        IPv6 Address:  Unknown
        Ipv4 Address:  100.100.0.22
           User-Name:  acct1
         Device-type:  RaspberryPi-Device
         Device-name:  RASPBERRY PI FOUNDATION
              Status:  Authorized
              Domain:  DATA
      Oper host mode:  multi-auth
     Oper control dir:  both
     Session timeout:  N/A
  Acct update timeout:  172800s (local), Remaining: 172794s
    Common Session ID:  94807C640000002210E0B46C
      Acct Session ID:  0x00000012
              Handle:  0x1f000016
      Current Policy:  PMAP_DefaultWiredDot1xClosedAuth_1X_MAB
```

```
Local Policies:


Server Policies:
          Vlan Group:  Vlan: 1021
          SGT Value:  17



Method status list:
       Method          State
          dot1x           Authc Success
```

As the output in Example 5-13 shows, the hr1 user is connected to interface GigabitEthernet 1/0/35, is connected using 802.1X with an IP address of 100.100.0.21 in Campus Users VLAN 1021, and has an SGT of 16 (hr).

Example 5-13 *hr1 User Connected Using 802.1X*

```
edge-1# show authentication sessions int gi1/0/35 details
          Interface:  GigabitEthernet1/0/35
            IIF-ID:  0x1A295E9C
        MAC Address:  b827.ebfd.c3e8
       IPv6 Address:  Unknown
       IPv4 Address:  100.100.0.21
          User-Name:  hr1
        Device-type:  RaspberryPi-Device
        Device-name:  RASPBERRY PI FOUNDATION
             Status:  Authorized
             Domain:  DATA
     Oper host mode:  multi-auth
    Oper control dir:  both
     Session timeout:  N/A
  Acct update timeout:  172800s (local), Remaining: 172729s
   Common Session ID:  94807C640000002310E64DE8
     Acct Session ID:  0x00000013
             Handle:  0x96000017
     Current Policy:  PMAP_DefaultWiredDot1xClosedAuth_1X_MAB


Local Policies:

Server Policies:
          Vlan Group:  Vlan: 1021
          SGT Value:  16



Method status list:
       Method          State
          dot1x           Authc Success
```

Step 7.   Configure policies that allow communication only by accounting users, and only to access the HR file server via FTP. Currently, ACME 802.1X accounting and hr users are able to communicate with each other on all ports, because no micro-segmentation policies are configured between the SGTs. As per the ACME corporate security policy, accounting users should be able to access the HR file server over FTP, and no other traffic should be allowed. In Figure 5-45, Cisco DNA Center is used to configure policies between acct SGT and hr SGT to allow FTP and ICMP. This policy will be pushed to ISE so that ISE can enforce the policy (SGACL) on the edge devices.

Figure 5-45   *SGACL Policies Allowing FTP from Acct to HR User in Cisco DNA Center*

In Example 5-14 with the outputs from an edge switch, the access policy created in Cisco DNA Center is downloaded from ISE, allowing FTP from the acct group to the hr group. The edge node downloads only the policies of the SGTs associated to the connected clients. The output of **show cts role-based permissions** indicates Allow_FTP-00 policy from the acct group to the hr group.

Example 5-14   *CTS Policy Download on Edge Switch*

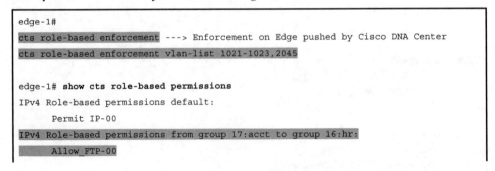

```
edge-1#
cts role-based enforcement ---> Enforcement on Edge pushed by Cisco DNA Center
cts role-based enforcement vlan-list 1021-1023,2045

edge-1# show cts role-based permissions
IPv4 Role-based permissions default:
      Permit IP-00
IPv4 Role-based permissions from group 17:acct to group 16:hr:
      Allow_FTP-00
```

```
RBACL Monitor All for Dynamic Policies : FALSE
RBACL Monitor All for Configured Policies : FALSE


edge-1# show cts role-based permissions from 17 to 16 det
IPv4 Role-based permissions from group 17:acct to group 16:hr:
    Allow_FTP-00
Details:
Role-based IP access list Allow_FTP-00 (downloaded)
    10 permit tcp dst eq ftp
    20 permit tcp dst eq 21000
    30 permit icmp
    40 deny ip
RBACL Monitor All for Dynamic Policies : FALSE
RBACL Monitor All for Configured Policies : FALSE
```

ACME has now deployed its wired LAN securely from Cisco DNA Center and ISE using the previous steps. ACME would like to make sure that its wireless LAN is also using the same policies as the wired LAN and that the employees are assigned the same policies coming from the wireless LAN. As part of the initial fabric, the WLC is already added to the fabric (as per Chapter 4). With an additional few steps, Cisco DNA Center can be configured to create an enterprise SSID and configure policies for the wireless network.

Step 8.   Use Cisco DNA Center to create the ACME enterprise SSID. Cisco DNA Center supports brownfield WLC configuration with fabric and non-fabric SSIDs.

Step 9.   In the Fabric Host Onboarding, the same Campus Users IP pool is assigned to the enterprise SSID, as shown in Figure 5-46. Until an IP pool is assigned to the SSID, the SSID status is shown as Disabled on the WLC. If there is a requirement to use a separate IP subnet for wireless users, a new IP pool can be created and assigned to the SSID. An IP pool that needs to be provisioned to a wireless SSID first needs to be mapped to a virtual network using the steps followed in Step 5. In fabric-enabled wireless, the wireless client data traffic follows the same path as the wired client data traffic through the edge and then the border. With IP pool to VN mapping, an SVI is provisioned on the fabric edge devices and the VLAN is added to the LISP instance. Depending on the IP pool requirements, Cisco SD-Access has the flexibility to provision the wired Campus IP pool to wireless campus users as well. Wireless campus users can also be provisioned with a separate IP pool. In either case, the wireless IP pool first needs to be mapped to the campus VN. IP pool to VN mapping results in SVI creation for the IP pool on the fabric edge nodes, and it will be made part of a LISP instance. An IP pool without a VN mapping won't be shown for selection for wireless SSID.

Figure 5-46   *Wireless SSID to IP Pool Mapping*

Step 10.   Conduct wireless client testing. A wireless user hr2 is connected to the ACME
wireless SSID SDA-Campus and can connect successfully. Because the policies
in ISE are configured for wired and wireless 802.1X, no additional configuration is needed in ISE. The SGT policies created are applicable to wireless users
as well because the policies are based on SGTs, not the IP address. The policy
enforcement still happens on the edge device, as the client wireless traffic uses
the underlying wired infrastructure, and the wireless Control and Provisioning
of Wireless Access Points (CAPWAP) is used only for the client association
traffic. Figure 5-47 shows that wireless client hr2 received an IP address of
100.100.0.23, which is the same IP pool used for the wired users.

Figure 5-47   *hr2 User Client Summary*

Figure 5-48 shows additional details for wireless user hr2 with the hr (tag value -16) SGT
assigned by Cisco ISE dynamically.

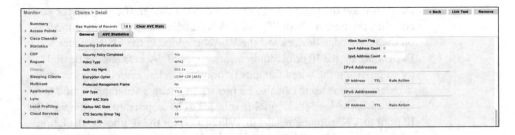

Figure 5-48   *hr2 User Client Authentication Details*

ACME has successfully deployed wired and wireless secure access in its Cisco SD-Access network.

Guest Access Use Case

ACME would like the guests visiting its campus to have a great experience by providing free Internet access. Guests should be provided with a hotspot page where they are asked to accept terms and conditions before they are provided Internet access. The security team would like to make sure that guests cannot have access to any of the corporate resources and cannot reach other guests via the network. Because ACME's network has already been working well for corporate users using Cisco SD-Access, ACME would like to leverage Cisco DNA Center to onboard the guest use case as well. The steps ACME needs to follow for this use case are presented here:

Step 1.   Per ACME security policies, place guest users in a separate network. Guests should be placed in their own virtual network so that they can be handed off to a DMZ network when they leave the fabric. Figure 5-49 shows the Guest VN created for ACME and the Guests SGT that will be used within this VN. As shown, the Guest Virtual Network checkbox should be checked for a Guest VN. Enabling the Guest VN checkbox helps you later in the workflow to map the Guest IP pool associated to this VN.

Figure 5-49   *Guest VN for ACME*

Step 2.   In Cisco DNA Center, create a fabric-enabled Guest SSID. As part of the Guest SSID creation, Cisco DNA Center has the capability to create the portals that are presented to the guest users. Guest flows include Self-Registered Guest, Sponsored-Guest, and Hotspot Guest. When the portals are created from Cisco DNA Center, they get pushed to Cisco ISE through the ERS API so that ISE can present these portals during client guest redirection. Figure 5-50 shows the Guest SSID created for ACME. The SDA-Guest SSID is created on the WLC but is not enabled because no IP pool is assigned to the SSID yet. Cisco DNA Center also creates the Hotspot Guest portal in ISE to present to guest users during their connection.

Figure 5-50   *Fabric-Enabled Guest SSID Creation*

Step 3.   Reserve the Guest IP pool for the guest users. Similar to the IP pool for corporate users, the Guest IP pool can be a subset of a larger global pool or can be individually configured at the global level and reserved at the fabric level. The IP pool reservation should always be done at the fabric level. Figure 5-51 shows the IP pool reservation for ACME; the pool type should be Generic (grayed out in the figure).

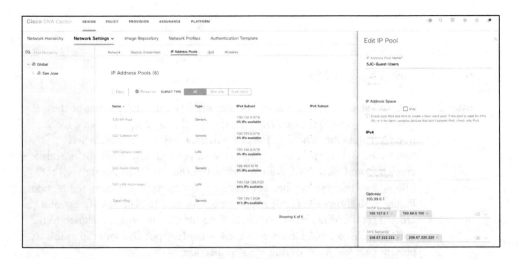

Figure 5-51   *IP Pool Reservation for Guest Users*

Step 4.   Map the IP pool created in Step 3 to the Guest VN. This step results in an SVI created for the IP pool on the edge nodes and adds LISP instances for the Guest VN on all the devices in fabric. This step also moves the status of the SSID to Enabled on the WLC. The IP pool should be enabled as a Wireless Pool, as shown in Figure 5-52, which creates a corresponding VLAN interface on the WLC. It also makes sure that the pool can be shown in the drop-down list for Guest SSID mapping.

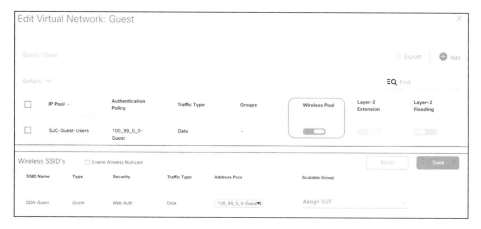

Figure 5-52   *VN to IP Pool Mapping for Guest SSID*

The Guest pool name is 100_99_0_0-Guest, which can be customized if needed. If a default SGT needs to be assigned just in case ISE does not push an SGT, the Assign SGT option can be used. ISE dynamic SGT assignment takes precedence over the static SGT assigned to the IP pool.

Step 5.   As part of the Guest SSID creation and the IP pool to SSID mapping, Cisco DNA Center automatically creates the authorization policies for the Guest SSID in ISE under the default policy set. Figure 5-53 shows the policies created by Cisco DNA Center under the default policy set in ISE. ACME can either continue using the policies pushed by Cisco DNA Center or customize the policies if it needs a separate policy set for Guest users. Two authorization rules are configured for guests: one rule for the initial guest redirection so that the guest users are presented with the redirection portal as soon as they connect to the Guest SSID, and a second rule to provide final Internet access and Guest SGT to the Guest users once a guest accepts the AUP on the portal page. ISE uses change of authorization (CoA) to move the guest from a redirection state to the final access state.

Figure 5-53   *Cisco ISE Guest Policies Pushed by Cisco DNA Center*

Step 6.   Now that all the policies are in place for ACME guest users, begin the testing phase. A wireless client is connecting to the SDA-Guest SSID. When the client is connected to the SSID, the guest redirect policy is matched, the client is in the CENTRAL_WEB_AUTH state, and the redirect URL is pushed, as shown in Figure 5-54. The client received an IP address of 100.99.0.22 from the Guest IP pool and is in the web authentication state with a redirection URL pointing to Cisco ISE. At this stage, when the client tries to access any traffic, a captive portal opens to the AUP page.

Figure 5-54   *Guest in Web Authentication State on WLC*

The guest accepts the AUP and the client is placed in a RUN state and given the Guests SGT. Figure 5-55 shows the client state on the WLC after successful guest connection. Figure 5-56 shows the authentication report from ISE. ISE logs indicate a guest policy pushed first, and then the final Internet access pushed to the client after change of authorization.

Figure 5-55   *Client State on WLC*

At this point, guests of ACME are able to connect to the network and receive Internet access. ACME's security policies indicate that guests should not be able to communicate with other guests. Cisco DNA Center can be leveraged to configure SGT policy to block traffic between guests.

Figure 5-56 *Wireless Client Report in ISE*

Step 7. Cisco DNA Center is used to configure deny policy (SGACL) between guests. The policy gets pushed to Cisco ISE, which then deploys the policy (SGACL) to the edge nodes for enforcement. Figure 5-57 shows the Guest policy created on Cisco DNA Center that will be pushed to the edge node. Even though the clients are wireless clients, the enforcement happens on the edge node to which the access point is connected, as wireless data traffic uses the same path as wired data traffic in Cisco SD-Access.

Figure 5-57 *Deny Policy for Inter-Guest Communication*

On Edge-1, the command **show cts role-based permissions** shows the policy downloaded and applied on the edge node for Guests SGT users, as shown in Example 5-15.

Example 5-15   *Inter-Guest Policy Based on Guest SGT*

```
edge-1# show cts role-based permissions
IPv4 Role-based permissions default:
     Permit IP-00
IPv4 Role-based permissions from group 6:Guests to group 6:Guests:
     Deny IP-00
RBACL Monitor All for Dynamic Policies : FALSE
RBACL Monitor All for Configured Policies : FALSE
```

Segmentation Outside the Fabric

Segmentation beyond the fabric site has multiple variations depending on the type of transit. In Cisco SD-Access for Distributed Campus and SD-WAN transits, the VN information is natively carried within the packet.

In an IP-based transit, due to the VXLAN de-encapsulation outside the Cisco SD-Access fabric, that SGT information can be lost. Two approaches exist to carry SGT information between fabric sites using an IP-based transit. The most straightforward approach, although the least deployed due to service provider equipment being beyond the engineer's administrative control, is to configure inline tagging (sending SGT in the Ethernet header) hop by hop between each fabric site. A second design option is to use SGT Transfer Protocol (SXP) to carry the IP-to-SGT bindings between sites. Using SXP, these bindings can be carried over Generic Routing Encapsulation (GRE), IP Security (IPsec), Dynamic Multipoint Virtual Private Network (DMVPN), and Group Encrypted Transport VPN (GETVPN) circuits between sites.

SXP has both scaling and enforcement point implications that must be considered. Between fabric sites, SXP can be used to enforce the SGTs at either the border nodes or at the routing infrastructure northbound of the border. If enforcement is done at the routing infrastructure, SGT needs to be carried from the border node all the way to the enforcement point in the traditional network.

Summary

Policy plays a vital role in Cisco SD-Access. Through integration of Cisco DNA Center and Cisco ISE, SGTs, access contracts, and policies are managed from Cisco DNA Center. Various levels of security are embedded into the campus fabric. The first level of defense is macro-segmentation via virtual networks. The second level of defense is micro-segmentation using scalable groups. Security has never been simple to implement, but Cisco DNA Center has made it much simpler through an interactive and flexible web GUI. The two use cases of the fictional ACME organization described several policy options in detail.

References in This Chapter

Cisco DNA Center End-User Guides: https://www.cisco.com/c/en/us/support/cloud-systems-management/dna-center/products-user-guide-list.html

Cisco Software-Defined Access Design Guides: https://www.cisco.com/c/en/us/solutions/enterprise-networks/software-defined-access/index.html#~resources

Cisco DNA Center Install and Upgrade Guides: https://www.cisco.com/c/en/us/support/cloud-systems-management/dna-center/products-installation-guides-list.html

Cisco TrustSec Design Guides: https://www.cisco.com/c/en/us/solutions/enterprise-networks/trustsec/design-guide-listing.html

Chapter 6

Cisco Software-Defined Access Operation and Troubleshooting

This chapter covers the following topics:

- **Cisco SD-Access Under the Covers:** This section discusses the underlying protocols used in the Cisco Software-Defined Access fabric.

- **Host Operation and Packet Flow in Cisco SD-Access:** This section covers how hosts connect to a Cisco Software-Defined Access fabric and how packets flow between fabric hosts and outside of the fabric.

- **Cisco SD-Access Troubleshooting:** This section focuses on troubleshooting common issues in Cisco Software-Defined Access.

- **Authentication/Policy Troubleshooting:** This section focuses on troubleshooting common issues with authentication and policy in a Cisco Software-Defined Access fabric.

Cisco SD-Access Under the Covers

Although a few of the biggest benefits of Cisco Software-Defined Access are automation and an abstraction of the underlying hardware and configuration, in some cases network engineers need to know what is happening "under the hood" to resolve issues or simply to understand the solution more completely.

Fabric Encapsulation

As discussed in Chapter 2, "Introduction to Cisco Software-Defined Access," Cisco SD-Access is a fabric-based (or overlay-based) solution that is built using two industry-standard encapsulation protocols:

- Locator/Identifier Separation Protocol (LISP) is used for the control plane in Cisco SD-Access and provides host and network reachability information to the nodes in the fabric.

- Virtual Extensible LAN (VXLAN) is used for the data plane in Cisco SD-Access and carries the host traffic between fabric nodes in its encapsulation.

Figure 6-1 illustrates a simplified view of encapsulation in which the original packet remains intact as LISP or VXLAN headers are applied.

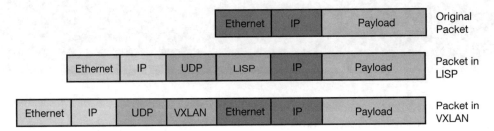

Figure 6-1   *Simplified Encapsulation Model*

The use of LISP and VXLAN provides many benefits over traditional networking using Layer 2 VLANs and Layer 3 routing protocols, including the following:

- **Elimination of Spanning Tree Protocol (STP):** Because VLANs are no longer spanned between connected Layer 2 switches, there are no loops that require the STP loop prevention mechanism. This also comes with the added benefit of no longer having a risk of broadcast storms.

- **Seamless mobility:** Because LISP uses primarily host routes and a "pull" model (covered later in this chapter), endpoint mobility is made easier and more efficient without the overloading of routing tables that would occur with traditional routing protocols.

- **Native support for segmentation using Scalable Group Tags (SGTs):** As discussed in Chapter 2, Cisco SD-Access leverages Cisco TrustSec SGTs for micro-segmentation, which are supported in the VXLAN header used in the solution.

- **Efficient use of redundant links:** Because Cisco SD-Access is a Layer 3–based solution, it can take advantage of parallel links between devices in the fabric using Layer 3 load-balancing mechanisms such as equal-cost multi-path (ECMP) routing.

LISP

In traditional IP-based networks, an endpoint IP address is composed of two parts: the network address and the host address. The endpoint's subnet mask is used to distinguish between these two parts so that the endpoint can differentiate between local traffic

(traffic on the same subnet) and remote traffic. This IP scheme is used globally within enterprises and the Internet, and although it is functional, it has limitations in terms of scalability and flexibility.

Locator/Identifier Separation Protocol (LISP) is an industry-standard protocol described in RFC 6830. LISP was originally conceived in 2006 as a potential solution to address the scalability and addressing limitations inherent to traditional IP-based networking used on the Internet. LISP solves these limitations by separating reachability information into routing locator (RLOC) and endpoint identifier (EID). This separation allows for better scale and more agile networks because the actual endpoint IP address can be abstracted and doesn't need to be known by the underlying network. LISP has many uses in networking today, including in WAN and data center applications, and its flexibility and scalability make it suitable for campus/branch network solutions such as Cisco SD-Access.

Due to this separation and LISP's on-demand functionality, the use of LISP in Cisco SD-Access allows for host mobility and the flexibility to span subnets across many switches without having to also span Layer 2 VLANs or utilize routing table space on every fabric node.

An appropriate analogy for this operation is how modern-day mobile phone networks work. Simply put, when a mobile phone is moved from area to area, it registers to its nearest cell tower/switch, which in turn updates a centralized database. That database is shared between mobile phone carriers globally. Therefore, when the number for the mobile phone is dialed from a different phone (mobile or landline), the tower/switch near the calling phone queries the centralized database to find out which tower/switch the receiving phone is connected to. Only when that is accomplished does the call establish. Similarly, in Cisco SD-Access, an endpoint (A) registers with its connected fabric edge switch, which updates the LISP control plane with this registration information. When a different endpoint (B) needs to communicate with the endpoint A, its fabric edge switch queries the LISP control plane to ask its location. The LISP control plane responds with the location of endpoint A's fabric edge switch, thus establishing the communication path.

All fabric devices that play a role in Cisco SD-Access (edge, control plane, and border nodes) are configured as RLOCs by Cisco DNA Center, with the Loopback0 interface address representing the RLOC address, while hosts/endpoint IP addresses in a fabric are tracked as EIDs. As discussed in Chapter 4, "Cisco Software-Defined Access Fundamentals," intermediate nodes are not technically part of the Cisco SD-Access or LISP process and are only responsible for routing packets between RLOCs in the fabric.

Figure 6-2 shows the LISP header format and demonstrates how it encapsulates the original packet header, allowing the packet to be routed between RLOCs. Other fields include Instance ID, which is used to identify which table the EID is in and maintain segmentation in the fabric. The result is that the underlay network needs to know only where the RLOCs are located and simply routes the encapsulated traffic between them.

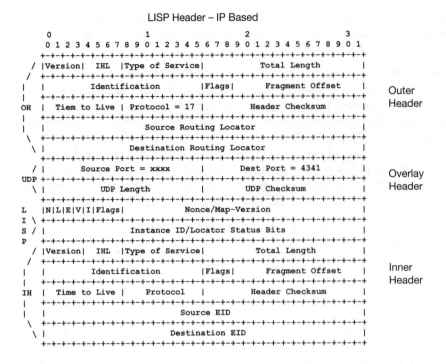

Figure 6-2 *LISP Header*

In Cisco SD-Access, the fabric roles in Table 6-1 are mapped to corresponding LISP roles.

Table 6-1 *Fabric Roles*

Cisco SD-Access Fabric Role	LISP Role	Function(s)
Edge	Egress Tunnel Router (ETR)/Ingress Tunnel Router (ITR)	Endpoint connectivity Registration of endpoints with control plane
Control plane	Map Resolver/Map Server	Endpoint/network registration database Responds to EID lookup requests from fabric edge and borders
Border	Proxy Egress/Ingress Tunnel Router (PETR/PITR)	Routes traffic between the fabric and non-fabric networks

Virtual networks (VNs) or virtual routing and forwarding instances (VRFs) in Cisco SD-Access are represented by LISP instance IDs, with each instance ID housing its own table of EIDs. This allows LISP to maintain macro-segmentation between its tables, which also makes troubleshooting easier.

VXLAN

Virtual Extensible LAN (VXLAN) is a network encapsulation solution that is described in RFC 7348. VXLAN allows for the transport of Layer 2 Ethernet frames over a Layer 3 infrastructure and is used in many data center applications to address scalability limitations present in traditional VLAN-based networks, including support for up to 16 million VLANs and the ability to span VLANs across geographic boundaries. It is also the data plane protocol used in the Cisco Application Centric Infrastructure (Cisco ACI) solution.

Note Cisco SD-Access technically uses VXLAN Group Policy Option (VXLAN-GPO) extension for encapsulation, which is a backward-compatible extension to VXLAN that adds support for the carrying of SGTs in its header. This extension allows for policy in the Cisco SD-Access fabric.

Figure 6-3 shows the VXLAN header format, which encapsulates similarly to how LISP encapsulates but can also carry Layer 2 Ethernet frames, enabling SGTs to be transported from end to end.

```
                        VXLAN Header - Ethernet Based

        0                   1                   2                   3
        0 1 2 3 4 5 6 7 8 9 0 1 2 3 4 5 6 7 8 9 0 1 2 3 4 5 6 7 8 9 0 1
        +-+-+-+-+-+-+-+-+-+-+-+-+-+-+-+-+-+-+-+-+-+-+-+-+-+-+-+-+-+-+-+-+
     / |Version|  IHL  |Type of Service|          Total Length         |
     /  +-+-+-+-+-+-+-+-+-+-+-+-+-+-+-+-+-+-+-+-+-+-+-+-+-+-+-+-+-+-+-+-+
    |  |          Identification        |Flags|      Fragment Offset   |    Outer
    |   +-+-+-+-+-+-+-+-+-+-+-+-+-+-+-+-+-+-+-+-+-+-+-+-+-+-+-+-+-+-+-+-+   Header
    OH |  Time to Live | Protocal = 17 |          Header Checksum       |
    |   +-+-+-+-+-+-+-+-+-+-+-+-+-+-+-+-+-+-+-+-+-+-+-+-+-+-+-+-+-+-+-+-+
    |  |                  Source Routing Locator                       |
    \   +-+-+-+-+-+-+-+-+-+-+-+-+-+-+-+-+-+-+-+-+-+-+-+-+-+-+-+-+-+-+-+-+
    \  |                Destination Routing Locator                    |
        +-+-+-+-+-+-+-+-+-+-+-+-+-+-+-+-+-+-+-+-+-+-+-+-+-+-+-+-+-+-+-+-+
     / |       Source Port = xxxx      |       Dest Port = 4789        |
    UDP +-+-+-+-+-+-+-+-+-+-+-+-+-+-+-+-+-+-+-+-+-+-+-+-+-+-+-+-+-+-+-+-+
    \  |          UDP Length           |         UDP Checksum          |
        +-+-+-+-+-+-+-+-+-+-+-+-+-+-+-+-+-+-+-+-+-+-+-+-+-+-+-+-+-+-+-+-+
     / |R|R|R|R|I|R|R|R|             Reserved                          |    Overlay
    VXLAN +-+-+-+-+-+-+-+-+-+-+-+-+-+-+-+-+-+-+-+-+-+-+-+-+-+-+-+-+-+-+-+   Header
    \  |             VXLAN Network Identifier (VNI) |   Reserved        |
        +-+-+-+-+-+-+-+-+-+-+-+-+-+-+-+-+-+-+-+-+-+-+-+-+-+-+-+-+-+-+-+-+
     / |           Inner Destination MAC Address                       |
     /  +-+-+-+-+-+-+-+-+-+-+-+-+-+-+-+-+-+-+-+-+-+-+-+-+-+-+-+-+-+-+-+-+
    |  | Inner Destination MAC Address | Inner Source MAC Address       |
    Eth +-+-+-+-+-+-+-+-+-+-+-+-+-+-+-+-+-+-+-+-+-+-+-+-+-+-+-+-+-+-+-+-+
    |  |               Inner Source MAC Address                         |
    \   +-+-+-+-+-+-+-+-+-+-+-+-+-+-+-+-+-+-+-+-+-+-+-+-+-+-+-+-+-+-+-+-+
Optional Ethertype = C-Tag [802.1Q]    | Inner.VLAN Tag Infromation    |    Inner
        +-+-+-+-+-+-+-+-+-+-+-+-+-+-+-+-+-+-+-+-+-+-+-+-+-+-+-+-+-+-+-+-+   Header
     / | Ethertype of Original Payload |                                |
     /  +-+-+-+-+-+-+-+-+-+-+-+-+-+-+-+-+                                +
    |  |                                    Original Ethernet Payload   |
Payload|                                                                 |
    |  | (Note that the original Ethernet Frame's FCS is not included)  |
    |   +-+-+-+-+-+-+-+-+-+-+-+-+-+-+-+-+-+-+-+-+-+-+-+-+-+-+-+-+-+-+-+-+
    \  |    New FCS (Frame Check Sequence) for Outer Ethernet Frame     |
    \   +-+-+-+-+-+-+-+-+-+-+-+-+-+-+-+-+-+-+-+-+-+-+-+-+-+-+-+-+-+-+-+-+
```

Figure 6-3 *VXLAN Header*

Similar to how LISP terminates its packets on RLOCs, VXLAN uses VXLAN tunnel endpoints (VTEPs), and in Cisco SD-Access, VTEPs are represented by the Loopback0 interface on each fabric node.

After an endpoint's location (RLOC) is looked up using the LISP control plane, a fabric node encapsulates all traffic destinated for that endpoint in VXLAN with a destination VTEP of the RLOC. This flow is described in detail later in this chapter.

MTU Considerations

An important design consideration when using a Cisco SD-Access fabric, or any overlay-based solution, is that the encapsulation protocol generally increases the total size of the packet that transits across the underlying network. In the case of LISP and VXLAN, up to 56 bytes could be added to every packet, which may cause fragmentation and connectivity issues if the underlying network is not configured to handle larger packets. For this reason, the recommended maximum transmission unit (MTU) for any Cisco SD-Access underlay is 9100 bytes end to end. This MTU size allows for any encapsulated traffic to properly route through the network without disruption.

Host Operation and Packet Flow in Cisco SD-Access

From an endpoint's perspective, host operation in Cisco SD-Access behaves identically to the way it does with traditional networking. If an endpoint needs to reach another endpoint on the same subnet, it will send an Address Resolution Protocol (ARP) request for the destination endpoint IP's MAC address. When an ARP reply is received, the source endpoint will send the traffic to the switch with the destination endpoint's MAC as the target. For a destination endpoint on a different subnet, the sending endpoint will send the packet to its default gateway with the destination endpoint's IP address as the target. The difference in Cisco SD-Access is that the LISP process on the fabric edge switch intercepts these processes so that it can encapsulate the traffic and send it through the fabric. The following section describes this flow and the processes involved.

DHCP in Cisco SD-Access

As described in Chapter 5, "Cisco Identity Services Engine with Cisco DNA Center," after an endpoint authenticates to the network, Cisco ISE or a third-party RADIUS server instructs the fabric edge to place the switch interface connected to the endpoint onto its authorized VLAN and to tag each packet from the endpoint with a specific SGT. After the endpoint is connected to the VLAN, unless configured with a static IP address, it broadcasts a Dynamic Host Control Protocol (DHCP) packet in order to receive an IP address from a DHCP server. In a traditional networking environment, the **ip helper-address** command is configured on the upstream Layer 3 or switch virtual interface (SVI), which encapsulates all DHCP requests and unicasts them to a DHCP server elsewhere in the network with itself as a source. In Cisco SD-Access, an anycast gateway is used, which replicates the same SVI address on all fabric edge nodes. As a result, the DHCP request must be specially handled in the fabric.

This process is facilitated by the fabric edge acting as a DHCP relay agent using the DHCP Option 82 field, which allows the fabric to locate the source of the DHCP request when the DHCP server replies.

Example 6-1 shows a sample of the DHCP configuration that is pushed to fabric edge switches from Cisco DNA Center. This configuration includes the **ip helper-address** command and enables the DHCP relay agent and DHCP snooping to intercept DHCP requests from the endpoints.

Example 6-1   *DHCP Configuration on Fabric Edge Switch*

```
ip dhcp relay information option
ip dhcp snooping vlan 1021-1023,2045
ip dhcp snooping

interface Vlan1021
 description Configured from Cisco DNA-Center
 vrf forwarding Campus
 ip address 100.100.0.1 255.255.0.0
 ip helper-address 100.127.0.1
 ip helper-address 100.64.0.100
```

The DHCP request process in Cisco SD-Access is as follows:

1. The client sends a broadcast DHCP request packet with its MAC address as a source to the fabric edge switch.

2. The fabric edge switch adds DHCP Option 82 containing the VXLAN Network Identifier (VNID), or instance ID along with its RLOC address and then encapsulates the request into a unicast packet with the IP address of the SVI/anycast gateway as its source and the DHCP server IP address as the destination.

3. This packet is routed in the overlay and sent via the fabric border to the DHCP server outside of the fabric.

Figure 6-4 shows the flow of the DHCP request sent from the endpoint. The fabric edge switch intercepts this request and adds DHCP Option 82 to the request containing instance ID 4099 and its RLOC address of 100.124.128.135. The fabric edge switch also changes the source of the DHCP request to its SVI address of 100.100.0.1 and sends the packet toward the fabric border in the overlay.

Example 6-2 is sample output of a debug captured on the fabric edge switch during the DHCP request process. It shows the fabric edge intercepting the request and adding Option 82 before forwarding it toward the DHCP server.

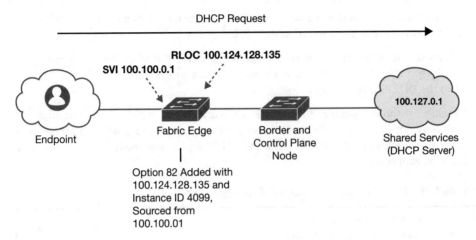

Figure 6-4 *DHCP Request Sent from Endpoint*

Example 6-2 *DHCP Debug on Fabric Edge Switch*

```
DHCP_SNOOPING: received new DHCP packet from input interface (GigabitEthernet1/0/36)
DHCP_SNOOPING: process new DHCP packet, message type: DHCPREQUEST, input interface:
  Gi1/0/36, MAC da: ffff.ffff.ffff, MAC sa: b827.eb07.5b9a, IP da: 255.255.255.255,
  IP sa: 0.0.0.0, DHCP ciaddr: 0.0.0.0, DHCP yiaddr: 0.0.0.0, DHCP siaddr: 0.0.0.0,
  DHCP giaddr: 0.0.0.0, DHCP chaddr: b827.eb07.5b9a, efp_id: 931069952, vlan_id:
  1021
DHCP_SNOOPING: add relay information option.
DHCP_SNOOPING: Encoding opt82 CID in vlan-mod-port format
LISP ID is valid, encoding RID in srloc format
DHCP_SNOOPING: binary dump of relay info option, length: 22 data:
0x52 0x14 0x1 0x6 0x0 0x4 0x3 0xFD 0x1 0x24 0x2 0xA 0x3 0x8 0x0 0x10 0x3 0x1 0x64
  0x7C 0x80 0x86
DHCP_SNOOPING: bridge packet get invalid mat entry: FFFF.FFFF.FFFF, packet is
  flooded to ingress VLAN: (1021)
DHCP_SNOOPING: bridge packet send packet to cpu port: Vlan1021.
```

The response from the DHCP server is sent back toward the endpoint and goes through the following process:

1. The DHCP reply is received by the fabric border, which has a loopback interface configured with the same IP address as the anycast gateway.

2. The fabric border sees Option 82 in the reply containing the fabric border's RLOC address and the instance ID and sends the DHCP response directly to the fabric edge.

3. The fabric edge receives the reply, de-encapsulates the packet, and then forwards the raw DHCP reply to the endpoint.

Figure 6-5 shows the flow of the DHCP reply sent from the DHCP server. The fabric border receives the reply and, after reading Option 82 in the packet, directs the reply to the fabric edge switch for forwarding to the endpoint.

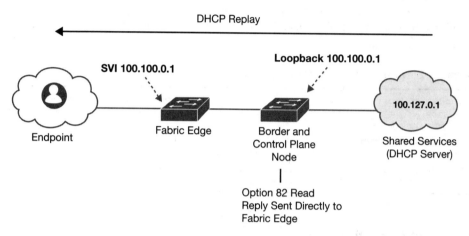

Figure 6-5   *DHCP Reply Sent from DHCP Server*

Wired Host Onboarding and Registration

After an authenticated wired endpoint connects to the Cisco SD-Access fabric and obtains an IP address via DHCP, the fabric edge switch performs two tasks:

1. It adds the endpoint's MAC and IP addresses in its local database.

2. It registers the endpoint's MAC and IP addresses with the fabric control plane(s). This registration is done via the LISP Map-Register message.

Figure 6-6 shows the fabric edge sending a LISP Map-Register message containing the IP/EID of the endpoint (100.100.0.22) and registering itself (100.124.128.134) as the RLOC.

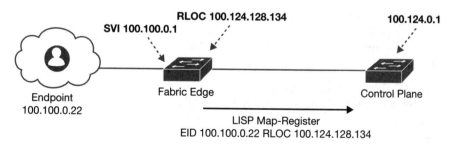

Figure 6-6   *LISP Map-Register Message*

These registrations are stored in the control plane's LISP table, which lists each MAC or IP address with a corresponding RLOC address of the fabric edge. As previously noted, these tables are stored as separate instance IDs in LISP to maintain segmentation. An example of these tables is presented later in the chapter.

Example 6-3 is sample output of a debug captured on the fabric edge switch during the LISP Map-Register process. It shows the fabric edge registering the EID 100.100.0.22 with the control plane at 100.124.0.1. It also shows the EID being added to the local LISP database of the fabric edge.

Example 6-3   *LISP Map-Register Debug on Fabric Edge Switch*

```
[XTR] LISP-0: Local dynEID Auto-L2-group-8188 IID 8188 prefix b827.eb07.5b9a/48,
  Creating AR entry 100.100.0.22 l3_iid 4099, now has 1 v4 and 1 v6 (state: active,
  rlocs: 1/1, sources: dynamic).
[XTR] LISP-0: IPv4 Map Server IID 4099 100.124.0.1, Built map-register, 1 records,
  first 100.100.0.22/32 last 100.100.0.22/32, DONE.
[XTR] LISP-0: IPv4 Map Server IID 4099 100.124.0.1, Sending map-register (src_rloc
  100.124.128.134) nonce 0xEA924B8B-0xF096DB7A.
```

Wired Host Operation

When a fabric endpoint needs to send traffic to another endpoint, the process on the fabric edge differs depending on where the destination endpoint is.

Intra-Subnet Traffic in the Fabric

If the destination endpoint is in the Cisco SD-Access fabric and in the same subnet as the source endpoint, the process is as follows:

1. The source endpoint (A) sends an ARP request for the MAC address of the destination endpoint (B).

2. The LISP process on endpoint A's fabric edge (A) intercepts this ARP request and asks the fabric control plane for the requested mapping of endpoint B's IP address to its MAC address.

3. The fabric control plane looks up endpoint B's IP address in its LISP address resolution table. This table is similar to a switch's ARP table but is specific to LISP. The fabric control plane then sends this MAC address to fabric edge A with a LISP ARP reply.

   Figure 6-7 shows endpoint A sending an ARP request message for 100.100.0.22 to fabric switch A. Fabric switch A intercepts the ARP request and sends a LISP ARP request to the fabric control plane. The fabric control plane replies with an entry from its LISP ARP table.

4. Fabric edge A stores this mapping in its local ARP cache and then queries the fabric control plane again for the location of endpoint B's MAC address.

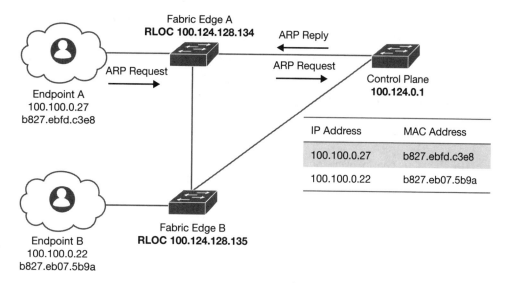

Figure 6-7 *LISP ARP Process*

5. The fabric control plane responds to fabric edge A with the RLOC address of endpoint B's fabric edge (B).

Figure 6-8 shows fabric edge A sending a LISP Map-Request message for MAC address b827.eb07.5b9a to the fabric control plane. The fabric control plane responds with the RLOC address of fabric edge B.

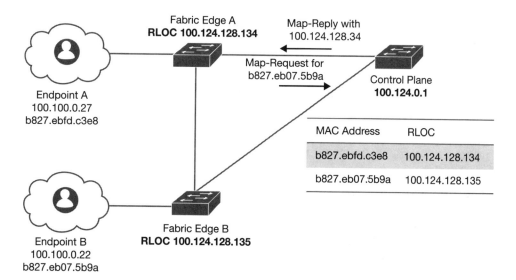

Figure 6-8 *LISP Layer 2 Map-Request/Reply*

6. Fabric edge A encapsulates the ARP request in VXLAN with fabric edge B's VTEP (RLOC) as the destination and sends it in the underlay.

7. Fabric edge B receives the VXLAN packet, de-encapsulates it, and forwards the ARP request to endpoint B.

8. Endpoint B sends an ARP reply to endpoint A's MAC address.

9. Fabric edge B queries the fabric control plane for the location of endpoint A's MAC address.

10. The fabric control plane looks up the location of endpoint A's MAC address and responds to fabric edge B with the RLOC address of fabric edge A.

11. Fabric edge B encapsulates the ARP reply in VXLAN with fabric edge A's VTEP (RLOC) address as the destination and sends it in the underlay.

Figure 6-9 shows fabric edge A sending the ARP request for endpoint B's MAC address to fabric edge B, which forwards it to endpoint B. Endpoint B sends a reply back to endpoint A, and after looking up b827.ebfd.c3e8's location with the fabric control plane, fabric edge B sends it to fabric edge A for forwarding to endpoint A.

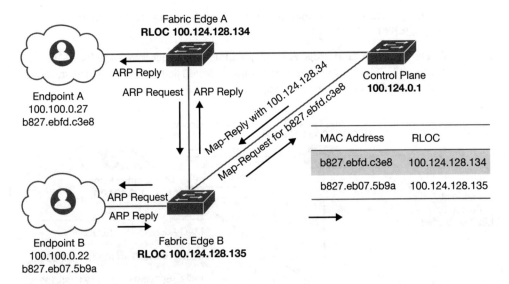

Figure 6-9 *LISP MAC Lookup and ARP Forwarding*

All subsequent traffic between endpoint A and endpoint B is sent in this same fashion, encapsulated in VXLAN, and sent directly between fabric edge A's and fabric edge B's VTEP (RLOC) addresses.

Inter-Subnet Traffic in the Fabric

If the destination endpoint is in the Cisco SD-Access fabric and in a different subnet than the source endpoint, the process is as follows:

1. The source endpoint (A) sends the traffic to its default gateway, which is the anycast gateway configured as an SVI on endpoint A's fabric edge (A).

2. Fabric edge A queries the fabric control plane for the location of the IP address of the destination endpoint (B).

3. The fabric control plane performs a lookup and forwards the message to endpoint B's fabric edge (B).

4. Fabric edge B responds to fabric edge A with its RLOC address.

   Figure 6-10 shows fabric edge A sending a LISP Map-Request for endpoint B's IP address (100.101.0.22) to the fabric control plane, which forwards it to fabric edge B after a lookup in its table. Fabric edge B then sends a LISP Map-Reply to fabric edge B with its RLOC address (100.100.0.27).

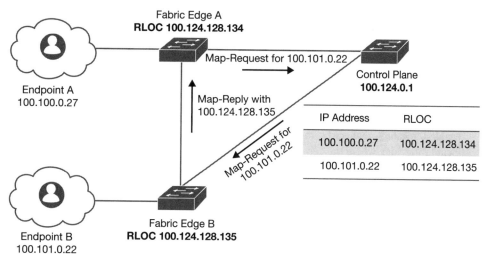

Figure 6-10 *LISP IP Lookup*

5. Fabric edge A installs the mapping in its map-cache table, encapsulates any traffic to endpoint B in VXLAN with fabric edge B's VTEP (RLOC) as the destination, and forwards the traffic through the underlay.

6. Return traffic is processed in the same way and all subsequent traffic between endpoints A and B is now encapsulated in VXLAN and forwarded through the underlay directly between fabric edge A and fabric edge B.

Traffic to Destinations Outside of the Fabric

Any traffic that is destinated outside of the fabric will be processed as follows:

1. The source endpoint (A) sends the traffic to its default gateway, which is the anycast gateway configured as an SVI on fabric edge (A).

2. Fabric edge A checks its LISP map-cache to find a match for the destination endpoint (B). If there is no match, it sends a LISP Map-Request to the fabric control plane.

3. The fabric control plane checks its LISP EID table for the IP address of the destination and, if there is no match, returns a "forward-natively" message to fabric edge A.

4. Fabric edge A encapsulates the packet in VXLAN with a destination VTEP (RLOC) of the fabric border, which is configured as a Proxy Egress Tunnel Router (PETR).

5. Return traffic via the fabric border is processed in the same way as traffic within the fabric is processed.

Note   The previous example is based on an external border as described in Chapter 4. Internal borders register non-fabric prefixes to the control plane, and traffic is processed similarly to how typical intra-fabric traffic is processed.

Wireless Host Operation

As discussed in Chapter 4, wireless endpoints in a Cisco SD-Access fabric are fabric-enabled, meaning that traffic to or from wireless endpoints is switched natively on the local fabric edge where the access point (AP) is connected. This means not only that traffic flows are more efficient than traditional centralized, or over-the-top (OTT), wireless, but also that policies and IP address pools can be used consistently regardless of whether an endpoint is wired or wireless.

Traffic for wireless endpoints in a fabric is processed identically to traffic for wired endpoints, with the major difference being the onboarding and registration process.

Initial Onboarding and Registration

When an AP is connected to a fabric edge node and receives an IP address, it learns the IP address of the fabric-enabled Cisco Wireless LAN Controller (WLC), which is connected outside of the fabric. The WLC IP address can be learned in a variety of ways, including via DNS, broadcast, and DHCP Option 43, which is the most common method.

Note   Some Cisco WLC types, such as the Cisco Catalyst 9800 Embedded Wireless Controller for Switch, are not connected outside of the fabric but are actually embedded on Cisco Catalyst 9300 switches that are inside of the fabric. The operations described in this section are identical regardless of the type of WLC being used.

The newly connected AP then forms a Control and Provisioning of Wireless Access Points (CAPWAP) tunnel to the WLC, which is used for control plane operations such as facilitating authentication and host registration for wireless endpoints. When the AP forms this CAPWAP tunnel, the WLC checks whether the AP supports Cisco SD-Access and verifies that it is in the fabric.

When a wireless endpoint associates with a fabric-enabled service set identifier (SSID) on the AP, the authentication process for the endpoint is completed via the WLC using the CAPWAP tunnel. After the wireless endpoint is authenticated, the WLC updates the AP with the endpoint's SGT and VLAN/VNID assignment. The WLC also updates the fabric control plane with the MAC address of the new endpoint, which will be associated in the EID table with the RLOC of the fabric edge where the AP is connected.

Figure 6-11 shows the process of the WLC sending VNID (or instance ID) and VLAN information to the AP for a new wireless endpoint over the CAPWAP tunnel. The WLC also registers with the fabric control plane the MAC address of the wireless endpoint along with the RLOC of the fabric edge.

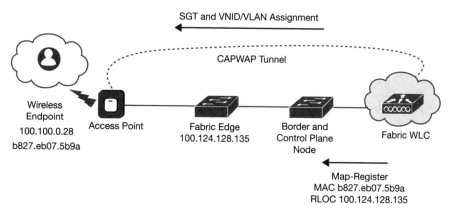

Figure 6-11 *AP and WLC Registration Operations During Onboarding*

This process allows traffic to flow from the wireless endpoint, through the AP, and directly to the fabric edge via a VXLAN tunnel that is established between the AP and the fabric edge.

All further IP host registration and traffic processing from this point is identical to the process described previously in the "Wired Host Operation" section.

Cisco SD-Access Troubleshooting

Cisco SD-Access is based on industry-standard protocols such as TrustSec, LISP, and VXLAN, which have existed on Cisco switch and router platforms for many years. As such, the various Cisco operating systems have a robust set of commands available for troubleshooting. The following sections illustrate some of the most common trouble-shooting commands and descriptions that are used for Cisco SD-Access. You can perform further troubleshooting in Cisco DNA Center using the Assurance application. Fabric Assurance in Cisco DNA Center is discussed in Chapter 9, "Cisco DNA Assurance."

Fabric Edge

Troubleshooting DHCP-related issues in a traditional network is typically straightforward because issues are usually on the client or the DHCP server. In Cisco SD-Access, however, extra steps may be required to troubleshoot DHCP problems due to the DHCP snooping and relay mechanisms that are used to provide DHCP services to endpoints in the fabric.

The first common thing to verify is whether the DHCP binding is stored on the fabric edge, using the **show ip dhcp snooping binding** command. Next, display which hosts are both connected to the fabric edge and in the device tracking database, which you can do with the **show device-tracking database** command.

Example 6-4 is sample output of the **show ip dhcp snooping binding** command, which displays any DHCP bindings that the fabric edge has facilitated along with the VLAN and interface each endpoint is connected to. Note that both wired (100.101.0.22) and wireless (100.100.0.26) endpoints are shown with this command.

Example 6-4 *Displaying DHCP Snooping Bindings*

```
edge-1# show ip dhcp snooping binding
MacAddress          IpAddress      Lease(sec) Type            VLAN  Interface
------------------  -------------  ---------- -------------   ----  ---------------
B8:27:EB:A8:96:BD   100.100.0.26   85355      dhcp-snooping   1021  AccessTunnel0
0C:D0:F8:94:19:38   100.123.0.25   73230      dhcp-snooping   2045  GigabitEthernet1/0/3
B8:27:EB:A8:96:BD   100.101.0.22   73306      dhcp-snooping   1023  AccessTunnel0
B8:27:EB:07:5B:9A   100.100.0.22   73492      dhcp-snooping   1021  GigabitEthernet1/0/36
B8:27:EB:FD:C3:E8   100.100.0.27   85407      dhcp-snooping   1021  GigabitEthernet1/0/35
Total number of bindings: 5
```

Example 6-5 is sample output of the **show device-tracking database** command, which displays connected endpoints along with their associated interfaces and VLANs.

Example 6-5 *Displaying Device Tracking Database*

```
edge-1# show device-tracking database
Binding Table has 10 entries, 6 dynamic (limit 100000)
Codes: L - Local, S - Static, ND - Neighbor Discovery, ARP - Address Resolution
    Protocol, DH4 - IPv4 DHCP, DH6 - IPv6 DHCP, PKT - Other Packet, API - API created
Preflevel flags (prlvl):
0001:MAC and LLA match      0002:Orig trunk          0004:Orig access
0008:Orig trusted trunk     0010:Orig trusted access 0020:DHCP assigned
0040:Cga authenticated      0080:Cert authenticated  0100:Statically assigned
```

Network Layer Address	Link Layer Address	Interface	vlan
DH4 100.123.0.25	0cd0.f894.1938	Gi1/0/3	2045
L 100.123.0.1	0000.0c9f.f85c	Vl2045	2045
DH4 100.101.0.22	b827.eba8.96bd	Ac0	1023
L 100.101.0.1	0000.0c9f.f45e	Vl1023	1023
DH4 100.100.0.22	b827.eb07.5b9a	Gi1/0/36	1021
L 100.100.0.1	0000.0c9f.f45c	Vl1021	1021
L 100.99.0.1	0000.0c9f.f45d	Vl1022	1022

As discussed earlier in the chapter, traffic between endpoints within the fabric and on the same subnet is switched as Layer 2 traffic but encapsulated in VXLAN. In some cases, it may be necessary to verify MAC addresses in the fabric edge's LISP table that are directly connected. The **show lisp instance-id** *instance-id* **ethernet database** command accomplishes this. To also look at MAC addresses in LISP learned from other fabric edge nodes, use the **show lisp instance-id** *instance-id* **ethernet map-cache** command.

Example 6-6 shows sample output from the **show lisp instance-id** *instance-id* **ethernet database** command with the fabric edge switch edge-1 listed as the RLOC for the MAC address b827.ebfd.c3e8. This is noted by the "site-self" tag in the output.

Example 6-6   *Displaying MAC Addresses Connected to Fabric Edge and in LISP*

```
edge-1# show lisp instance-id 8188 ethernet data
LISP ETR MAC Mapping Database for EID-table Vlan 1021 (IID 8188), LSBs: 0x1
Entries total 2, no-route 0, inactive 0

b827.ebfd.c3e8/48, dynamic-eid Auto-L2-group-8188, inherited from default
  locator-set rloc
  Locator          Pri/Wgt  Source    State
  100.124.128.135  10/10    cfg-intf  site-self, reachable
```

Example 6-7 shows sample output from the **show lisp instance-id** *instance-id* **ethernet map-cache** command, which shows that MAC address b827.eb07.5b9a is associated with the fabric edge at RLOC 100.124.128.134.

Example 6-7   *Displaying MAC Addresses Learned from Fabric Control Plane and in LISP*

```
edge-1# show lisp instance-id 8188 ethernet map-cache
LISP MAC Mapping Cache for EID-table Vlan 1021 (IID 8188), 1 entries

b827.eb07.5b9a/48, uptime: 00:52:24, expires: 23:07:36, via map-reply, complete
  Locator          Uptime    State   Pri/Wgt   Encap-IID
  100.124.128.134  00:52:24  up      10/10     -
```

When troubleshooting issues between endpoints within the fabric but in different subnets, pay attention to the Layer 3 LISP EID tables, including both the tables that display the locally connected EIDs and the ones learned from the fabric control plane. The commands to display these tables are **show lisp instance-id** *instance-id* **ipv4 database** and **show lisp instance-id** *instance-id* **ipv4 map-cache**, respectively.

Example 6-8 is sample output from the **show lisp instance-id** *instance-id* **ipv4 database** command, which shows two locally connected endpoints that are associated with fabric edge switch edge-1 as their RLOCs. This is reflected by the "site-self" tag in the output.

Example 6-8 *Displaying IP Addresses Connected to Fabric Edge and in LISP*

```
edge-1# show lisp instance-id 4099 ipv4 database
LISP ETR IPv4 Mapping Database for EID-table vrf Campus (IID 4099), LSBs: 0x1
Entries total 2, no-route 0, inactive 0

100.100.0.22/32, dynamic-eid 100_100_0_0-Campus-IPV4, inherited from default
  locator-set rloc
  Locator          Pri/Wgt  Source      State
  100.124.128.135  10/10    cfg-intf    site-self, reachable
100.101.0.22/32, dynamic-eid 100_101_0_0-Campus-IPV4, inherited from default
  locator-set rloc
  Locator          Pri/Wgt  Source      State
  100.124.128.135  10/10    cfg-intf    site-self, reachable
```

Example 6-9 is sample output from the **show lisp instance-id** *instance-id* **ipv4 map-cache** command showing EID 100.100.0.27 associated with the fabric edge at RLOC 100.124.128.134. This output also shows EIDs learned from the fabric control plane that should use a PETR for reachability. PETR verification is covered in this example.

Example 6-9 *Displaying IP Addresses Learned from Fabric Control Plane and in LISP*

```
Edge-1# show lisp instance-id 4099 ipv4 map-cache
LISP IPv4 Mapping Cache for EID-table vrf Campus (IID 4099), 7 entries

0.0.0.0/0, uptime: 03:31:10, expires: never, via static-send-map-request
  Encapsulating to proxy ETR
0.0.0.0/2, uptime: 00:00:02, expires: 00:14:57, via map-reply, forward-native
  Encapsulating to proxy ETR
100.64.0.0/11, uptime: 00:06:11, expires: 00:08:48, via map-reply, forward-native
  Encapsulating to proxy ETR
100.100.0.0/16, uptime: 03:31:10, expires: never, via dynamic-EID, send-map-request
  Encapsulating to proxy ETR
100.100.0.27/32, uptime: 00:00:12, expires: 23:59:47, via map-reply, complete
  Locator          Uptime    State    Pri/Wgt    Encap-IID
  100.124.128.134  00:00:12  up         10/10       -
```

```
100.101.0.0/16, uptime: 03:31:10, expires: never, via dynamic-EID, send-map-request
  Encapsulating to proxy ETR
100.112.0.0/12, uptime: 00:06:11, expires: 00:08:48, via map-reply, forward-native
  Encapsulating to proxy ETR
```

As discussed, the host registration process for wireless endpoints is actually initiated by the WLC until the endpoint receives an IP address. To display the MAC addresses for wireless clients that are connected via the fabric edge and were registered by a WLC, use the **show lisp instance-id** *instance-id* **ethernet database wlc** command. Example 6-10 is sample output of this command showing three MAC addresses that have been registered by the WLC.

Example 6-10 *Displaying Wireless Endpoint MAC Addresses Learned from WLC*

```
edge-1# show lisp instance-id 8188 ethernet data wlc


WLC clients/access-points information for router lisp 0 IID 8188


Hardware Address   Type    Sources   Tunnel Update


----------------   ------  -------   -------------
  b827.eb52.0ecf   client     2        Signalled
  b827.eba8.96bd   client     2        Signalled
  b827.ebfd.c3e8   client     2        Signalled
```

When an AP is connected to a fabric edge switch and its session is established with the WLC, a VXLAN tunnel is created between the AP and the fabric edge that is used for wireless endpoint traffic. To verify this tunnel, use the **show access-tunnel summary** command. Example 6-11 is sample output of this command showing a tunnel between the fabric edge switch and an AP with IP address 100.123.0.25.

Example 6-11 *Displaying Access Tunnels to APs*

```
edge-1# show access-tunnel summary

Access Tunnels General Statistics:
  Number of AccessTunnel Data Tunnels      = 1


Name   RLOC IP(Source)  AP IP(Destination)  VRF ID  Source Port  Destination Port
------ ---------------  ------------------  ------  -----------  ----------------
Ac0    100.124.128.135  100.123.0.25          0      N/A          4789


Name   IfId         Uptime
------ ----------   --------------------
Ac0    0x0000005B   0 days, 00:15:34
```

In some cases, during troubleshooting, you may want to query the fabric control plane directly, without needing to use an endpoint. In this case, use the LISP Internet Groper (**lig**) command to specify an IP address to query. Example 6-12 shows the output of the **lig instance-id** *instance-id ip address* command querying for IP address 10.4.21.1. In this case, the PETR is used for reachability.

Example 6-12   *LISP Internet Groper (lig) Output*

```
edge-1# lig instance-id 4099 10.4.21.1
Mapping information for EID 10.4.21.1 from 100.124.128.146 with RTT 1 msecs
0.0.0.0/2, uptime: 00:00:00, expires: 00:14:59, via map-reply, forward-native
  Encapsulating to proxy ETR
```

To verify the configured PETR(s) that the fabric edge uses to reach destinations outside of the fabric, use the **show running-config | include use-petr** command to parse the configuration on the fabric edge. Example 6-13 shows that the fabric edge switch is configured to use PETRs at 100.124.0.1 and 100.124.128.146 for traffic destinated outside of the fabric.

Example 6-13   *Displaying Configured Proxy Edge Tunnel Routers*

```
Edge-1# show running-config | include use-petr
  use-petr 100.124.0.1
  use-petr 100.124.128.146
```

Fabric Control Plane

Although most connectivity issues are resolved by troubleshooting from the fabric edge, some common commands can be used on the fabric control plane to verify the operation of LISP in Cisco SD-Access.

For Layer 2 connectivity issues, verify the fabric control plane's Layer 2 EID table with the **show lisp instance-id** *instance-id* **ethernet server** command. Example 6-14 is sample output from this command showing three MAC addresses and their associated fabric edge RLOCs (displayed in the "Who Last Registered" column).

Example 6-14   *Displaying MAC Addresses Learned on Fabric Control Plane via LISP*

```
cp-border-1# show lisp instance-id 8188 ethernet server
LISP Site Registration Information
* = Some locators are down or unreachable
# = Some registrations are sourced by reliable transport

Site Name      Last      Up    Who Last        Inst      EID Prefix
               Register        Registered      ID
```

```
site_uci      never     no     --                        8188      any-mac
              01:03:00  yes#   100.124.128.134:4108 8188           b827.eb07.5b9a/48
              00:47:01  yes#   100.124.128.135:1468 8188           b827.eba8.96bd/48
              01:03:51  yes#   100.124.128.135:1468 8188           b827.ebfd.c3e8/48
```

You can collect similar data for Layer 3 reachability issues using the **show lisp instance-id** *instance-id* **ipv4 server** command. This command displays all EID prefixes (IP addresses) learned from the entire fabric in the given instance ID.

Example 6-15 is sample output from the **show lisp instance-id** *instance-id* **ipv4 server** command showing three IP addresses and their associated fabric edge RLOCs (displayed in the "Who Last Registered" column).

Example 6-15 *Displaying IP Addresses Learned on Fabric Control Plane via LISP*

```
cp-border-1# show lisp instance-id 4099 ipv4 server
LISP Site Registration Information
* = Some locators are down or unreachable
# = Some registrations are sourced by reliable transport

Site Name     Last      Up     Who Last              Inst      EID Prefix
              Register         Registered            ID
site_uci      never     no     --                    4099      100.100.0.0/16
              01:09:51  yes#   100.124.128.134:4108  4099      100.100.0.22/32
              00:53:48  yes#   100.124.128.135:1468  4099      100.100.0.26/32
              01:10:35  yes#   100.124.128.135:1468  4099      100.100.0.27/32
              never     no     --                    4099      100.101.0.0/16
```

As discussed earlier in the chapter, LISP has its own ARP table that is used for processing ARP requests from fabric endpoints. You can display this ARP table on the fabric control plane with the **show lisp instance-id** *instance-id* **ethernet server address-resolution** command. Example 6-16 is sample output from this command displaying three mappings of IP to MAC addresses.

Example 6-16 *Displaying LISP Address Resolution Protocol (ARP) Mappings*

```
cp-border-1# show lisp instance-id 8188 ethernet server address-resolution

Address-resolution data for router lisp 0 instance-id 8188

L3  InstID    Host Address                            Hardware Address
    4099      100.100.0.22/32                         b827.eb07.5b9a
    4099      100.100.0.26/32                         b827.eba8.96bd
    4099      100.100.0.27/32                         b827.ebfd.c3e8
```

Authentication/Policy Troubleshooting

Although most troubleshooting of authentication and policy issues can be accomplished in the Cisco ISE GUI, as discussed in Chapter 5, there are some commands that you can use on the CLI of the fabric edge and WLC to verify that endpoints have authenticated to the network and that policies have been applied properly.

Authentication

During the Host Onboarding workflow in Cisco DNA Center, a default authentication template is selected and applied to the entire fabric, but it can also be overridden on a per-port basis. This authentication template specifies the rules that apply to endpoints connecting to the fabric edge switch. This template can be verified by looking at the running configuration of the fabric edge switch—specifically, the interface and template sections.

Example 6-17 shows that the DefaultWiredDot1xClosedAuth template is applied to interface GigabitEthernet 1/0/34. The contents of the template are then displayed showing the default authentication settings in the template.

Example 6-17 *Displaying the Authentication Template*

```
edge-1# show running-config interface GigabitEthernet 1/0/34
Building configuration...

Current configuration : 226 bytes
!
interface GigabitEthernet1/0/34
 switchport mode access
device-tracking attach-policy IPDT_MAX_10
 dot1x timeout tx-period 7
 dot1x max-reauth-req 3
 source template DefaultWiredDot1xClosedAuth
 spanning-tree portfast
end

edge-1# show run | begin template DefaultWiredDot1xClosedAuth
template DefaultWiredDot1xClosedAuth
 dot1x pae authenticator
 switchport access vlan 2047
 switchport mode access
 switchport voice vlan 2046
 mab
 access-session closed
 access-session port-control auto
 authentication periodic
 authentication timer reauthenticate server
 service-policy type control subscriber PMAP_DefaultWiredDot1xClosedAuth_1X_MAB
```

You can use the **show authentication sessions** command on the fabric edge to display any endpoints that are authenticated to the switch. You can then use this output to get details about the authenticated endpoints, for further investigation.

Example 6-18 is sample output from the **show authentication sessions** command on a fabric edge switch that shows an endpoint on interface GigabitEthernet 1/0/36 that is authenticated using 802.1X.

Example 6-18 *Displaying Any Active Authentication Sessions*

```
edge-1# show authentication sessions
Interface                MAC Address     Method  Domain   Status
--------------------------------------------------------------------
Gi1/0/3                  0cd0.f894.1938 mab      DATA     Auth
Gi1/0/23                 701f.5301.43c7 N/A      UNKNOWN Unauth
Gi1/0/24                 701f.5301.43d7 N/A      UNKNOWN Unauth
Gi1/0/36                 b827.eb07.5b9a dot1x    DATA     Auth
Gi1/0/21                 f87b.2076.5947 N/A      UNKNOWN Unauth
Gi1/0/22                 f87b.2076.5957 N/A      UNKNOWN Unauth
```

Example 6-19 shows further details for the endpoint connected to the GigabitEthernet 1/0/36 interface, including IP address(es), username, and type of device.

Example 6-19 *Displaying Authentication Session Details on Interface*

```
edge-1# show authentication sessions interface gig 1/0/36 details
            Interface:  GigabitEthernet1/0/36
              IIF-ID:  0x173A89EB
          MAC Address:  b827.eb07.5b9a
         IPv6 Address:  fe80::ba27:ebff:fe07:5b9a
         IPv4 Address:  100.100.0.22
            User-Name:  acct1
          Device-type:  RaspberryPi-Device
          Device-name:  RASPBERRY PI FOUNDATION
               Status:  Authorized
               Domain:  DATA
       Oper host mode:  multi-auth
      Oper control dir:  both
      Session timeout:  N/A
  Acct update timeout:  172800s (local), Remaining: 170717s
    Common Session ID:  87807C640000001007EBC160
      Acct Session ID:  0x00000005
               Handle:  0xf1000006
       Current Policy:  PMAP_DefaultWiredDot1xClosedAuth_1X_MAB
```

Even though data plane traffic is switched directly on the fabric edge switch, wireless endpoints in Cisco SD-Access are authenticated via the WLC over the CAPWAP tunnel that is established between the AP and WLC. On AireOS-based WLCs, you can use the **show client detail** *MAC address* command to gather authentication details for wireless endpoints.

Example 6-20 shows the output of the **show client detail** *MAC address* command on a WLC, which displays authentication details for a wireless endpoint, including username, IP address, SSID, RLOC, and SGT.

Example 6-20 *Displaying Wireless Endpoint Authentication Details on WLC*

```
(Cisco Controller) > show client detail b827.eba8.96bd
Client MAC Address............................... b8:27:eb:a8:96:bd
Client Username ................................. hr2
Client Webauth Username ......................... N/A
Hostname: ....................................... client1
Device Type: .................................... Workstation
AP MAC Address................................... 0c:d0:f8:95:30:20
AP Name.......................................... AP0CD0.F894.1938
AP radio slot Id................................. 0
Client State..................................... Associated
User Authenticated by ........................... RADIUS Server
Client User Group................................ hr2
Client NAC OOB State............................. Access
Wireless LAN Id.................................. 17
Wireless LAN Network Name (SSID)................. SDA-PoV-Enterprise
Wireless LAN Profile Name........................ SDA-PoV-En_Global_F_1e9bd381
IP Address....................................... 100.101.0.22
Security Group Tag............................... 16


Fabric Configuration
--------------------
Fabric Status: .................................. Enabled
Vnid: ........................................... 8191
Client RLOC IP registered to MS: ................ 100.124.128.135
Clients RLOC IP  : .............................. 100.124.128.135
```

Policy

Policy in Cisco SD-Access is enforced on egress, meaning that it is enforced by the fabric edge switch of the destination endpoint. Some policy information that can be gathered from the fabric edge switch includes any Security Group ACL (SGACL) names and summaries of the SGACLs, along with the SGTs that will be affected.

Example 6-21 shows the output of the **show cts role-based permissions** command, which displays any SGACLs pushed to the fabric edge switch by ISE. In this case, an SGACL named AllowWeb is applied to any traffic from the acct SGT (17) destined to the hr SGT (16).

Example 6-21 *Displaying SGACLs on Fabric Edge*

```
edge-1# show cts role-based permissions
IPv4 Role-based permissions default:
      Permit IP-00
IPv4 Role-based permissions from group 17:acct to group 16:hr:
      AllowWeb-00
RBACL Monitor All for Dynamic Policies : FALSE
RBACL Monitor All for Configured Policies : FALSE
```

Example 6-22 shows the content of the AllowWeb ACL using the **show cts rbacl** *SGACL* command. The AllowWeb SGACL permits TCP traffic to ports 80 and 443 and UDP traffic to port 443. The SGACL also has a default deny, so any other traffic is dropped.

Example 6-22 *Displaying SGACL Details*

```
edge-1# show cts rbacl AllowWeb
CTS RBACL Policy
================
RBACL IP Version Supported: IPv4 & IPv6
  name    = AllowWeb-00
  IP protocol version = IPV4, IPV6
  refcnt = 2
  flag    = 0xC1000000
  stale  = FALSE
  RBACL ACEs:
    permit tcp dst eq 80
    permit tcp dst eq 443
    permit udp dst eq 443
    deny ip
```

Scalable Group Tags

Although most of the fabric and policy configuration is done in Cisco DNA Center, Cisco SD-Access uses ISE as its policy engine. ISE is responsible for pushing any SGTs and policies to the fabric edge switch. You can verify that the SGTs have been pushed from ISE properly with the **show cts environment-data** command.

Example 6-23 is sample output of the **show cts environment-data** command, which shows that the ISE server at 100.64.0.100 is communicating with the fabric edge switch and has pushed a number of SGTs to the switch.

Example 6-23   *Displaying Scalable Group Tags Available on the Fabric Edge*

```
edge-1# show cts environment-data
CTS Environment Data
====================
Current state = COMPLETE
Last status = Successful
Local Device SGT:
  SGT tag = 0-00:Unknown
Server List Info:
Installed list: CTSServerList1-0001, 1 server(s):
 *Server: 100.64.0.100, port 1812, A-ID 81CB54142B404DD9CAA62F57A06F5CBD
          Status = ALIVE
          auto-test = TRUE, keywrap-enable = FALSE, idle-time = 60 mins,
  deadtime = 20 secs
Security Group Name Table:
    0-00:Unknown
    2-00:TrustSec_Devices
    3-00:Network_Services
    4-00:Employees
    5-00:Contractors
    6-03:Guests
    7-00:Production_Users
    8-00:Developers
    9-00:Auditors
    10-00:Point_of_Sale_Systems
    11-00:Production_Servers
    12-00:Development_Servers
    13-00:Test_Servers
    14-00:PCI_Servers
    15-00:BYOD
    16-00:hr
    17-00:acct
    18-00:Campus_Quarantine
    100-00:finance_user
    200-00:PCI_user
    255-00:Quarantined_Systems
    911-00:RestrictedVN_QUARANTINED
Environment Data Lifetime = 86400 secs
Last update time = 21:57:33 UTC Sun Feb 2 2020
Env-data expires in   0:23:06:33 (dd:hr:mm:sec)
Env-data refreshes in 0:23:06:33 (dd:hr:mm:sec)
Cache data applied           = NONE
State Machine is running
```

Summary

This chapter covered the various technologies used in Cisco SD-Access, including the details of the LISP and VXLAN implementations. It also demonstrated a typical packet flow for both wired and wireless endpoints, from host onboarding and registration to end-to-end conversations. In addition, this chapter discussed common troubleshooting commands for Cisco SD-Access and provided examples for each.

References in This Chapter

draft-smith-vxlan-group-policy-05, "VXLAN Group Policy Option," Oct. 2018, M. Smith, L. Kreeger: https://tools.ietf.org/id/draft-smith-vxlan-group-policy-05.txt

RFC 6830, "The Location ID/Separation Protocol (LISP)," Jan. 2013, D. Farinacci, V. Fuller, D. Meyer, D. Lewis: http://www.ietf.org/rfc/rfc6830.txt

RFC 7348, "Virtual eXtensible Local Area Network (VXLAN): A Framework for Overlaying Virtualized Layer 2 Networks over Layer 3 Networks," Jan. 2013, M. Mahalingam et al: http://www.ietf.org/rfc/rfc7348.txt

Advanced Cisco Software-Defined Access Topics

This chapter covers the following topics:

- **Cisco Software-Defined Access Extension to IoT:** This section covers the extension of Cisco SD-Access into the Internet of Things world, the types of extended nodes, the supported deployments, and their packet flows in Cisco Software-Defined Access campus networks.

- **Multicast Flows in Cisco SD-Access:** This section provides an overview of multicast and the various multicast options available with Cisco Software-Defined Access.

- **Layer 2 Flooding in Cisco SD-Access:** This section provides details about flooding options available in Cisco SD-Access to accommodate applications using traditional one-to-all or one-to-many traffic flows.

- **Layer 2 Border in Cisco SD-Access:** This section covers the Layer 2 border feature that allows a Layer 2 segment to reside in a traditional network as well as a Cisco SD-Access network. The feature makes the Campus SD-Access migrations less impactful to users for phased rollouts.

- **Cisco SD-Access for Distributed Campus Deployments:** This section analyzes the high-level design and deployment of Cisco SD-Access in different customer verticals.

- **Cisco SD-Access Design Considerations:** This section covers the design considerations when moving the network toward the next-generation software-defined campus solution.

- **Cisco SD-Access Policy Extension to Cisco ACI:** This section covers the simplified policy integration in a multidomain environment extending policy from campus to data center and vice versa.

Cisco Software-Defined Access Extension to IoT

In the modern world, computing devices are compact and smart. Each user carries an average of three smart devices with them, such as a smartphone, a smart watch, and a tablet, among many other possibilities. The total installation base of Internet of Things (IoT)-connected devices is projected to grow to 75.44 billion devices worldwide by 2025, a fivefold increase in ten years (source: https://www.statista.com). These IoT devices may or may not be connected to the edge devices. Considering that edge devices are expensive, are not small in size, and are racked in a wired closet or in the data center, edge devices may not be the best place to connect IoT devices to the network.

There is a need to extend network connectivity to IoT devices placed in nontraditional environments that have new networking requirements. Here are some examples of connecting IoT devices in different customer environments:

- A hotel room has access points to provide Internet connectivity. Multiple smart devices, such as the TV, temperature control, and smart lights, are connected to a compact switch that is backhauled into the main network so that it can be monitored and controlled.

- A casino has a cluster of slot machines connected to a switch that is backhauled into the main network for control and analytics.

IoT devices such as cameras that are powered by Power over Ethernet (PoE) connect to the network and need to stay up even if the switch reloads so that the live feed is not interrupted. The switches need to be compact, secure, and noiseless, have PoE capabilities, and withstand non–data center environments. There are many uncarpeted or outdoor spaces such as factory floors, manufacturing plants, and parking garages where network devices are used to connect machines. These network devices must withstand harsh environments such as high temperatures, wind, and so forth. Some IoT endpoints require the first hop to run specific protocols so that they can onboard onto the network immediately and start transmitting captured data.

As the world moves into a "smart" era where all the devices need to be controlled, most endpoints are data collectors. Nontraditional spaces are becoming more common and need to be integrated into the enterprise environments. The standard requirements of a traditional network—security, automation, and network insights—apply to IoT networks as well. The network must block hackers from gaining entry to the network from any smart connected IoT devices (for example, a monitored air conditioning unit). There is a growing need in the IoT space for ease of management, onboarding IoT devices automatically, securing east-west communication, redundancy, and faster convergence.

With Cisco Identity Services Engine (Cisco ISE) integrated into the architecture of Cisco SD-Access, network segmentation and policy based on the endpoints' identity is integrated into the network. Cisco DNA Center automates the deployment of a Campus Fabric that can be extended to IoT devices. The IoT switches can be made part of the fabric, and the switches can be managed and monitored by Cisco DNA Center. Figure 7-1 depicts an IoT extension into the Campus Fabric built in the previous chapters. These IoT switches are officially called *extended nodes* in the Cisco Campus Fabric world.

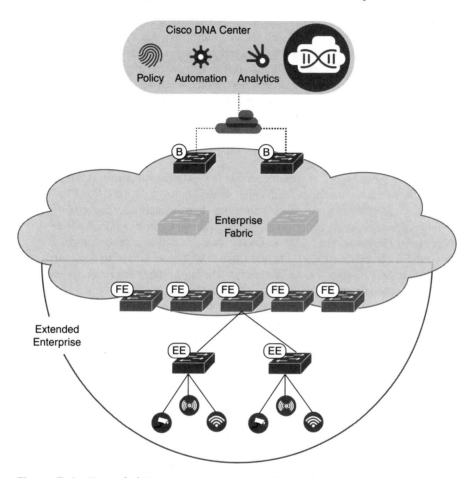

Figure 7-1   *Extended Enterprise in a Campus Network*

An extended node usually runs in a Layer 2 switch mode, connects the IoT endpoints, and does not support fabric technology natively. An extended node is configured by an automated workflow from Cisco DNA Center. Depending on the type of extended node, the packet forwarding, authentication, and policy application happen either at the fabric edge layer above the extended node or on the extended node itself (as discussed in the next section). Security is the top priority for any network, including IoT networks. By integrating IoT networks into the fabric, security from the fabric is automatically applied to the IoT networks. Cisco DNA Center capabilities include onboarding extended nodes from the factory reset state using Plug and Play (PnP), integrating the extended nodes into the fabric, enabling security controls on the extended network, and enforcing fabric policies to the endpoints connecting into the extended nodes.

Types of Extended Nodes

Extended nodes always connect to the fabric edge. The fabric edge has 802.1X or MAC Authentication Bypass (MAB) authentication enabled to authenticate with an authentication server, which can be Cisco ISE or a third-party AAA server. There are two types of extended nodes: *extended node* and *policy extended node*. An extended node is designated as a policy extended node if it includes authentication features that are available only on the latest IoT switches. Refer to the Cisco SD-Access Product Compatibility matrix (the URL for which is provided at the end of the chapter) for the supported model numbers of the extended nodes and policy extended nodes.

Extended Nodes

An extended node is a Layer 2 switch connecting IoT endpoints. It performs 802.1X or MAB authentication with the authentication server. Dynamic virtual LAN (VLAN) assignments are feasible with an extended node based on the attributes pushed by Cisco ISE. A Scalable Group Tag (SGT) cannot be assigned to the extended node client port even if ISE pushes the SGT. End devices connected to an extended node are placed in an SGT based on their VLAN, and Cisco DNA Center is used to configure the static VLAN-to-SGT mapping on the fabric edge. The fabric edge performs Location Identifier Separation Protocol (LISP), Virtual Extensible LAN (VXLAN), and Scalable Group Access Control List (SGACL) enforcement for the clients connecting to the extended nodes. An extended node can handle multicast to allow the multicast traffic to be received only on the intended ports at the extended node, where the receivers are connected. Cisco DNA Center takes care of onboarding the extended node, orchestration of the AAA configuration, SGT-to-VLAN mapping, and multicast configuration on the connected ports.

Policy Extended Nodes

A policy extended node has 802.1X/MAB authentication enabled to communicate to Cisco ISE and to dynamically apply VLAN and SGT attributes to the endpoints. A policy extended node performs security (SGACL) enforcement, unlike an extended node, where SGACL enforcement happens on the fabric edge. Cisco DNA Center configures inline SGT tagging between the fabric edge and the policy extended node as part of provisioning the extended node. The SGACL enforcement happens on the destination policy extended node, and the source SGT is carried all the way to the destination through the inline tagging.

Figure 7-2 illustrates the differences between an extended node, policy extended node, and fabric edge. The hardware and the software version need to be compatible for an extended node to act as a policy extended node.

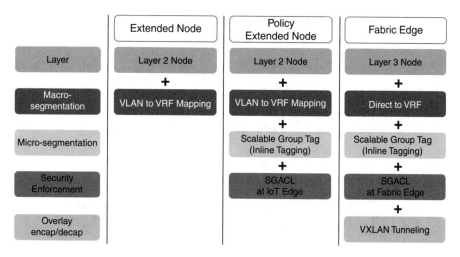

Figure 7-2 *Features Supported by Various Types of Extended Nodes*

With Cisco DNA Center 1.3.x, a fabric edge can be a standalone switch or a stack. An extended node can connect with a single interface to the fabric edge, as shown on the left in Figure 7-3, but this is a potential single point of failure isolating the extended node from the fabric. An extended node can be connected to the fabric edge over a port channel, as shown in the center of Figure 7-3, and the port channel can be spread across multiple switches in the stack to ensure redundancy. The port channel has to support Port Aggregation Protocol (PAgP). Some extended nodes in the supported device list do not support PAgP; for these devices, on mode, also known as static mode, is supported. If an organization has separate operational technology (OT) network and enterprise network management teams and the organization's policies specify that each team must manage its own switches, a ring topology is supported. The switches connecting in the ring can be managed by the OT team. When the traffic from the OT switches hits the fabric edge, the policy can be applied. This is shown on the right in Figure 7-3, where the extended nodes are in a REP ring. Resilient Ethernet Protocol (REP) is used for faster convergence, resiliency, and high availability.

Following are the supported Resilient Ethernet Protocol topologies in an extended node Cisco SD-Access deployment:

- Extended node ring to StackWise Virtual (SVL) fabric edge. REP edge on the fabric edge. Two ways out of extended node ring. No single point of failure.

- Extended node ring to stacked fabric edge. Two ways out of extended node ring. Stacked fabric edge might cause a potential single point of failure.

- Extended node open ring to SVL fabric edge.

- Extended node open ring to stacked fabric edge.

- Single extended node ring to dual-homed stacked fabric edge.

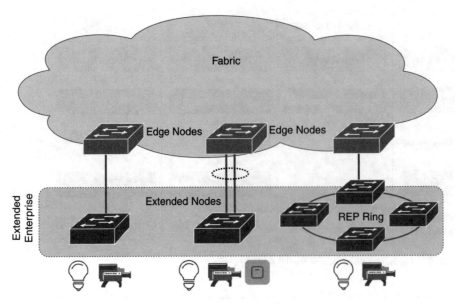

Figure 7-3 *Supported Extended Node Deployments*

Configuration of Extended Nodes

Cisco DNA Center automates onboarding and configuration of the extended nodes to make sure the fabric policies are applied to IoT networks. Before selecting a node as an extended node, refer to the Cisco SD-Access Product Compatibility matrix to view the supported hardware for extended nodes. Following are the steps for configuring the extended node from Cisco DNA Center. Some of the steps are similar to the steps in the configuration of the fabric covered in the previous chapters; the following steps are based on the assumption that the fabric is already provisioned at the network.

Step 1. Apply device credentials (CLI credentials and Simple Network Management Protocol settings) to the site level on Cisco DNA Center where the extended node needs to be provisioned. This will be part of Design settings in the site hierarchy on Cisco DNA Center.

Step 2. Add an IP address pool for the extended node management. Because the extended node is going to be automatically onboarded using PnP, configure an IP pool for Cisco DNA Center to assign a loopback interface address for the discovered extended node.

Step 3. If an IoT pool is used for the clients connecting to the extended node, configure an IoT pool for the clients. Reserve the IP pool at the fabric site level where the extended node is assigned.

Step 4. Create a virtual network (VN) for IoT devices if the security requirement is to place all the IoT devices in a separate VN. Virtual network creation is not necessary if the IoT devices will be part of the existing virtual network as the campus users. Leverage SGTs to apply segmentation policies if the IoT devices are in the same VN as campus users.

Step 5.   (Optional) Configure a port channel on the fabric edge for the extended node link. Starting with DNA Center 1.3, the extended node and fabric edge are always connected using a port channel (even for a single port). For No Authentication mode, a port channel is created automatically. For Cisco Catalyst IE3300/3400 Rugged Series switches, the port channel should be created in static mode. For all other extended devices, the port channel should be created in PAgP mode.

Create the port channel on the fabric edge on the Port Channel tab and select the interface to which the extended node is connected, along with the PAgP protocol, as shown in Figure 7-4.

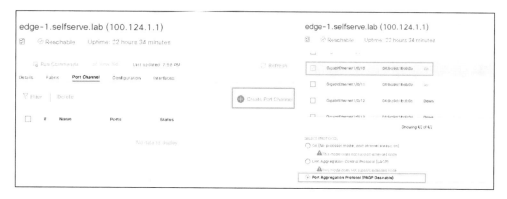

Figure 7-4   *Port Channel Creation on Fabric Edge*

Step 6.   Assign the extended node management IP address pool (created in Step 2) under the **Fabric > Host Onboarding** tab, scroll to the Virtual Networks section, click **INFRA_VN**, click **Pool Type**, and choose **Extended**, as shown in Figure 7-5. An extended node is an infrastructure device and is placed in the INFRA_VN similar to the access points, as shown in Figure 7-5. This step results in an SVI creation of the IP pool. The SVI is placed in the INFRA_VN.

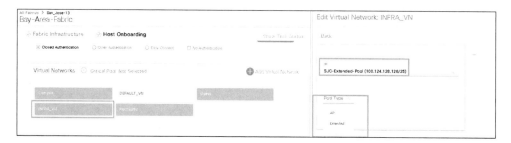

Figure 7-5   *IP Pool Assignment for Extended Nodes*

Example 7-1 shows the configuration pushed on the fabric edge.

Example 7-1   *IP Pool Configuration Pushed by Cisco DNA Center*

```
FE2-9300-04# sh run int Vlan1024
interface Vlan1024
 description Configured from Cisco DNA-Center
 mac-address 0000.0c9f.f45f
 ip address 100.124.128.129 255.255.255.128
 ip helper-address 10.5.130.12
 no ip redirects
 ip route-cache same-interface
 no lisp mobility liveness test
 lisp mobility 100_124_128_128_INFRA_VN_IPV4
end
```

Step 7.   On the Host Onboarding tab, select the port channel and assign it as an extended node, as shown in Figure 7-6.

Figure 7-6   *Port Channel Assignment for Extended Node*

Example 7-2 shows the configuration pushed on the fabric edge with the port channel creation and assignment of the extended node for the port channel.

Example 7-2   *Port Channel Configuration Pushed for the Extended Node Link from Cisco DNA Center*

```
FE2-9300-04# sh run int gig 1/0/2
interface GigabitEthernet1/0/2
 switchport mode trunk
 channel-group 1 mode desirable
end
```

```
FE2-9300-04# sh run int port-channel 1
interface Port-channel1
 switchport mode trunk
end
```

Extended nodes are discovered using PnP and are added to the Inventory, site, and fabric topology automatically. The following section provides details of the packet flow involved in onboarding the extended node.

Onboarding the Extended Node

Extended nodes are discovered using Plug and Play. For PnP to work, the node should not have an existing configuration. Execute **write erase** and reload the extended node so that it is at the following factory default prompt:

Would you like to enter the initial configuration dialog? [yes/no]:

Behind the scenes, Cisco DNA Center uses a series of protocols and checks to discover the extended node. An extended node in a factory default state is powered on and connected to the fabric edge. Autoconf on the edge switch recognizes that the port is connected to an extended node based on the product ID (PID) information exchanged in the Cisco Discovery Protocol (CDP) packet received from the extended node. All the fabric edges have a SWITCH_INTERFACE_TEMPLATE configured that is triggered based on the extended node PID. The template enables the port connected to the extended node as a trunk port, as shown in Example 7-3.

Example 7-3 *Template to Auto-Configure the Switchport as Trunk*

```
FE2-9300-04# sh run | sec parameter
--------output_ommitted------------

150 map device-type regex "CDB*"
10 interface-template SWITCH_INTERFACE_TEMPLATE
160 map device-type regex "WS-C3560CX*"
10 interface-template SWITCH_INTERFACE_TEMPLATE


--------output_terminated------------


FE2-9300-04# sh run | inc  SWITCH_INTERFACE_TEMPLATE
template SWITCH_INTERFACE_TEMPLATEswitchport mode trunk
```

The extended node receives CDP information from the fabric edge. CDP information consists of Type-Length-Values (TLV) attributes of neighboring devices. A TLV consists of information such as IP address, device ID, and platform embedded in the CDP information. On the extended node, a CDP packet received from the edge node has a TLV with a pnp_startup-vlan, meaning the extended node receives information about the VLAN from which it will receive an IP address. The PnP agent on the extended node configures the VLAN Trunking Protocol (VTP) mode to transparent and the interface connecting to the edge node is configured to trunk. The extended node negotiates to get a DHCP IP address on the pnp_startup-vlan configured. The extended node IP address pool on the DHCP server should be configured with DHCP Option 43 pointing toward Cisco DNA Center. In summary, the extended node receives an IP address from the DHCP server with Option 43 pointing toward Cisco DNA Center. With Option 43, the extended node registers to Cisco DNA Center, as shown in Figure 7-7.

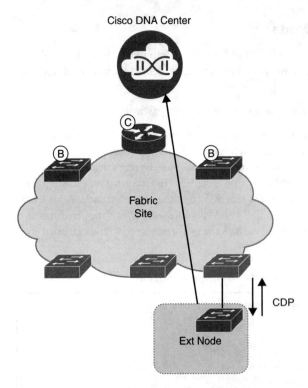

Figure 7-7   *Extended Node Onboarding Flow*

If the extended node is connected via multiple interfaces, Cisco DNA Center configures the port channel on the extended node. To check the status of the extended node, go to **Provision > Devices > Plug and Play.** A loopback IP address is assigned for management of the extended node. On Cisco DNA Center, the extended node gets added to the Inventory and the extended node ports can now be managed by Cisco DNA Center. If the extended node discovered is a policy extended node based on the hardware, inline SGT tagging is configured between the policy extended node and the fabric edge.

Example 7-4 shows the configuration commands pushed on the edge node downlink interface connected to the extended node. SGT 8000 is assigned to the packets received from the policy extended nodes without any SGT value.

Example 7-4 *Extended Node Link Configuration on Edge Node*

```
FE2-9300-04# sh run int gig 1/0/2
interface GigabitEthernet1/0/2
 cts manual
  policy static 8000 trusted
 channel-group 1 mode desirable
end
```

Packet Walk of Extended Cisco SD-Access Use Cases

This section discusses various packet flows for the hosts connected within a fabric. The hosts in a fabric could be communicating with other fabric endpoints or could be initiating traffic to destinations outside the fabric.

Use Case: Hosts in Fabric Communicating with Hosts Connected Outside the Fabric

In an enterprise network, hosts connected to extended nodes or in an IoT network probably need to communicate to hosts or servers outside the fabric. For example, IP cameras need to communicate with the feed server to provide live feeds. Figure 7-8 shows the packet flow steps, described next, for a host connected to the extended node where the destination resides outside the fabric.

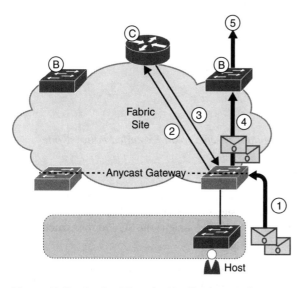

Figure 7-8 *Packet Flow for Traffic from Fabric to Non-Fabric*

1. A host connects to the extended node. It gets authenticated and dynamically placed in the VLAN assigned by Cisco ISE. The host initiates traffic outside the fabric. The traffic reaches the anycast gateway on the edge nodes.

2. The edge node checks with the control plane node to find the next hop to forward the traffic to.

3. The control plane node does not have the non-fabric destination in the host database. The edge node will receive a negative lookup response from the control plane node. Any unknown host traffic will be sent to the border by the fabric edge.

4. The edge node forwards the packet to the border node over a VXLAN tunnel with the source host SGT and VN inserted in the VXLAN header.

5. The border node decapsulates the VXLAN packet and forwards the packet out of the fabric to the next hop.

Use Case: Traffic from a Client Connected to a Policy Extended Node

In this use case, Host 1 is connected to a policy extended node and initiates traffic to Host 2, which is connected to the fabric edge node FE2, as shown in Figure 7-9.

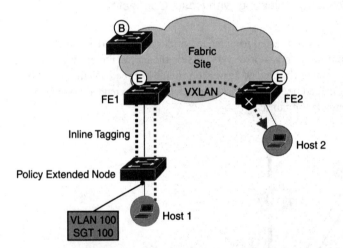

Figure 7-9   *Traffic Flow Initiated by Client Connected to an Extended Policy Node*

Here is the packet flow for this traffic:

1. When Host 1 connects to the policy extended node, it is authenticated, dynamically assigned to a VLAN (VLAN 100), and assigned an SGT (SGT 100) by Cisco ISE. The policy extended node understands SGTs and assigns the SGT to the switchport attached to the host.

2. Host 1 initiates traffic to Host 2, which is connected to FE2. Traffic from Host 1 has source SGT 100 assigned at the policy extended node. SGT 100 is carried inline to FE1.

3. FE1 checks with the control plane node to find the next hop to forward the traffic to. The control plane responds with the next hop as FE2.

4. FE1 forwards the packets to FE2 over a VXLAN tunnel with the SGT 100 and the VN (VRF) of the VLAN 100 the user is part of.

5. FE2 enforces the SGACL policy.

Use Case: Traffic to a Client Connected to a Policy Extended Node

In this use case, Host 2 is connected to fabric edge FE2 and initiates traffic destined to Host 1, which is connected to the policy extended node, as shown in Figure 7-10.

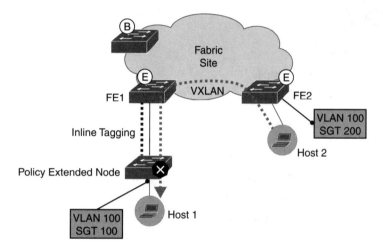

Figure 7-10   *Traffic to a Client Connected to a Policy Extended Node*

Here is the packet flow for this use case:

1. Host 1 and Host 2 connect, get authenticated, and are assigned a VLAN and SGT dynamically from Cisco ISE.

2. Host 2 initiates traffic to Host 1 connected to the policy extended node. Traffic from Host 2 has source SGT 200 assigned at FE2.

3. FE2 checks with the control plane to find the next hop to forward the traffic to. The control plane responds with the next hop as FE1.

4. FE2 forwards the packets to FE1 over a VXLAN tunnel with the source SGT 200 and VN inserted. The VXLAN packet is decapsulated at FE1, and the traffic is forwarded to the policy extended node along with the SGT with inline tagging.

5. The SGACL is applied at the policy extended node.

Use Case: Traffic Flow Within a Policy Extended Node

In this use case, Host 1 and Host 2 are connected to the policy extended node. Figure 7-11 illustrates the packet flow for traffic between the hosts connected to the same policy extended node.

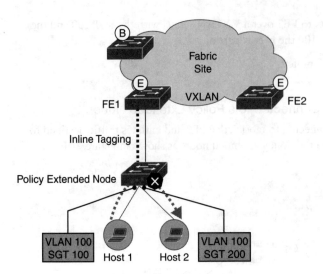

Figure 7-11   *Traffic Within the Policy Extended Node*

Here is the packet flow in detail for this use case:

1. Host 1 and Host 2 connect to the policy extended node, get authenticated, and are assigned a VLAN and SGT dynamically from Cisco ISE.

2. Host 1 initiates traffic destined to Host 2. Traffic is received at the policy extended node.

3. The policy extended node sees the destination hop as itself. It is aware of the source and destination SGT.

4. Policy (SGACL) enforcement is applied on the policy extended node.

In summary, Cisco DNA Center simplifies the deployment of extended nodes and applies unified security policies in a Campus Fabric to the fabric extension. With the introduction of policy extended nodes, dynamic micro-segmentation is applicable. Micro-segmentation and macro-segmentation security policies can be leveraged for an IoT network that are based on the enterprise security requirements, and Cisco DNA Center eases the deployment of the security policies. Cisco DNA Center features include running a recommended release on all the extended nodes during the discovery phase. The device replacement flow of Cisco DNA Center to replace the devices without any hassle is applicable to extended nodes as well.

Multicast in Cisco SD-Access

Multicast involves one source and multiple destinations, unlike broadcast or unicast. Several applications use multicast in traditional IP networks. This section provides a brief overview of IP multicast in traditional networks and describes IP multicast delivery modes to lay the foundation for understanding the multicast flow in a Cisco SD-Access campus network, which is the topic of the subsequent section.

Multicast Overview

Multicast technology reduces traffic bandwidth consumption by delivering a single stream of information simultaneously to potentially thousands of destination clients. Applications that offer services such as video conferencing, corporate communications, distance learning, distribution of software, stock quotes, news, and so on make use of multicast.

IP multicast is a technique for one-to-many communication over an IP network. IP multicast routing enables a host (source) to send packets to a group of hosts (receivers) anywhere within the IP network by using the multicast group address. The sending host inserts the multicast group address into the IP destination address field of the packet, and IP multicast devices such as routers and switches forward incoming IP multicast packets out all interfaces that lead to the receivers of the multicast group. Any host, whether a member of the multicast group or not, can send traffic to the multicast group. The multicast group address has a dedicated Class D space addressed by IANA. The Class D address range is 224.0.0.0 to 239.255.255.255.

Multicast uses IGMP and can be run in any of the Protocol Independent Multicast (PIM) modes that are listed after the following description of IGMP:

- **Internet Group Management Protocol (IGMP):** IGMP is used by the hosts and their access devices to establish multicast group membership. PIM is a family of multicast routing protocols used between network devices so that the devices can track which multicast packets to forward to each other and to their directly connected LANs. PIM does not have its own routing table but instead relies on the unicast routing protocol running in the IP network. Hence, PIM is protocol independent. PIM has the following four variants or modes that determine how multicast traffic is forwarded to the recipients.

- **PIM dense mode (PIM-DM):** This mode uses a push model, which floods the multicast traffic to all the network segments even if the receiver has not requested the data. PIM-DM initially floods multicast traffic throughout the network. Routers that have no downstream neighbors prune back the unwanted traffic. PIM-DM is not commonly used or recommended because the traffic is flooded to unwanted devices, causing unnecessary bandwidth utilization.

- **PIM sparse mode (PIM-SM):** This mode uses a pull model that sends the multicast traffic to the network segments that have active receivers explicitly requesting the traffic. In sparse mode, when hosts join a multicast group, the directly connected routers send PIM Join messages toward the rendezvous point (RP), which is the meeting point for multicast sources and receivers. In PIM-SM mode, sources send the traffic to the RP, which forwards the traffic to the receivers via a shared distribution tree (SDT). The RP keeps track of multicast groups. By default, when the first-hop device of the receiver learns about the source, it sends a Join message directly to the source, creating a source-based distribution tree from the source to the receiver. This source tree does not include the RP unless the RP is located within the shortest path between the source and receiver. The RP is needed only to start new sessions with sources and receivers for the control traffic in multicast and usually is not involved in the data plane. Consequently, the RP experiences little overhead from traffic flow or processing.

■ **PIM sparse-dense mode:** Some use cases require some multicast groups to be in sparse mode and other multicast groups to be in dense mode. PIM sparse-dense mode enables the interface mode based on the multicast group. The interface will be in dense mode if the multicast group is in dense mode, and vice versa with sparse mode.

■ **Bidirectional PIM:** This mode builds shared bidirectional trees. It is designed for efficient many-to-many communications within an individual PIM domain. Multicast groups in bidirectional mode can scale to an arbitrary number of sources with only a minimal amount of additional overhead.

IP Multicast Delivery Modes

IP multicast delivery modes apply only to the receiver hosts, not to the source hosts. A source host sends an IP multicast packet with its own IP address as the IP source address of the packet and a group address as the IP destination address of the packet. In the subsequent sections, the first-hop router is the router connecting to the multicast source, and the last-hop router is the first hop connecting to the multicast receiver.

Two different types of service models support multicast delivery from a source to the multicast receivers:

■ Any Source Multicast (ASM)

■ Source-Specific Multicast (SSM)

In ASM, the receiver does not have knowledge of the multicast source. The receiver is only aware of the multicast group the source uses. This model can have multiple sources on the same group or channel, meaning multiple applications or sources can be in the same group. ASM is an older form of multicast but is more commonly used than SSM.

In SSM, the multicast receiver receives packets delivered from the source that it has to receive packets from. SSM requires the receiver to specify the multicast source address, and it uses IGMPv3. Different applications running on the same source host must use different SSM groups. Different applications running on different source hosts can arbitrarily reuse SSM group addresses without causing any excess traffic on the network.

Multicast Flows in Cisco SD-Access

This section discusses in detail the three most common scenarios of multicast use in Cisco SD-Access.

Scenario 1: Multicast in PIM ASM with Head-End Replication (Fabric RP)

In scenario 1, PIM ASM runs in the overlay with the rendezvous point in the fabric and the multicast source outside the fabric. Figure 7-12 illustrates the initial steps for the control plane interaction.

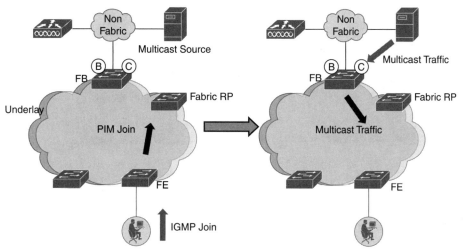

Figure 7-12   *Control Plane Interaction with Fabric RP in PIM ASM Head-End Replication*

The following steps detail the process of the RP discovering the receiver and the source IP address:

1. The multicast client is in the overlay and sends an IGMP Join for a specific multicast group to its first-hop device fabric edge (FE). PIM ASM runs in the overlay in this use case, and the multicast source is outside the fabric, as shown in Figure 7-12.

2. The FE node receives the IGMP Join and sends a PIM Join toward the fabric RP. The RP is registered with the control plane because it is part of the overlay in this scenario. The FE asks the control plane node for the location of the RP address (stored in the IP address-to-RLOC table) and, based on the reply, sends the PIM Join in the overlay to the RP.

3. The RP now has the receiver information of the multicast group.

4. The multicast source sends multicast traffic toward the fabric border (FB) because it is the designated router (DR) for that segment.

5. The FB receives the multicast traffic and sends it toward the RP. The FB queries the control plane for the location of the RP address (IP address-to-RLOC table) and sends the traffic in the overlay to the RP, as shown on the right side in Figure 7-12.

6. The RP now has the source and receiver information for that multicast group.

   The right side of Figure 7-12 shows the final control plane interaction where the RP is made aware of the source and the destination multicast group.

As shown in Figure 7-13, data plane traffic flow slightly differs from the control plane connection steps discussed earlier.

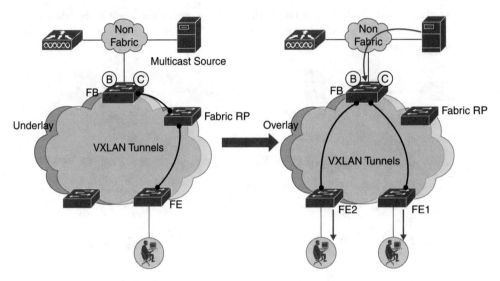

Figure 7-13   *Head-End Replication Multicast Data Plane Interaction in Fabric: PIM ASM*

Data plane interaction of multicast traffic in the fabric in PIM ASM is described in the following steps:

1. From the previous flow, the RP has the source and receiver information of the multi-cast group. The FB forwards the multicast traffic from the source to the RP over the VXLAN tunnel. The RP forwards this traffic to the FE over the VXLAN tunnel, as shown on the left side in Figure 7-13.

2. The FE receives the VXLAN packets, decapsulates them, applies the policy, and sends the original IP multicast packet to the port on which the multicast client is connected.

3. The FE is now aware that the border owns the multicast source based on the first multicast packet received and sends a PIM Join directly to the border for that mul-ticast group. With the PIM Join from the FE on the FB, the FB knows the FEs with clients that requested the specific multicast group.

4. Multicast shortest-path tree (SPT) forwarding kicks in after the first multicast packet; multicast traffic is forwarded between the FB and the FEs directly subsequently.

5. The fabric border performs head-end replication and the VXLAN tunnel encapsu-lates the multicast traffic and unicasts it to the FEs with the receivers. The multicast traffic is sent in the overlay, as shown on the right side in Figure 7-13.

6. The FE receives the VXLAN packets, decapsulates them, applies the policy, and then sends the original IP multicast packet to the port on which the receiver is connected.

Scenario 2: Multicast in PIM SSM with Head-End Replication

Scenario 2 has a topology with PIM SSM in the overlay and the multicast source outside the fabric. Figure 7-14 provides a flow visualization of the control steps involved for multicast traffic in this scenario. In PIM SSM mode, no RP is required because the client is aware of the multicast source.

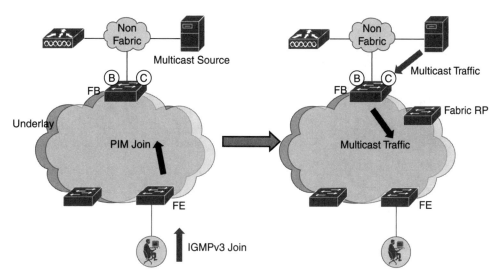

Figure 7-14   *Head-End Replication PIM SSM Control Plane Interaction*

The following steps detail the flow for control plane interaction with head-end replication in PIM SSM mode:

1. The multicast client (receiver) is in the overlay. The multicast source can be outside the fabric or in the overlay; in this scenario, the multicast source is outside the fabric. PIM SSM is running in the overlay and does not need an RP.

2. The client sends an IGMPv3 Join for a specific multicast group, and the source address is part of the IGMPv3 Join.

3. The fabric edge (FE) receives the IGMPv3 Join and, because the IGMPv3 Join has the source address information for that multicast group, the FE sends a PIM Join toward the source directly. In this scenario, the source is reachable through the border, and the FE sends the PIM Join to the border. The FE queries the control plane node for the RLOC of the source address, which is the RLOC of the fabric border (FB). The PIM Join is sent in the overlay from the FE to the FB. This flow is illustrated on the left side in Figure 7-14.

4. The multicast source sends the multicast traffic on the interfaces toward the FB because it is the DR for that segment.

5. The FB receives the multicast traffic and sends it toward the FE, because the PIM Join is coming directly from the FE to the FB in an SSM deployment.

As shown in Figure 7-15, data plane traffic flow slightly differs from the control plane flow discussed earlier.

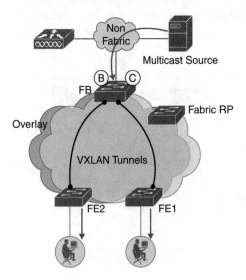

Figure 7-15 *Head-End Replication Multicast Data Plane Interaction in Fabric: PIM SSM*

Data plane interaction of multicast traffic in the fabric in PIM SSM is described in the following steps:

1. The fabric border knows which FEs have receivers that requested the specific multicast group.

2. The FB performs head-end replication, encapsulates the multicast traffic in VXLAN packets, and unicasts it to the interested FEs. The multicast traffic is sent in the overlay.

3. The FE receives the VXLAN packets, decapsulates them, applies the policy, and then sends the original IP multicast packet to the port on which the receiver is connected.

4. The flow works exactly the same for wireless fabric deployments.

Scenario 3: Cisco SD-Access Fabric Native Multicast

The head-end replication scenarios previously discussed do not scale well. Native multicast enhances Cisco SD-Access multicast scaling over head-end replication because it significantly reduces replication load at the head end, improves scale, and reduces latency. The existing multicast control plane overlay behavior remains the same, and PIM ASM or PIM SSM can be used in the overlay. Native multicast is a site-wide setting; that is, each site can only use either native multicast or head-end replication. In native multicast, each multicast group in the overlay is mapped to a corresponding (PIM SSM) multicast underlay group (the underlay multicast should be PIM SSM only). Multicast distribution happens natively within the underlay network. Incoming multicast traffic for a given VN is encapsulated in VXLAN and then sent with {Source IP = Fabric node RLOC,

Destination IP = Underlay Multicast Group} as the outer IP addresses. Native multicast supports a maximum of 1000 multicast groups in the overlay, across all VNs per fabric site. An overlay group is mapped to an underlay group, starting with 232.0.0.1 (thus, 232.0.3.232 is the high-end group). Cisco DNA Center version 1.3.3 and later provides the option to configure the underlay group.

A Campus Fabric built on LAN Automation by Cisco DNA Center automatically enables multicast in the underlay. Brownfield deployments need to manually enable multicast in the underlay to leverage the native multicast in the Cisco SD-Access Campus Fabric. Cisco recommends using the Template Editor in Cisco DNA Center to provision the native multicast configuration for brownfield deployments. When the native multicast is enabled on Cisco DNA Center, VNs that have multicast turned on are instructed to move over to native multicast for the data path.

Example 7-5 shows the configuration pushed under the LISP interface for the respective VNs. The multicast groups in that VN will be mapped to underlay SSM groups for data transport.

Example 7-5   *LISP Configuration for Native Multicast Pushed by Cisco DNA Center*

```
interface LISP0.4096
 ip pim lisp transport multicast
 ip pim lisp core-group-range 232.0.0.1 1000
```

Figure 7-16 shows an example topology with the RP in the fabric and the multicast source outside the fabric. The topology is provided to help you understand the packet flow of multicast when native multicast is used in Cisco SD-Access. In this example, the overlay uses ASM with a group address of 238.0.0.1. The SSM mapping for the group in the underlay is 232.0.0.9.

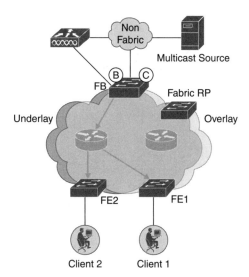

Figure 7-16   *Packet Flow for Native Multicast in Cisco SD-Access Fabric*

With SSM in the underlay for native multicast, there is no prebuilt multicast tree for any given group in the overlay.

Packet flow for native multicast is described in the following steps:

1. Client 1 (multicast receiver) sends an IGMP Join to the fabric edge of group 238.0.0.1, which is mapped to the group 232.0.0.9 in the underlay.

2. The FE1 node sends one PIM Join to the RP in the overlay to address 238.0.0.1, while also sending one PIM Join in the underlay to SSM group 232.0.0.9. The source address in the underlay Join is the RLOC address, because SSM always needs a source IP address (S). Multicast entries for (*,G) joins in the overlay (in this case, * refers to any source IP address and G is the Multicast Group address) and (S,G) joins in the underlay are created.

3. When the fabric border (FB) receives multicast source traffic, it sends a source registration message in the overlay for group address 238.0.0.1 to the RP and forwards the traffic in the overlay for the group address 238.0.0.1 to the RP. The FB also forwards the traffic in the underlay on the mapped group 232.0.0.9 to the RP. The traffic is sent to the RP because the overlay group is still ASM. This creates the S,G state in the underlay for the overlay group. (If SSM were used in the overlay, the RP would have no role for this multicast group.)

4. Multicast entries in the underlay are now complete to replicate the traffic to the needed devices for the multicast group.

Cisco SD-Access Multicast Configuration in Cisco DNA Center

Enabling multicast in Cisco SD-Access involves a series of steps from Cisco DNA Center. Here are the steps on Cisco DNA Center version 1.3.3:

Step 1. Navigate to **Provision > Fabric > Fabric Site**, click the gear icon, and choose **Enable Multicast** from Cisco DNA Center.

Step 2. Select the type of multicast to be enabled: Native Multicast or Head-End Replication. For this example, select Native Multicast, as shown in Figure 7-17.

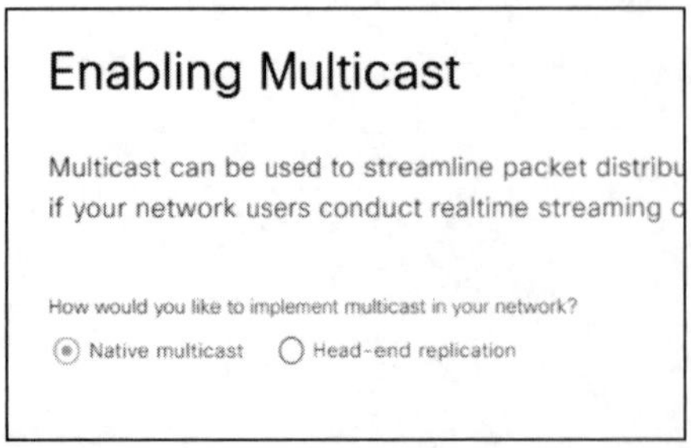

Enabling Multicast

Multicast can be used to streamline packet distribu
if your network users conduct realtime streaming c

How would you like to implement multicast in your network?
◉ Native multicast   ○ Head-end replication

Figure 7-17 *Enabling Multicast on a Cisco SD-Access Fabric*

Step 3.   Select the virtual networks on which multicast needs to be enabled. In this example, enable multicast for both VNs, Campus and IoT, as shown in Figure 7-18.

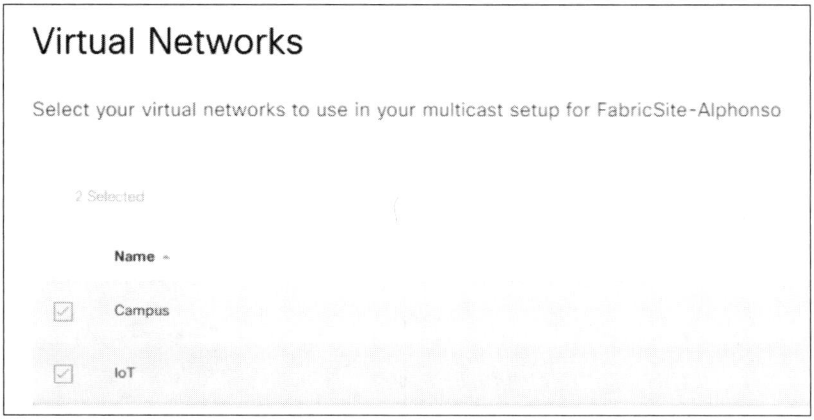

Virtual Networks

Select your virtual networks to use in your multicast setup for FabricSite-Alphonso

2 Selected

	Name ⌃
☑	Campus
☑	IoT

Figure 7-18   *Enabling Multicast on VNs*

Step 4.   Assign multicast IP pools for each selected VN.

Step 5.   Select the multicast mode: SSM or ASM. For ASM mode, an RP needs to be configured. The RP can reside within a fabric or can be an external RP from Cisco DNA Center 1.3.3. For an external RP of 20.20.20.20 for Campus CN, the following CLI configuration is pushed:

```
ip pim vrf Campus rp-address 20.20.20.20
```

For SSM mode, a valid network address for the SSM range for every VN needs to be provided. Prior to Cisco DNA Center 1.3.3, no option exists to customize the range, and a default SSM range of 232.0.0.0 0.255.255.255 is pushed. With 1.3.3, customization of the SSM range is possible, and the valid SSM Range is 225.0.0.0 to 239.255.255.255.

Example 7-6 provides the configuration pushed for a custom SSM range.

Example 7-6   *Custom SSM Range Multicast Pushed by Cisco DNA Center*

```
ip access-list standard SSM_RANGE_Campus
10 permit 232.127.0.0 0.0.255.255
ip pim vrf Campus ssm range SSM_RANGE_Campus
```

Step 6.   Verify the details and click **Save**. Figure 7-19 shows an example multicast configuration with ASM and RP configured.

Figure 7-19   *Multicast Configuration Summary*

Layer 2 Flooding in Cisco SD-Access

Cisco SD-Access fabric provides many optimizations to improve unicast traffic flow and to reduce the unnecessary flooding of data such as broadcasts and Address Resolution Protocol (ARP) flooding. One such optimization is to disable ARP flooding and broadcasts in the fabric. Some traffic and applications require broadcasts to be enabled, especially legacy devices such as door locks, card readers, and silent hosts that still use broadcast. ARP flooding is common in traditional networks at small sites, but it may cause load issues if implemented in larger networks. Cisco SD-Access addresses this problem by implementing Layer 2 flooding efficiently to accommodate broadcasts, link-local multicasts, and ARP flooding. The Layer 2 flooding feature is disabled by default in a Cisco SD-Access fabric. If broadcast, link-local multicast, or ARP flooding is required, it must be specifically enabled on a per-subnet basis using the Layer 2 flooding feature.

Layer 2 Flooding Operation

Silent hosts reside in the Cisco SD-Access fabric connecting into the edge node, as shown in Figure 7-20. Broadcast and link-local multicast is also expected to traverse the fabric.

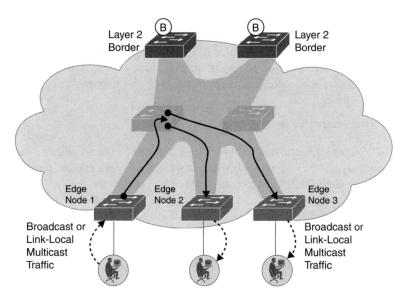

Figure 7-20   *Layer 2 Flooding*

Here is the order of operations when Cisco DNA Center enables Layer 2 flooding:

1. Layer 2 (L2) flooding is enabled per IP subnet. With flooding enabled, the IP subnet is mapped to a dedicated multicast address in the underlay. Because the multicast group is an ASM group, all the PIM Joins are sent to the RP in the underlay. Example 7-7 shows L2 flooding for an IP subnet and its corresponding instance-id. The VLAN 1021 instance-id is automatically placed in the underlay group 239.0.0.1. All the fabric nodes with the VLAN 1021 IP subnet configured will be made part of the multicast group.

Example 7-7   *L2 Flooding Configuration Pushed by Cisco DNA Center*

```
instance-id 8188
 remote-rloc-probe on-route-change
 service ethernet
   eid-table vlan 1021
   broadcast-underlay 239.0.0.1 //VLAN 1021 part of underlay multicast group
   database-mapping mac locator-set xxx
  exit-service-ethernet
exit-instance-id
```

2. All fabric nodes that have the IP subnet configured have sent the PIM Joins on their respective multicast group, and a multicast tree is prebuilt for that particular IP subnet. The traffic is flooded on this prebuilt multicast tree.

3. The fabric edge intercepts any ARP flooding or broadcast or link-local multicast from the client and sends it over the dedicated multicast group in the underlay. The fabric edge encapsulates the client traffic in the VXLAN tunnel and then sends it with {Source IP = FE node RLOC, Destination IP = Underlay Multicast Group} as the outer IP address. The underlay based on normal multicast functionality is responsible for replicating the traffic as needed. The source tree failover also happens based on regular multicast working.

4. All the fabric edges receive the traffic sent by Edge Node 1.

Prior to Cisco DNA Center 1.3.3, enabling L2 flooding for a given IP pool creates a multicast group in the underlay. Fabric with multiple IP pools with L2 flooding enabled results in multiple multicast route entries, leading to exhaustion of memory on the device. To alleviate this problem, Cisco DNA Center 1.3.3 and later creates a unique multicast group for the entire fabric site, which is configured for all the IP pools marked for L2 flooding for a given site. All the IP pools in the fabric will share the same multicast group for a given fabric site. Traffic is segmented by VLAN tag on the encapsulated Layer 2 packets being flooded, so there isn't a need to segment by multicast address.

Example 7-8 shows the configuration pushed by Cisco DNA Center when L2 flooding is enabled on VLAN 1022 and VLAN 1024. As shown, both the IP subnets use the same underlay multicast group 239.0.17.2.

Example 7-8 *L2 Flooding Configuration Pushed with Same Multicast Group*

```
instance-id 8189
  remote-rloc-probe on-route-change
  service ethernet
  eid-table vlan 1022
  broadcast-underlay 239.0.17.2 //Same multicast group
    flood unknown-unicast
  database-mapping mac locator-set <xxx>
   exit-service-ethernet
  !
  exit-instance-id
 !
instance-id 8190
  remote-rloc-probe on-route-change
  service ethernet
    eid-table vlan 1024
```

```
broadcast-underlay 239.0.17.2 // Same multicast group
 flood unknown-unicast
database-mapping mac locator-set <xxx>
 exit-service-ethernet
!
 exit-instance-id
!
```

To enable Layer 2 flooding in Cisco DNA Center, navigate to **Provision > Fabric**, select
the name of the fabric-enabled site, click the Host Onboarding tab, scroll to the Virtual
Networks section to select the VN, select the IP pool, click Actions, and select Enable
Layer-2 Flooding, as shown in Figure 7-21.

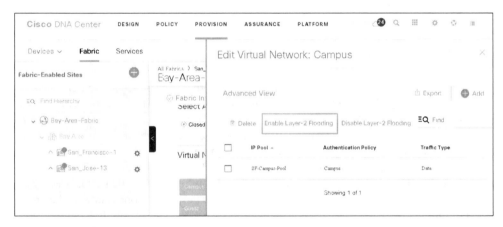

Figure 7-21 *Layer 2 Flooding Enablement*

Layer 2 Border in Cisco SD-Access

Traditional networks work based off of Layer 2 networks mainly using VLANs. For
migration purposes for scenarios where customers are moving from a traditional network
to a Cisco SD-Access fabric network, the Layer 2 border option is available with Cisco
SD-Access to help transition the users in traditional VLANs to fabric-enabled VLANs.
The same host subnet resides in the fabric and the traditional network. The Layer 2 border translates the traditional VLAN to the VLAN within the fabric. Figure 7-22 provides
a classic example of the same subnet residing in a fabric and a traditional network. As
shown, one of the fabric borders acts as a Layer 2 border. Host 3 in the traditional network is in the same subnet (10.1.1.0/24) as that of hosts in the fabric network.

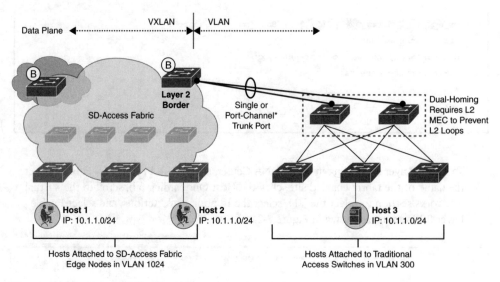

Figure 7-22 *Layer 2 Border Solution Overview*

In Figure 7-22, the fabric pool is in VLAN 1024, and the corresponding traditional network is in VLAN 300. The Layer 2 border maps VLAN 1024 in the fabric to VLAN 300 in the non-fabric. The SVI of VLAN 300 becomes the Layer 2 border by Cisco DNA Center configuration, meaning the default gateway of the endpoints in the traditional network is the Layer 2 border. The SVI for VLAN 300 needs to be present only on one device: the Layer 2 border. Be sure to remove the VLAN 300 SVI on any other devices. The Layer 2 border has the same configuration as the edge nodes except VLAN 1024 is replaced by VLAN 300 on the Layer 2 border. Cisco DNA Center pushes the configurations shown in Examples 7-9 and 7-10 on the fabric edge and L2 border, respectively. In Example 7-9, the fabric edge has VLAN 1024 configured as part of the fabric. Example 7-10 shows the configuration on VLAN 300 on the L2 border with a traditional VLAN 300 with the configuration and IP address the same as VLAN 1024 on the fabric edge.

Example 7-9 *Fabric Edge VLAN 1024 Configuration*

```
Fabric Edge#

instance-id 8188
  remote-rloc-probe on-route-change
  service ethernet
    eid-table vlan 1024
    broadcast-underlay 239.0.0.1
    database-mapping mac locator-set xxx
  exit-service-ethernet
exit-instance-id
!
```

```
interface Vlan1024
 description Configured from apic-em
 mac-address 0000.0c9f.f45c
 vrf forwarding Corp
 ip address 8.6.53.1 255.255.255.0
 ip helper-address 10.121.128.101
 no ip redirects
 ip route-cache same-interface
 no lisp mobility liveness test
 lisp mobility 8_6_53_0-Corp
```

Example 7-10   *Layer 2 Border Traditional VLAN 300 Configuration*

```
Fabric Border#

instance-id 8188
  remote-rloc-probe on-route-change
  service ethernet
    eid-table vlan 300
    broadcast-underlay 239.0.0.1
    database-mapping mac locator-set xxx
  exit-service-ethernet
exit-instance-id
!
interface Vlan300
 description Configured from apic-em
 mac-address 0000.0c9f.f45c
 vrf forwarding Corp
 ip address 8.6.53.1 255.255.255.0
 ip helper-address 10.121.128.101
 no ip redirects
 ip route-cache same-interface
 no lisp mobility liveness test
 lisp mobility 8_6_53_0-Corp
```

The L2 border registers all the endpoints in the non-fabric side to the fabric control plane node; hence, the fabric site needs to have a control plane and border node configured. There are scalability restrictions in terms of the endpoints supported by the L2 border. It supports only 4000 host registrations across all the external VLANs. The Layer 2 border does not support multihoming; it can connect the non-fabric network to an access port or a trunk port to just one fabric device.

Layer 2 Intersite

Large campus networks may consist of multiple fabric sites. Each fabric site consists of a border, control, and edge nodes. Cisco DNA Center 1.3.3 and later offers the Layer 2 intersite feature to extend the Layer 2 segment across fabric sites. The same Layer 2 subnet extension can be done across multiple fabric sites and the traditional network. The main use case of the feature is to allow ARP, broadcast, and link-local multicast communication for a subnet spanned across multiple sites. Legacy applications such as card readers, slot machines, printers, and so forth depend on Layer 2, and if the end clients for these applications reside in multiple fabrics and/or traditional networks, the Layer 2 intersite feature allows them to communicate with each other.

Figure 7-23 shows an example of a Layer 2 172.16.8.0/24 network dispersed across fabric sites and a traditional network. The fabric VLAN is 1021, and the equivalent traditional VLAN is 300. The fabric sites are connected using an IP network (IP transit), as shown in Figure 7-23. The endpoints may be connected to the fabric edges or connected using extended nodes.

Layer 2 Intersite Design and Traffic Flow

The following list describes the prerequisites, design, and traffic flow details for the example topology shown in Figure 7-23:

- Layer 2 flooding needs to be enabled to use the Layer 2 border feature.

- The Layer 2 border needs to be configured across every fabric site for a specific VLAN. Cisco DNA Center automatically creates a trunk between the fabric sites. Figure 7-23 shows the trunk link configured by Cisco DNA Center between the Layer 2 borders at Fabric Site 1 and Fabric Site 2 and shows that VLAN 300 is allowed on the trunk link. VLAN 300 is external to the fabric; it is the traditional VLAN with the same subnet as that of fabric VLAN 1021.

- In this example, an external VLAN 300 is configured by Cisco DNA Center. The Layer 2 VNIs/fabric VLAN for the same IP subnets across sites can be different. A common external VLAN is used to merge them.

- The Layer 3 border at every fabric site advertises the /32 prefixes to the external fusion routers. No summarized routes are sent because the traffic for a given host might return to the wrong side.

- When Host 1 in Fabric Site 1 sends traffic to Host 2 in Fabric Site 2, the control plane in Fabric Site 1 sends the traffic to the Layer 2 border in Fabric Site 1. The Layer 2 border translates VLAN 1021 to external VLAN 300 and sends it over the trunk link to the Layer 2 border at Fabric Site 2.

- The Fabric Site 2 Layer 2 border translates the external VLAN 300 to the fabric-provisioned VLAN 1021 in Fabric Site 2 and forwards the packet to the RLOC (fabric edge) of Host 2. Traffic flow is similar for traffic between fabric sites and traditional network hosts.

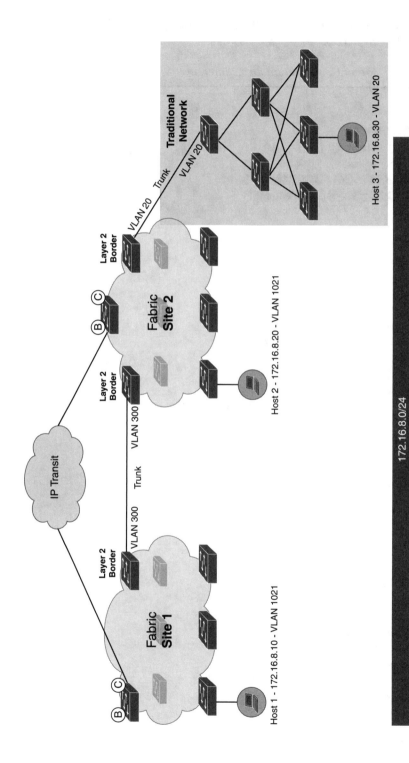

Figure 7-23 *Layer 2 Intersite Host Onboarding*

Example 7-11 provides an excerpt of the configuration pushed to the Layer 2 borders in Cisco DNA Center 1.3.3.

Example 7-11 *Border Configuration for L2 Intersite*

```
L2 Border#

interface Loopback1022
 description Loopback Border
 vrf forwarding Hosts
// Shared IP pool with loopback on L2 borders
 ip address 172.16.8.1 255.255.255.255
end
instance-id 4100
  remote-rloc-probe on-route-change
  dynamic-eid 172_16_8_0-Hosts-IPV4
<misc>
 instance-id 8189
  remote-rloc-probe on-route-change
  service ethernet
// L2 flooding enabled with Vlan 300
   eid-table vlan 300
   broadcast-underlay 239.0.17.1
   flood unknown-unicast
   database-mapping mac locator-set rloc_223e6de0-2714-4ad8-bef6-d11f76cd1574
   exit-service-ethernet
router bgp 422
 bgp router-id interface Loopback0
<misc>
address-family ipv4 vrf Campus
  bgp aggregate-timer 0
  network 172.16.90.0 mask 255.255.255.252
  network 172.16.91.1 mask 255.255.255.255
  aggregate-address 172.16.91.0 255.255.255.0 summary-only
<misc>
exit-address-family
  !
 address-family ipv4 vrf Servers
  bgp aggregate-timer 0
network 172.16.93.0 mask 255.255.255.0
// No network summarization for shared Pool
   aggregate-address 172.16.93.0 255.255.255.0
  redistribute lisp metric 10
 exit-address-family
 !
```

Note In topologies where there is a common DHCP server for both the fabric sites and the Layer 2 intersite feature is in use, when a host in Site 1 requests an IP address via DHCP, the DHCP offer from the data center can also reach the L3 border of Site 2. The L3 border in Site 2 cannot send the reply packet to the RLOC of the FE of the host in Site 1. The workaround is to have underlay connectivity between L3 borders of all the sites and the RLOCs of the FEs of all sites.

Note With IP transit, L3 borders advertise /32 routes to the fusion router; a larger fusion router should be considered in case of a greater number of common IP subnets across the sites. More L2 borders should be considered to spread the load with a rise in the number of common IP subnets.

Fabric in a Box in Cisco SD-Access

Deployments in some sectors often have branch sites with few end hosts, such as in the healthcare, manufacturing, and retail industries. Some of the branch sites might not be manned, and the end clients could be IoT devices. For a site to be fabric enabled, it needs edge, border, and control plane nodes. This may not be cost efficient for small sites. Fabric in a Box (FiaB) enables a single device to be configured as a fabric border, fabric control plane, and fabric edge. Figure 7-24 illustrates a Fabric in a Box deployment where the endpoints are in a fabric that consists of only one node.

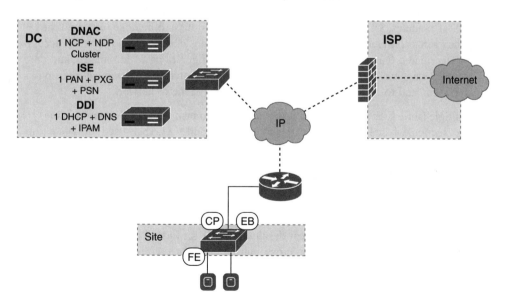

Figure 7-24 *Fabric in a Box in Cisco SD-Access*

Fabric in a Box is supported on Cisco Catalyst 9000 Series switches only. Fabric in a Box is supported only on one device that is standalone or a switch stack. Fabric in a Box cannot be combined with any other non-fabric devices as part of the fabric site. Cisco Catalyst 9000 switches have embedded wireless controller features to provision wireless networks for small sites. Embedded wireless is supported on FiaB.

In Figure 7-24, the access points connecting to the FiaB switch register to the embedded wireless controller. The scale for FiaB deployment is the fabric edge scale for the given Cisco Catalyst 9000 Series device. For remote, unmanned deployments or non-IT branches, the Cisco DNA Center Plug and Play feature is useful to discover and provision the FiaB switch. Fabric in a Box needs a gateway out of the fabric network similar to any fabric site. It supports IP transit and SD-Access transit, discussed in the following section. Most common FiaB deployments use the shared services present in the local data center that are accessible through the IP transit or SD-Access transit. Extended nodes can connect to the Fabric in a Box.

Cisco SD-Access for Distributed Campus Deployments

Cisco SD-Access for Distributed Campus deployment is a metro-area solution that connects multiple, independent fabric sites while maintaining the security policy constructs (virtual routing and forwarding and SGTs) across these sites. Multisite deployments have been supported for a while, but they were not completely automated by Cisco DNA Center. For example, SGT Transfer Protocol (SXP) configuration needs to be configured manually on the fabric borders to propagate the SGT into the IP transit. IP-SGT bindings, SXP, and complex ISE configurations have to be done to extend the policy across different sites. Because policy extension is possible with Cisco SD-Access for Distributed Campus, SXP is not required, the configurations are automated, and the complex mappings are simplified. This solution enables intersite communication using consistent, end-to-end automation and policy across the metro network.

Multiple fabric sites are connected using SD-Access Transit which is discussed in the next section, where LISP is used as the control plane and VXLAN is used for data encapsulation. SD-Access Transit makes the VXLAN encapsulation possible across multiple sites by retaining the VN and SGT information when traffic flows between fabric sites. Cisco DNA Center automates the configuration and policy enforcement across multiple sites by applying micro- and
macro-segmentation policies agnostic of the IP addressing.

This section focuses on the different designs available for various needs and scale, along with ways of extending the policy across multiple sites. As a refresher, the following keywords that have been discussed in detail in earlier chapters appear frequently in the ensuing design discussion:

- **Fabric site:** Consists of a fabric edge, fabric control plane node, and fabric border, usually with an ISE Policy Services Node (PSN) and fabric-mode WLC. A fabric border connects the fabric site to the rest of the network. A fabric site can be a single physical location, such as a building in a campus, or multiple locations. Fabric in a Box is an example of a fabric in a single device.

■ **Fabric domain:** Contains one or more individual fabric sites and any corresponding transit(s) associated with those sites managed by Cisco DNA Center. The fabric sites in a fabric domain are connected by a transit network for cross-site communication or external network communication.

■ **Transit:** Connects one or more fabric sites or connects a fabric site to the rest of the network.

Types of Transit

There are three types of transit that connect fabric sites with each other or to the rest of the network. The type of transit to select in a network depends on the scale, cost, policy, and resiliency requirements.

IP Transit

IP transit offers IP connectivity without native Cisco SD-Access encapsulation and functionality, potentially requiring additional VRF and SGT mapping for stitching together the macro- and micro-segmentation needs between fabric sites. It leverages the traditional network that uses VRF-LITE or the MPLS network. Even though IP transit does not carry VN and SGT information, IP transit is typically used for the following use cases:

■ Organizations have an existing WAN in place and would like to use the WAN as the transit without additional devices needed.

■ Internet handoff is a use case where the existing IP network is used as an IP transit for the fabric site(s) to communicate with the rest of the world.

■ IPsec tunnel termination is needed, and IP transit leverages the existing IP network for point-to-point IPsec encryption.

■ Policy-based routing is possible with IP transit, especially when the circuit speed is high from the providers.

■ IP transit could be the only option for a few geographically dispersed sites that are connected through a backhaul mobile LTE network with high latency.

Figure 7-25 shows the protocols involved when a fabric site with IP transit communicates with an external peer network. The control plane uses LISP in the fabric up to the fabric border. The border uses the Border Gateway Protocol (BGP) to hand off to the non-fabric handoff router (also known as a fusion router) for IP transit. Cisco DNA Center has the capability to automate the handoff using BGP on the borders connecting to the traditional network. However, Cisco DNA Center does not automate the BGP configuration on the northbound device to the border. It needs to be done manually on the fusion router. The fusion router can connect to the rest of the external domain using any Interior Gateway Protocol.

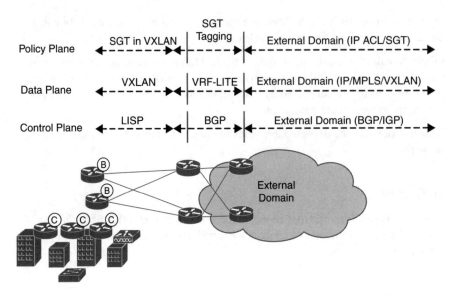

Figure 7-25 *Fabric Site Using IP Transit to External Domain*

The data plane uses VXLAN encapsulation in the fabric. Traffic leaving the fabric border destined to the fusion router uses the traditional VRF-lite, which Cisco DNA Center automates. From the fusion router, the traffic follows the data plane protocol used in the external domain, such as IP, MPLS, or VXLAN. Cisco SD-Access introduces an additional plane, called the *policy plane*, where the SGT is carried in the VXLAN header. The SGT is retained in VXLAN in the fabric, where it gets stripped off at the fabric border using IP transit. If the goal is to enforce policies based on SGT, the SGT needs to be propagated outside the fabric using IP transit. SGT propagation methods such as SXP or SGT inline tagging need to be implemented between the fabric border and the fusion router or the rest of the external domain. The SGT propagation configuration is manual, and Cisco DNA Center templates can be leveraged to push the manual configuration needed on the fabric border nodes. Inline SGT tagging is a scalable option because the SGT can be carried in the data packet.

Fabric Multisite or Multidomain with IP Transit

IP transit can be used to connect multiple fabric sites or fabric domains. Healthcare, financial, and federal government networks usually have security requirements such as encryption between various sites. Dynamic Multipoint Virtual Private Network (DMVPN) is a common VPN tunneling mechanism used for communication between various sites. Figure 7-26 shows a commonly used topology of two fabric sites communicating using DMVPN on an IP network (IP transit). As shown, LISP is used for the control plane within each fabric site. The fabric sites use DMVPN/GRE terminating on fabric borders for the control plane across sites.

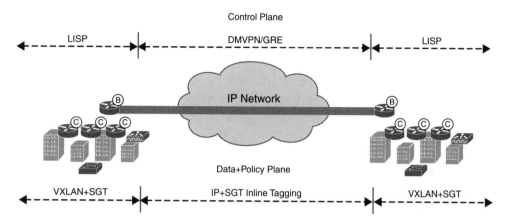

Figure 7-26 *Fabric Sites Connecting with DMVPN on IP Transit*

In this topology, the data plane and policy plane are the same because they are contained in the same packet. Within the fabric sites, VXLAN carrying the SGT is used for the data plane. The fabric border de-encapsulates the VXLAN packet for the traffic before sending it through the DMVPN tunnel. A DMVPN tunnel can carry SGTs inline, meaning the SGT from the VXLAN header on the fabric border is placed in the IP packet that is sent through the DMVPN tunnel, which the remote fabric site will be able to de-encapsulate and propagate in VXLAN within its fabric. The DMVPN configuration on both the fabric borders should be done manually or using Cisco DNA Center templates. The topology is scalable because the policy is carried inline in the data packet.

Figure 7-27 shows a topology of fabric sites using the traditional WAN as IP transit. There is no DMVPN running between the fabric sites in this topology, unlike the previous use case. This topology is common for retail networks with multiple branches connected over WAN links. The control plane uses LISP within the fabric sites, and the fabric border hands off using BGP to the fusion router. WAN link control protocols are used for the transit. For the data plane, VXLAN is used within the fabric site and contains the SGT and VN information. The fabric border strips off the SGT and uses VRF-lite for data plane communication with the fusion router. The SGT cannot be carried natively in a WAN transit. To propagate SGTs, SXP can be run between Cisco ISE and both the site borders, where ISE pushes the IP address-to-SGT mappings to both the fabric site borders. In this case, ISE is the SXP speaker, and both fabric site borders are SXP listeners. Another option is to run SXP directly between the fabric site borders, where one fabric border is the SXP speaker and the other fabric border is the SXP listener. Cisco DNA Center does not automate the SXP configuration on the fabric border nodes. The SXP configuration can be pushed using Cisco DNA Center templates. Scale numbers play a vital role when SXP is in use. Refer to the Cisco TrustSec platform compatibility matrix for the SXP-supported Cisco platforms.

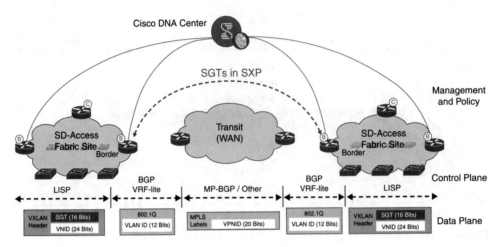

Figure 7-27   *Fabric Sites Connecting on WAN Transit*

Cisco SD-Access Transit

Cisco SD-Access transit interconnects fabric sites with the native Cisco SD-Access encapsulation, basically extending the logic in a fabric site to across the fabric sites for end-to-end automation and policy. The key consideration for the Distributed Campus design using Cisco SD-Access transit is that the network between fabric sites and to Cisco DNA Center should be high bandwidth, low latency, and able to accommodate the Maximum Transmission Unit (MTU) setting used for Cisco SD-Access (typically 9100 bytes). The physical connectivity can be direct fiber connections, leased dark fiber, or metro Ethernet systems (VPLS, etc.) supporting similar bandwidth, port rate, delay, and MTU connectivity capabilities. Cisco SD-Access transit is the transit of choice if policy and end-to-end segmentation using VNs and SGTs is a requirement. Cisco SD-Access transit provides a single view of the entire network, horizontally scales the networks, and contains the failure domain within the fabric site instead of extending to multiple fabric sites. Cisco SD-Access transit has multiple options such as Direct Internet Access (DIA) for each site if there are multiple paths outside the fabric.

Figure 7-28 shows two fabric sites connected using a Cisco SD-Access transit. LISP is used for the control plane all along within the fabric and for control plane traffic between the fabric sites. The data plane uses VXLAN throughout the traffic flow within the transit as well. VXLAN contains the SGT that allows the policy to be carried to multiple fabric sites.

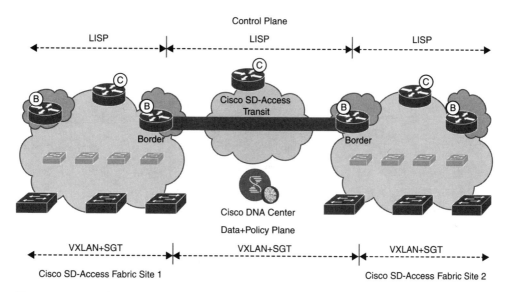

Figure 7-28 *Fabric Sites Connecting with Cisco SD-Access Transit*

A control plane node resides in the transit in the topology shown in Figure 7-28. Cisco SD-Access transit uses a transit control plane node. Transit control plane nodes receive aggregate routes from the fabric site borders for the fabric domain. They track all the aggregate routes and associate the routes to the fabric sites. In the topology, the control plane node in Fabric Site 1 contains prefixes of its site only; similarly, the control plane node in Fabric Site 2 contains the prefixes of its site only. The transit control plane node contains the aggregate of the prefixes of both Fabric Sites 1 and 2. The role of transit control plane nodes is to learn which prefixes are associated with each fabric site and to direct traffic to these sites across the Cisco SD-Access transit using control-plane signaling.

Traffic Flow for Multisite Fabric with Cisco SD-Access Transit

The transit control plane, as the name suggests, is involved in the control plane for traffic flow between fabric sites. Figure 7-29 shows two fabric sites with hosts that are connected using a Cisco SD-Access transit.

Following is the list of operations performed when Host 1, which is connected to Fabric Site 1, sends traffic to Host 2, which is connected to Fabric Site 2:

- Host 1 initiates traffic to Host 2. The fabric edge in Fabric Site 1 requests the fabric control plane node for the RLOC of Host 2. The fabric control plane responds to the fabric edge to send traffic to the fabric border in Fabric Site 1.

- The fabric edge in Fabric Site 1 sends Host 1 traffic to the fabric border in Fabric Site 1.

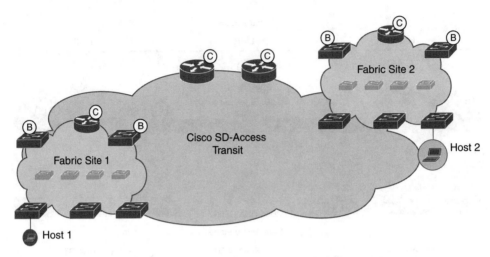

Figure 7-29 *Traffic Fabric Sites Connecting with Cisco SD-Access Transit*

- After receiving the traffic, the fabric border in Fabric Site 1 queries the transit network fabric control plane node for the destination host. This occurs because Cisco DNA Center configures the fabric border in Fabric Site 1 to query its fabric control plane node for the prefixes in Fabric Site 1 and query the transit control plane node for any other prefixes.

- The fabric transit control plane node responds to the query with the destination address of the fabric border in Fabric Site 2.

- The fabric border in Fabric Site 1 forwards the traffic to the fabric border in Fabric Site 2 using VXLAN with the SGT in the header.

- After receiving the traffic, the fabric border in Fabric Site 2 queries the fabric control plane node of Fabric Site 2 for the destination host. This occurs because Cisco DNA Center configures the fabric border in Fabric Site 2 to query its fabric control plane node for the prefixes in Fabric Site 2 and query the transit control plane node for any other prefixes.

- The fabric control plane in Fabric Site 2 responds with the destination address as the fabric edge in Fabric Site 2.

- The fabric border in Fabric Site 2 forwards the traffic to the fabric edge in Fabric Site 2 using VXLAN encapsulation with SGTs embedded. The fabric edge in Fabric Site 2 allows or denies traffic based on the SGACL enforced for the SGTs assigned to Host 1 and Host 2.

Internet Access Use Case with Multisite Cisco SD-Access Transit

The fabric sites can have different egress paths depending on the destination. Direct Internet Access is one of the common topologies, where the fabric site has one path out to the Internet directly and another path to communicate with other fabric sites.

Figure 7-30 illustrates a deployment of three fabric sites connected using Cisco SD-Access transit. Fabric Sites 2 and 3 have a direct connection to the Internet, whereas Fabric Site 1 has only one egress path using the Cisco SD-Access transit. A Direct Internet Access (DIA) topology ensures the traffic from the branch can be routed directly to the Internet. DIA helps reduce IT spending, increase application experience through better uplink and downlink speeds as the traffic is not backhauled to the main campus.

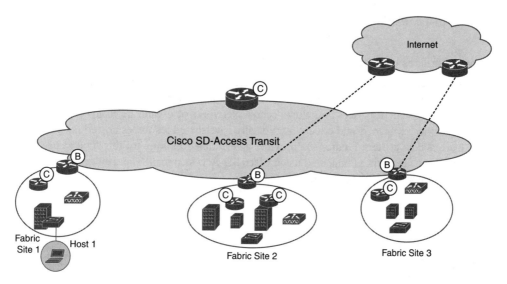

Figure 7-30 *Internet Access in Cisco SD-Access Distributed Deployment*

The following is the list of steps taken when Host 1 in Fabric Site 1 sends traffic to the Internet:

1. Host 1 in Fabric Site 1 initiates traffic to the Internet. The edge node in Fabric Site 1 sends a request to the Fabric Site 1 control plane for the destination RLOC.

2. The Fabric Site 1 control plane node sends a negative reply because the destination IP address is not registered in its database.

3. The negative reply prompts the edge node to send the traffic to the Fabric Site 1 border.

4. Upon receiving the traffic, the Fabric Site 1 border sends a request to the transit control plane node for the destination IP address information.

5. The transit control plane node does not have the Internet prefix in its database and sends a negative reply.

6. Based on the negative reply, the Fabric Site 1 border now knows to forward the traffic to the Fabric Site 2 or Fabric Site 3 border because they are connected to the Internet. This configuration is pushed by Cisco DNA Center.

7. Upon receiving the traffic again, the Fabric Site 2 border sends a request to the transit control plane node for the destination IP address information.

8. The transit control plane node again sends a negative reply because it does not have the destination IP address registered in its database.

9. The Fabric Site 2 border uses traditional routing lookup to evaluate the next hop to send the traffic, which usually is the default router. Traffic is sent to the default router, which then forwards further.

Shared Services Use Case with Multisite Cisco SD-Access Transit

Shared services such as DNS, DHCP, Cisco ISE, Cisco DNA Center, and internal web servers usually reside in the data center. This use case covers the traffic flow of fabric sites using shared services in the data center. Networks of organizations in sectors such as healthcare, finance, and education typically have shared resources hosted in the headquarters data centers. Figure 7-31 provides an example topology for this type of use case with three fabric sites connected using Cisco SD-Access transit. The data center is connected directly to Fabric Site 1.

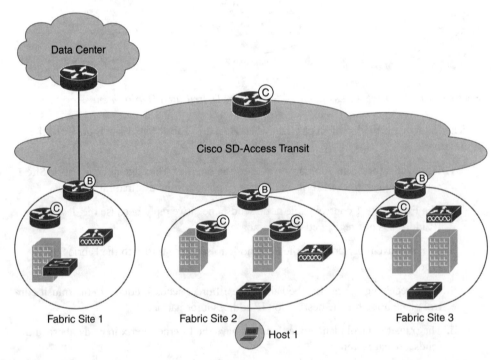

Figure 7-31 *Shared Data Center in Cisco SD-Access Distributed Deployment*

Host 1 is connected to Fabric Site 2 and is trying to access a resource in the data center. Here is the traffic flow:

1. Host 1 in Fabric Site 2 initiates traffic to the data center. The edge node in Site 2 sends a request to the Fabric Site 2 control plane for the destination RLOC.

2. The Fabric Site 2 control plane node sends a negative reply because the destination IP address is not registered in its database.

3. The negative reply prompts the edge node to send the traffic to the Fabric Site 2 border. The Fabric Site 2 border receives the traffic and sends a request to the transit control plane node for the destination IP address information.

4. The transit control plane node has the destination IP address information in its database because the data center aggregate address was registered by the Fabric Site 1 border. The transit control plane sends the destination IP address of the Fabric Site 1 border to the Fabric Site 2 border.

5. The Fabric Site 2 border forwards the DC traffic to the Fabric Site 1 border using VXLAN. The Fabric Site 1 border receives the traffic and sends a request to the transit control plane node for the destination IP address information.

6. The transit control plane node sends a reply to the Fabric Site 1 border noting that the destination RLOC is its own IP address. The Fabric Site 1 border forwards the traffic to the data center.

Cisco recommends deploying two dedicated transit control plane nodes for redundancy and load balancing. They need IP reachability through the underlay to all the site borders and could be located physically at different sites or in a centralized data center. Macro-segmentation using VNs and micro-segmentation using SGTs is possible, and consistent policies can be applied throughout the fabric domain agnostic of the IP addressing. The configuration is completely automated by Cisco DNA Center. Refer to the Cisco SD-Access Product Compatibility matrix for scale details of transit control plane nodes.

Cisco SD-WAN Transit

Organizations are rapidly moving toward digitizing their networks, and Cisco SD-WAN is digitizing wide-area networks at a rapid pace. Cisco SD-WAN can be used as a transit for connecting fabric sites. This is mainly for customers who have already implemented Cisco SD-WAN. Cisco SD-WAN transit introduces consistent policy and end-to-end segmentation using VNs and SGTs in Cisco SD-WAN encapsulation. Similar to Cisco SD-Access transit, Cisco SD-WAN transit has smaller and isolated fault domains and is resilient and scalable.

Figure 7-32 shows the protocols used in a multisite deployment with Cisco SD-WAN transit connecting the fabric sites. Cisco DNA Center and vManage sit in the management plane orchestrating the configuration. Cisco DNA Center and vManage communicate with each other using APIs. Cisco DNA Center automates the Campus Fabric configuration, and vManage orchestrates the Cisco SD-WAN configuration. The SD-WAN edges are fabric borders, and only one management point can exist for each device. Cisco DNA Center does not manage the fabric borders that are also the SD-WAN edges. Using APIs, Cisco DNA Center instructs vManage to push the Cisco SD-Access–relevant configuration on the border devices.

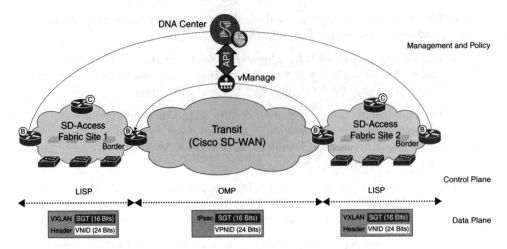

Figure 7-32 *Fabric Sites Connecting with Cisco SD-WAN Transit*

LISP is the control plane with the Campus Fabric sites. Overlay Management Protocol (OMP) is used in Cisco SD-WAN for the control plane. VXLAN encapsulation with SGT embedded is used for the data plane in fabric sites. VXLAN de-encapsulation happens on the fabric border, and the SGT and VN information is embedded in the IPsec header for the data plane in the Cisco SD-WAN transit to enable end-to-end segmentation.

Policy Deployment Models in Cisco SD-Access Distributed Deployment

Cisco ISE deployment plays a vital role in Cisco SD-Access deployments because the endpoints and devices connected in Cisco SD-Access deployments are performed by ISE. ISE also manages and provisions SGACL policies to the fabric edges for enforcement. The choice of which ISE deployment model to use depends on scale, redundancy, latency, and security requirements. Figure 7-33 shows a network with multiple fabric sites that are connected using a transit. In this topology, Cisco ISE is deployed in a distributed deployment with a Primary Administration Node (PAN), a Monitoring (MnT) node, and pxGrid distributed in each of two data centers, with Policy Services Nodes (PSNs) behind load balancers in each data center.

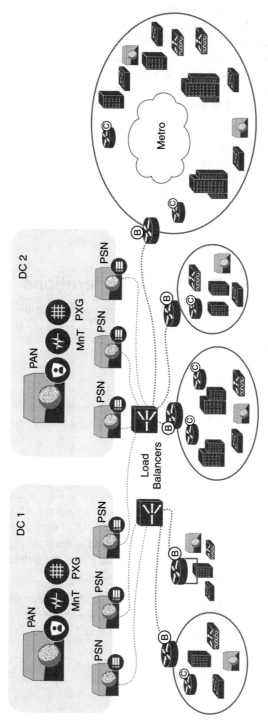

Figure 7-33 *Cisco ISE Distributed Deployment for Multisite*

The Cisco ISE distributed deployment shown in Figure 7-33 is optimal for resiliency and fault tolerance. Cisco DNA Center automates the configuration of the AAA settings and points them to the load-balancer VIP. If a PSN goes down behind a load balancer, the load balancer automatically detects it and forwards the authentication request to the next available PSN. If a data center is unreachable, authentication requests can be forwarded to the other data center. The only latency requirement is to ensure the ISE nodes have a round-trip time (RTT) of 300 ms or less.

Another Cisco ISE distributed deployment model often used is the localized PSN with centralized PAN, MnT, and pxGrid. The PSNs are local to each site and perform the authentication, and the authentication response is faster because the PSNs are deployed in the same location as the end clients. As of version 1.3.3, Cisco DNA Center can push only two PSN server IP addresses as part of the site settings. For small deployments with less than 20,000 clients, two-node ISE deployment is supported. Refer to the ISE scaling guide published by Cisco for the scale numbers supported by various specifications of ISE.

Cisco SD-Access Design Considerations

For a successful deployment of a Cisco SD-Access solution, various factors need to be considered prior to deployment. This section highlights some key factors to consider in Cisco SD-Access design and implementation.

Latency Considerations

Cisco DNA Center is the point of configuration and management of the Cisco SD-Access fabric. For management and operations, Cisco DNA Center needs to interact consistently with the components that make up the fabric.

Latency numbers play a vital role in Cisco SD-Access deployments, just like with traditional deployments. The fabric access points are in local mode in the Cisco SD-Access fabric. Figure 7-34 shows the latency requirements to consider in any fabric deployment. The AP requires an RTT of 20 milliseconds or less between the AP and the Wireless LAN Controllers (WLCs). This generally means that the WLC is deployed in the same physical site as the APs. Usually, APs and WLCs are deployed in the same physical site to meet the 20-ms latency requirement. Positioning APs and WLCs in different locations is not recommended if they are connected through WAN links.

Cisco DNA Center appliances support standalone or three-node clusters. A clustered deployment must have an RTT of 10 ms or less between the nodes in the cluster. The nodes in the cluster need to be in the same Layer 2 network and, because of this requirement, cannot be geographically apart.

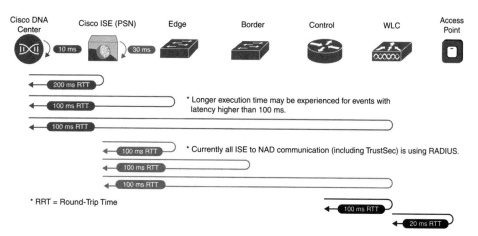

Figure 7-34   *Cisco DNA Center Latency Requirements*

Cisco DNA Center communicates with Cisco ISE over the External RESTful Services (ERS) API and pxGrid. To execute the TrustSec policy and configuration changes, Cisco DNA Center and Cisco ISE communication should not be limited to a maximum RTT of 200 ms. Cisco ISE nodes in a deployment should have a maximum RTT of 300 ms. Cisco ISE nodes can be geographically dispersed as long as the RTT requirement is met. Network access devices (NADs) communicate with Cisco ISE by using RADIUS or TACACS+, and the timeout between NADs and Cisco ISE is a configurable option.

Cisco DNA Center communicates with network devices for automation, fabric provisioning, inventory collection, Software Image Management (SWIM), and analytics over Secure Shell (SSH), Telnet, and Netconf. The maximum supported latency is 200 ms. Latency between 100 ms and 200 ms is supported, but a few operations, such as SWIM and inventory collection, might see some delay in execution.

Cisco SD-Access Design Approach

Cisco SD-Access design can be categorized into four types depending on the scale of the network. The scale numbers discussed in the following sections are based on Cisco DNA Center 1.3.3 and may differ in subsequent Cisco DNA Center releases.

Very Small Site

Very small site Cisco SD-Access design mainly consists of border, control, wireless, and edge nodes on a single device, also called Fabric in a Box, introduced earlier in the chapter. Figure 7-35 shows the FiaB switch deployed in a branch site as an example topology. The FiaB switch can be deployed in a stack. Very small site design is a cost-friendly solution for branch sites with limited survivability, meaning full redundancy or limited redundancy is available in case of a link or device failure.

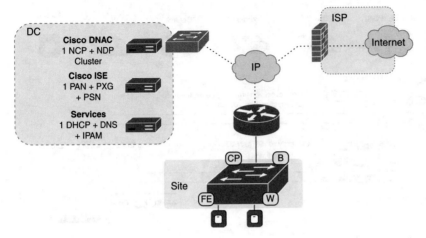

Figure 7-35 *Very Small Site Cisco SD-Access Design*

Small Site

In a small site design, border and control plane nodes are co-located on the same device with one or more fabric edges. Limited survivability is possible with the redundant co-located border and control plane node. Figure 7-36 illustrates an example of a small site Cisco SD-Access design. Only two co-located border and control plane nodes are allowed. Small site design benefits are limited survivability with the option to use a local WLC or embedded WLC with Catalyst 9000 Series switches.

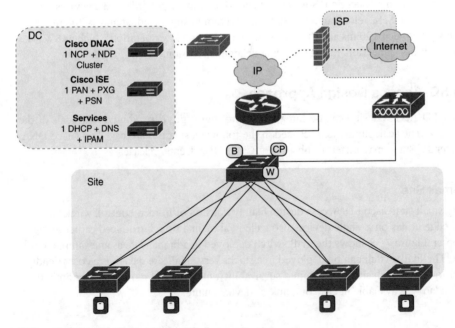

Figure 7-36 *Small Site Cisco SD-Access Design*

Medium Site

Medium site Cisco SD-Access design can have a maximum of six dedicated control plane nodes for wired networks and four control plane nodes for wireless (two enterprise CP nodes and two guest CP nodes) for higher survivability, as shown in Figure 7-37. The design can have up to two co-located control plane and border nodes. Dedicated edges are supported in this site model. Cisco ISE is a standalone deployment in a medium site design. A dedicated WLC or an embedded WLC in High Availability (HA) can be enabled in the medium site deployment.

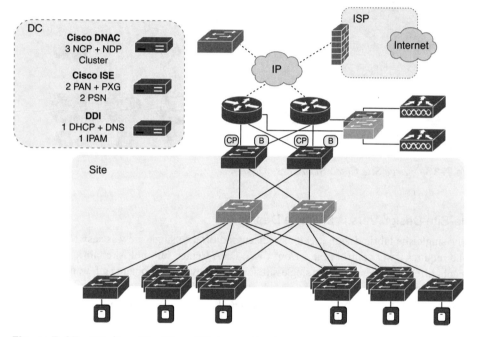

Figure 7-37 *Medium Site Cisco SD-Access Design*

Large Site

Figure 7-38 illustrates an example of large site Cisco SD-Access design. Large site design supports a maximum of six control plane nodes (wired) and four border nodes for site exits. In large site design, there is full survivability for the control plane and full redundancy for the border. Large site design can have dedicated edges. It supports a local WLC or an embedded WLC in HA.

Cisco DNA Center can be present in a local or remote data center as long as the latency requirements are met.

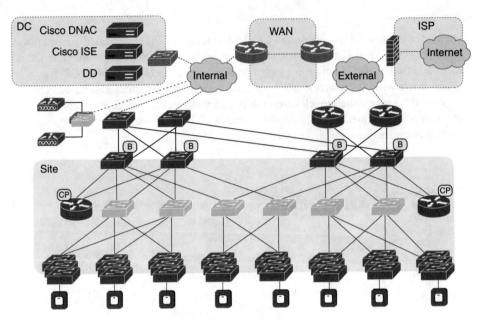

Figure 7-38 *Large Site Cisco SD-Access Design*

Single-Site Design Versus Multisite Design

The single-site fabric design previously discussed offers a single view, is easy to manage, and requires fewer control points from Cisco DNA Center, but multisite fabric deployments offer some benefits over single-site fabric deployments. To name a few, multisite deployments have smaller or isolated failure domains, increased scale in the endpoints, wireless client roaming because of the 20-ms RTT between AP and WLC, and local breakout at each site for direct Internet access. The total wireless scale is better in a multisite deployment where a local WLC is provisioned at every site to accommodate more APs and wireless clients.

As an example of the advantages of multisite over single-site design, consider a hospital emergency response network, the main requirement of which is survivability. With a single-site fabric deployment where all departments are in the same site, survivability is a concern. Best design for this use case would be two fabric sites in a fabric domain—one fabric site just for the emergency response network and another fabric site for the remaining networks. The two fabric sites can be part of the same fabric domain by connecting using a transit. This ensures better survivability for the ER network because of the smaller fault domain and by placing redundant control plane and border nodes locally.

Multiple factors affect the per-site scale parameters. IP subnets are present on the edge nodes. A single site consists of multiple IP subnets, and all the edge nodes are provisioned with the IP subnet even when there are no clients or client traffic for all the subnets on edge node(s). Some customers may need a few of the IP subnets across edge nodes for end-to-end mobility, but not all. The greater the number of IP subnets in a fabric site, the more time that is required for provisioning. Another parameter is the TCAM scale on the border. For every /32 edge client that the border needs to send traffic to, a /32 host entry is added in the TCAM table. In a dual-stack environment with IPv4 and IPv6, each endpoint would take two /32 entries in the TCAM table. In a single large site, the border TCAM limit needs to be considered when choosing the correct platform for the border. The greater the number of edge nodes in a site, the more time that is required for provisioning, similar to IP subnets. The total number of VNs (VRFs) supported in a fabric site depends on the platform used in the fabric site.

Table 7-1 shows the total scale parameters supported by various appliance versions of Cisco DNA Center XL. These parameters need to be accounted for when designing Cisco SD-Access, along with the provisioning times required. Apart from the discussed parameters, SGACL policy scale is another consideration for single-site versus multisite deployments.

Table 7-1   *Single-Site Scale Limit for Cisco DNA Center Appliances*

Parameters	DN2-HW-APL	DN2-HW-APL-L	DN2-HW-APL-XL
Number of fabric devices* per fabric site	500	600	1000
Number of IP pools per fabric site	100	300	600
Number of endpoints per fabric site	25,000	40,000	100,000
Number of virtual networks per fabric site	64	64	256
Number of fabric sites per Cisco DNA Center cluster	500	1000	2000
Number of total devices supported per Cisco DNA Center cluster	1000 (stacks)	2000 (stacks)	5000 (stacks)
Number of APs per Cisco DNA Center cluster	4000	6000	12,000

* An extended node is counted as a fabric device

Cisco SD-Access Component Considerations

While deploying Cisco SD-Access in a Campus network for a greenfield or a brownfield deployment, a robust design ensures a stable and smooth transition for end users and administrators. Design considerations are a big part of the planning phase, and each component has its own design options based on the network requirements. This section covers the design aspects of a Cisco SD-Access campus network viewed from each architecture component.

Cisco SD-Access uses virtual networks (overlay networks or fabric overlay) running on a physical network (underlay network) as discussed in Chapter 2, "Introduction to Cisco Software-Defined Access."

Underlay Network

The underlay network defines the physical switches and routers used to deploy a Cisco SD-Access network. The underlay network provides IP connectivity using a routing protocol (static routing is supported but not scalable) and carries the traffic encapsulated as part of the overlay network. A scalable, simple, reliable routing protocol is recommended in the underlay for a Cisco SD-Access network because the underlay is mainly used for transport purposes. Endpoints such as users, access points, IoT devices, and extended nodes connect to the underlay network. Endpoints connected to the underlay network are physically connected to the underlay, but they are part of the overlay network in Cisco SD-Access.

Underlay Network Design Considerations

The underlay network is used for transport of the encapsulated traffic, so it should be reliable, simple, scalable, and resilient to deploy a Cisco SD-Access network. Cisco DNA Center can be used to deploy an automated underlay. For brownfield deployments where there is an existing underlay, Cisco DNA Center discovers the existing underlay and provisions a fabric overlay.

Here are some of the design considerations for an underlay network in Cisco SD-Access deployments:

- **Layer 3 routed network:** A Layer 3 routed network is highly recommended for the Campus Fabric underlay network. Spanning Tree Protocol or any loop-prevention Layer 2 protocols are avoided by using a Layer 3 routed network. Cisco DNA Center LAN Automation automatically provisions the Intermediate System to Intermediate System (IS-IS) routing protocol for the underlay network. A dedicated Interior Gateway Protocol (IGP) in the underlay network is beneficial to logically differentiate between the underlay network and the overlay network to ease with the troubleshooting.

- **Point-to-point link with ECMP:** Point-to-point links are the most efficient way to achieve faster convergence because there is little dependency on the upper-layer protocol timeouts. Equal-cost multi-path (ECMP) routing, as the name suggests, takes multiple best paths for packet forwarding to a destination. Cisco Express Forwarding (CEF) takes care of load balancing between the ECMP paths, and the routing protocol used in the underlay should be ECMP-aware. LAN Automation configures ECMP and Bidirectional Forwarding Detection (BFD) with the IS-IS routing protocol for fault detection and faster convergence.

- **MTU:** Cisco SD-Access uses VXLAN for encapsulation in the data plane, which adds 50 bytes in the VXLAN header. The server MTUs typically are 9000 bytes, meaning the underlay should be able to carry 9050 bytes to avoid fragmentation issues inside or outside the fabric. LAN Automation by Cisco DNA Center automatically provisions an MTU of 9100 bytes in the underlay. In case of a manual underlay, MTU consideration is important. The **tcp-adjust-mss** command should be used if the underlay device cannot handle jumbo frames.

- **Loopback reachability:** Cisco DNA Center requires and communicates with the devices using their loopback address in the Campus Fabric. Cisco DNA Center resides outside the fabric, and shared services such as DNS, DHCP, and the AAA server usually reside outside the fabric. The underlay devices' loopback address should be routable outside the fabric for reachability to shared services and Cisco DNA Center. For RLOC reachability, /32 host masks are required, and the default route cannot be used. To avoid the hassle of prefix lists, tag the host routes to easily create policies to propagate the host routes outside the fabric.

- **Fabric-enabled WLC:** Cisco SD-Access consists of a fabric-enabled WLC that resides outside the fabric. Similar to loopback address /32 routes, a default route in the underlay cannot be used by the access points to reach the WLC. A specific route to the WLC IP address must exist in the global routing table (GRT) at each fabric edge where the APs are physically connected.

- **LAN Automation:** For greenfield deployments, leverage LAN Automation to create the underlay. LAN Automation enables unicast using IS-IS as the IGP and multicast in the underlay. LAN Automation creates point-to-point Layer 3 links and enables ECMP, NSF, BFD, and 9100 MTU on the Layer 3 links using a seed device. As part of LAN Automation workflow, the network devices can be provisioned with site-specific CLI, SNMP credentials, and the site-specific software image.

Overlay Network

An overlay network is created on top of the underlay to create a virtualized network. An overlay network is a logical topology used to virtually connect devices, built over an arbitrary physical underlay topology. An overlay network often uses alternate forwarding attributes to provide additional services that are not provided by the underlay. The data plane traffic and control plane signaling are contained within each virtualized network, maintaining isolation among the networks as well as independence from the underlay network, also known as macro-segmentation. Layer 2 overlays run a LAN segment to transport Layer 2 frames over the Layer 3 underlay.

Overlay Fabric Design Considerations

In the Cisco SD-Access fabric, the overlay networks carry user traffic in a fabric. The overlay packet contains the VN and the SGT of the user traffic. Following are some design considerations for an efficient overlay fabric:

- **Reduce subnets and simplify DHCP management:** Overlay subnets simplify the network, and the idea of Cisco SD-Access is to move away from the IP address–based policies and avoid L2 loops. Reduce the number of overlay user subnets and use larger DHCP scopes instead of assigning smaller subnets per location. Convert the security policies based on IP addressing to policies based on the user roles.

■ **Micro- and macro-segmentation:** Macro-segmentation is possible in Cisco SD-Access using virtual networks. Inter-VN communication is not possible by default in Cisco SD-Access fabric. Users or endpoints that would never talk to each other could be in their individual VN. If traffic policies need to be set for certain traffic flows or users, place the traffic in one VN and leverage SGTs to enforce the security policies.

■ **No overlapping IP subnets:** Overlapping subnets are supported in overlay networks, but in scenarios with shared services or for inter-VN communication scenarios, overlapping subnets can create additional complexities. Avoid overlapping IP subnets in the overlay to maintain a simplified overlay network.

Fabric Control Plane Node Design Considerations

The fabric control plane is the map server with the host database to identify the location of the endpoint. The mapping database is critical for fabric operation, and an overloaded, sluggish control plane node could result in traffic loss on the initial packet. Failure of a control plane node results in endpoints being unable to communicate with remote endpoints that do not have a cached RLOC entry in the database. Redundant control plane nodes ensure high availability of the fabric, meaning the host mapping database copy is present on a second control plane node.

The control plane node can be co-located with the border node if the endpoint scale requirements are honored. When there is a possibility of several mobility events in the network, co-locating the control plane and border nodes is not recommended. Every time a wireless user roams, the WLC sends notifications to the control plane node, and high roam rates result in hundreds of mobility events per second or thousands of mobility events per minute, which is why a dedicated control plane node works better.

A Cisco SD-Access fabric site can support up to six control plane nodes in a wired-only deployment. Cisco AireOS and Catalyst WLCs can communicate with four control plane nodes in a fabric site. To use four control plane nodes in a site with a Cisco SD-Access wireless deployment, two control plane nodes are dedicated to the guest and two are dedicated to local site traffic. If the dedicated guest border/control plane nodes feature is not used, WLCs can communicate with only two control plane nodes per fabric site.

The transit control plane node in case of Cisco SD-Access transit has to be a dedicated box.

Fabric Border Node Design Considerations

The fabric border connects the fabric network to the external network. The design of the fabric border depends on how the fabric connects to the outside network. Virtual networks in a fabric are mapped to VRFs using VRF-lite in the outside network. Fabric edges forward the traffic to the fabric border for the destinations outside the fabric. Internet services and other shared services usually reside outside the fabric, and the fabric endpoint /32 details are added to the TCAM table on the border. The border TCAM should be able to handle the /32 host entries in a fabric site. In the Cisco SD-Access distributed deployments discussed in the earlier sections, shared services might be interconnected through a transit control plane. Depending on the scale requirements, the fabric border can be co-located with a fabric control plane.

Infrastructure Services Design Considerations

Cisco SD-Access does not require changes to the existing shared services such as DHCP and DNS. The DHCP traffic flow in a fabric is slightly different from the traditional DHCP flows. In a typical DHCP relay design, the unique gateway IP address determines the subnet address assignment for an endpoint, in addition to the location to which the DHCP server should direct the offered address. In a fabric overlay network, the gateway is not unique, as the fabric edges use the same anycast IP address. When the DHCP server sends an offer, the offer is seen by the fabric border, and the fabric border can't determine from the anycast gateway address which fabric edge to forward the request to. Special handling of DHCP is required wherein advanced DHCP options need to be inserted by the relay agent (fabric edge) when the DHCP discovery packet is forwarded. To identify the specific DHCP relay source, Cisco DNA Center automates the configuration of the relay agent at the fabric edge with DHCP Option 82 including the information option for circuit ID insertion. Adding the information provides additional suboptions to identify the specific source relay agent. DHCP relay information embedded in the circuit ID is used as the destination for DHCP offer replies to the requestor by the fabric border in Cisco SD-Access. The fabric edge inserts the Option 82 for circuit ID insertion, sent to the DHCP server. The DHCP server should send the offer preserving the DHCP options. The fabric border receives the DHCP offer, looks at the circuit ID, and forwards the DHCP offer to the correct fabric edge. Do not use a DHCP server such as Windows 2008, as it cannot preserve the DHCP options in the DHCP offer sent.

Fabric Wireless Integration Design Considerations

The RTT between the fabric WLC and the APs should be less than or equal to 20 ms. The APs are connected to the fabric edges and are part of the fabric overlay. The APs belong to an overlay AP VLAN that is part of the INFRA_VN in the fabric that is mapped to a global routing table. In fabric mode, an AP joins the WLC in a local mode. Fabric WLCs do not actively participate in the data plane traffic-forwarding role, and fabric mode APs are responsible for delivering wireless client traffic into and out of the wired fabric. The WLC is connected outside the fabric (AireOS WLC). The WLC is involved in the control plane communication with the CP nodes. An AireOS WLC can have two CP nodes for the enterprise network and two CPs for the guest network. Because of latency and CP restrictions, the WLC can be part of only one fabric site.

The WLC typically is connected to the shared services that are reachable through the underlay. WLC single sign-on (SSO) is supported in fabric deployments for high availability. A brownfield WLC can be added to a Cisco SD-Access fabric.

Wireless Over-the-Top Centralized Wireless Option Design Considerations

Over-the-top centralized wireless is an option where the APs are not in a fabric mode and use the native CAPWAP for control and data communication with the WLC. The APs connect in to the fabric edge but do not use the overlay network, as the wireless client traffic is sent through the CAPWAP tunnel. No fabric benefits could be leveraged in over-the-top deployment. This is mainly used when there is a legacy service set identifier (SSID) or when there is an existing non-Cisco wireless network. Over-the-top centralized wireless can be used as a migration step to full Cisco SD-Access.

An over-the-top centralized design still provides IP address management, simplified configuration and troubleshooting, and roaming at scale. In the centralized model, the WLAN controller and APs are located within the same fabric site. The WLC can connect to a data center or shared services adjacent to the campus core. APs can reside inside or outside the fabric without any change to the recommended centralized WLAN design, keeping in mind that the benefits of fabric and Cisco SD-Access are not extended to and integrated with the wireless when the fabric is used only as an over-the-top transport.

Mixed SD-Access Wireless and Centralized Wireless Option Design Considerations

The mixed Cisco SD-Access wireless design has a mix of fabric and non-fabric (centralized) SSIDs. Customers may initially deploy over-the-top centralized wireless as a transition step before integrating Cisco SD-Access wireless into the fabric. A dedicated WLC should be used for enabling Cisco SD-Access wireless, which enables the use of the same SSID in fabric and non-fabric domains without modifying any existing centralized wireless deployment. If a dedicated WLC cannot be allocated for Cisco SD-Access, the same WLC can be used to be discovered by Cisco DNA Center to automate the configuration to support both fabric and non-fabric SSIDs. Cisco DNA Center does not modify any existing configuration on the centralized WLC; it only adds new configuration as per the migration requirements.

Wireless Guest Deployment Considerations

In a Cisco SD-Access fabric, the guest VN uses the same control plane node and border node for the guest traffic as any other fabric virtual network. This workflow is automated by Cisco DNA Center, it's simple, and the guest VN can be mapped to a guest VRF through VRF-lite as part of the L3 border handoff. Organizations in verticals, such as healthcare and federal government, have guest requirements that mandate the guest traffic use a dedicated path, such as through a DMZ, where the rest of the organization traffic does not flow. For such use cases, a dedicated guest border and guest control plane are set up for the guest VN. They can be co-located or dedicated nodes. Figure 7-39 illustrates a topology where the guest VN has a dedicated guest border and a guest control plane configured.

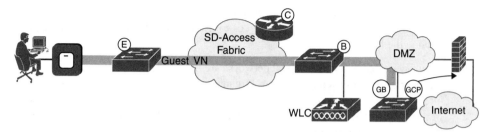

Figure 7-39 *Guest Border and Guest Control Plane with Cisco SD-Access*

The guest border RLOC should be reachable in the underlay. The end-to-end MTU should be 9100 because of the additional VXLAN header. The guest endpoint IDs are going to be registered with the guest control plane (GCP). In this topology, all guest traffic terminated on a dedicated guest border (GB) and the east to west isolation can be achieved by micro-segmentation using SGTs.

Security Policy Design Considerations

As introduced earlier in the chapter, Cisco SD-Access has a new policy plane to carry the user role in the VXLAN header. The security policies play a key role in the campus design, and the policy scale is one of the parameters in choosing a design. The following parameters need to be considered when designing a Cisco SD-Access network:

- **Network device administration:** Network devices in the infrastructure need equal security as the end users because they are common targets for security attacks. TACACS+ is the most secure device administration protocol to ensure administrators are authenticated, authorized, and provided the right level of access. Command authorization with TACACS+ takes security up a notch by ensuring each command entered by the administrator/operator is validated by the AAA server. Cisco DNA Center automates TACACS+ configuration except for the command authorization as of version 1.3.3.

- **Device-based policy:** Enterprise networks are adapting to the bring your own device (BYOD) network trend of allowing employees to connect to the network with their own devices, but this could also allow security holes, as the organization has no control over the software running on each BYOD device. Depending on the enterprise's BYOD security policy, the BYOD users can be placed in a dedicated virtual network or can be provided an SGT that only has access to resources allowed to BYOD users.

- **Network access control:** NAC ensures that the endpoints connecting to the network are authenticated and authorized with the correct VN, VLAN, and SGT dynamically. The number of VNs and SGTs to be deployed in a Cisco SD-Access fabric depends on the NAC authorization requirements. Users, endpoints, or traffic flows that do not communicate should be in their dedicated virtual network, as inter-VN communication is not enabled by default. SGTs within a VN are leveraged to enforce security policies within the VN. SGACL policies need not be applied at the access layer, but they can be applied at the border or close to the data center if the destination is in the data center. SGT propagation needs to be considered when policies are applied outside the fabric.

- **Security device audit:** Traditional networks are used to applying security controls on security devices such as firewalls. Organizations might have requirements that inter-VN communication restrictions need to be implemented on a security device. In those cases, the Cisco SD-Access design needs to include a firewall as the handoff device and implement policy enforcements on the firewall for auditing and visibility purposes.

- **Data integrity and confidentiality:** Federal government and financial verticals often use encryption between devices to avoid any man-in-the-middle attacks. Media Access Control Security (MACsec) encryption provides device-to-device encryption. Cisco DNA Center does not automate MACsec encryption, but the configuration can be provisioned using templates.

- **Number of fabric sites:** Networks with a larger number of SGTs factor in the type of Cisco SD-Access design to choose: either single site or multisite fabric deployment.

Cisco SD-Access Policy Extension to Cisco ACI

Cisco SD-Access is the fabric for campus networks where Cisco DNA Center is the orchestrator to automate the configuration of the fabric. The Campus Fabric supports end-to-end segmentation, host mobility, and open and programmable interfaces for integration with third-party solutions. Many customer verticals such as financial, healthcare, manufacturing, and retail have multiple domains, with critical applications residing in the data center and accessible only to authorized campus endpoints. These critical applications should not be accessible by all the campus users, but only by a few user roles. For example, HR users should be able to access only the HR application, and finance users should be able to access only finance applications, not development servers. The policy applied in the Cisco SD-Access fabric is not carried over to the data center, as the data center is not part of the fabric. Extending the policy from the fabric to the data center is possible with the integration of Cisco SD-Access and Cisco Application Centric Infrastructure (Cisco ACI).

Similar to Cisco SD-Access, Cisco ACI is the software-defined networking offering for data centers and cloud networks. Cisco Application Policy Infrastructure Controller (Cisco APIC) is the main architectural component of the Cisco ACI solution. It is the unified point of automation and management for the Cisco ACI fabric, policy enforcement, and health monitoring, similar to Cisco DNA Center in campus networks. Cisco ACI shares similar concepts to those of Cisco SD-Access. It uses Multiprotocol BGP (MP-BGP) with Ethernet VPN (EVPN) for the control plane operations and VXLAN for data plane operations. For policy application, Cisco ACI uses endpoint groups (EPGs), similar to SGTs in Cisco SD-Access. Integration between the two domains allows interoperability between EPGs and SGTs so that policies can be applied within the data center leveraging groups using context from Cisco SD-Access. The integration involves the following steps:

Step 1.   Integrate Cisco DNA Center and ISE over pxGrid to exchange SGT information.

Step 2.   Integrate Cisco ISE and Cisco ACI. The Cisco ISE PAN integrates with Cisco APIC over SSL and uses APIs to synchronize the SGTs and EPGs. Cisco APIC details are added on Cisco ISE so that IP address-to-SGT mappings from Cisco ISE and IP address-to-EPG mappings from Cisco APIC are exchanged over SXP. Whenever the SXP protocol is used, scale needs to be accounted for in terms of the number of mappings that can be shared between Cisco ISE and Cisco ACI.

As shown in Figure 7-40, LISP is used for the control plane and VXLAN is used for the data plane in the Campus Fabric, which is connected to the Cisco ACI fabric using BGP/IGP and VRF-lite. The controllers automate the respective fabric domain configuration, but the configuration and integration between the domains is achieved manually. A fusion device is required for route leaking and connecting to the Cisco ACI fabric.

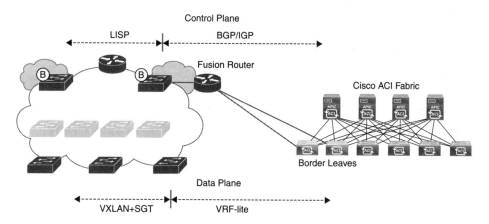

Figure 7-40   *Cisco SD-Access and Cisco ACI Interaction*

Cisco SD-Access uses a blacklist model for SGT policies by default, meaning traffic between SGTs is allowed by default unless blocked explicitly. Cisco ACI uses a whitelist model where the traffic by default between EPGs is blocked unless explicitly allowed. After the SGTs and EPGs are exchanged and the IP address-to-SGT/EPG mappings are exchanged across domains, the policies in each domain have to be manually created in their own fashion.

Note   The integration only works with a single Cisco ACI fabric with a single Cisco ACI tenant. Single L3out in ACI tenant and shared L3out are not supported. Cisco SD-Access uses SGACL for policies, and Cisco APIC uses access contracts for policies between EPGs.

Summary

Cisco SD-Access deployment designs vary based on the scale, resiliency, policy, multicast, type of nodes, and all the parameters discussed in detail in this chapter. Enterprises can chose to deploy a Campus fabric using a single fabric site deployment or multi-site fabric deployment. Depending on the network scale, device platforms, their software versions, round trip time, and a single fabric site model may work for some customers. Single fabric site brings in ease of use and one policy across the whole Campus fabric. Multi-site fabric deployment could be an option for large customers with a bigger scale who are distributed geographically with higher RTTs. To retain end-to-end segmentation with minimal manual work in multisite deployments, using Cisco SD-Access transit or Cisco SDWAN transit is recommended. Cisco DNA Center 1.3.3 introduces flexible features such as policy extended nodes, Layer 2 intersite, and Layer 2 flooding. Layer 2 flooding leverages native multicast in the underlay to allow legacy applications depending on ARP, broadcast, and link-local multicast in fabric deployments. Multidomain deployments are inevitable in customer networks where applications reside not in the campus network but in a data center or cloud. Cisco SD-Access integration with Cisco ACI provides the flexibility of exchanging groups between the domains so that policies can be applied based on user roles or endpoint groups.

References in This Chapter

Cisco DNA Center User Guide: https://www.cisco.com/c/en/us/td/docs/cloud-systems-management/network-automation-and-management/dna-center/1-3/user_guide/b_cisco_dna_center_ug_1_3/b_cisco_dna_center_ug_1_3_chapter_01011.html

Cisco SD-Access Product Compatibility: https://www.cisco.com/c/en/us/solutions/enterprise-networks/software-defined-access/compatibility-matrix.html

Cisco SD-Access (SDA) Integration with Cisco Application Centric Infrastructure (ACI): https://community.cisco.com/t5/networking-documents/cisco-sd-access-sda-integration-with-cisco-application-centric/ta-p/3909344

IP Multicast Technology Overview: https://www.cisco.com/c/en/us/td/docs/ios-xml/ios/ipmulti_pim/configuration/xe-16/imc-pim-xe-16-book/imc-tech-oview.pdf

Software-Defined Access for Distributed Campus Deployment Guide: https://www.cisco.com/c/en/us/td/docs/solutions/CVD/Campus/SD-Access-Distributed-Campus-Deployment-Guide-2019JUL.html

Software-Defined Access Solution Design Guide: https://www.cisco.com/c/en/us/td/docs/solutions/CVD/Campus/sda-sdg-2019oct.html#CiscoDigitalNetworkArchitectureandSoftwareDefinedAccess

Statista, "Internet of Things (IoT) Connected Devices Installed Base Worldwide from 2015 to 2025": https://www.statista.com/statistics/471264/iot-number-of-connected-devices-worldwide/

Chapter 8

Advanced Cisco DNA Center

This chapter covers the following topics:

- **Cisco DNA Center Architecture and Connectivity:** This section discusses an overview of the Cisco DNA Center appliance along with some deployment best practices.

- **Software Image Management:** This section discusses the Software Image Management tool in Cisco DNA Center that allows for easy, efficient, and reliable software upgrades to be pushed to network devices.

- **Cisco DNA Center Templates:** This section discusses the templating features of Cisco DNA Center, which enable network operators to deploy configuration changes to many devices simultaneously.

- **Plug and Play:** This section discusses the Plug and Play application, which provides the capability to automatically onboard and configure network devices from a factory default state.

- **Cisco DNA Center Tools:** This section discusses some of the other tools available in Cisco DNA Center that can be handy for day-to-day network operations.

The focus of this book so far has been on Cisco Software-Defined Access; however, it is important to remember that Cisco Software-Defined Access is just one application included in Cisco DNA Center's application suite. This chapter covers some of the other workflows and tools in Cisco DNA Center that can increase efficiency, lower risk, and provide agility in enterprise networks.

Cisco DNA Center Architecture and Connectivity

Although Cisco DNA Center is designed to be an "off-the-shelf" solution with very little effort required to get it up and running, it is still a powerful controller for the network and thus requires careful attention during the initial installation and configuration to avoid any issues in the future.

Hardware and Scale

Cisco DNA Center is an appliance-based solution running on the Cisco Unified Computing System (UCS) platform. The exact Cisco UCS model depends on the appliance size (entry-level, midsize, or large), and as of this writing, the models are the Cisco UCS C220 M5 or Cisco UCS C480 M5 chassis.

The size of the Cisco DNA Center appliance should be selected based on current and anticipated scale of the network, including the number of physical network devices, endpoints, and Cisco SD-Access fabrics. Table 8-1 is a sample of supported scale numbers of each size of Cisco DNA Center appliance as of this writing. Current and more detailed scale support can be found on Cisco.com.

Table 8-1 *Cisco DNA Center Scale Numbers*

Appliance Size	Entry	Midsize	Large
Number of network devices	1000	2000	5000
Number of wireless access points	4000	6000	13,000
Number of concurrent endpoints	25,000	40,000	100,000
Number of fabric sites	500	1000	2000

Network Connectivity

Because the Cisco DNA Center solution runs on a Cisco UCS server, it features a variety of network connectivity options that can be selected depending on the environment. Before configuring the interfaces during installation, it is important to understand exactly which resources need to be reachable on Cisco DNA Center and which resources it needs to be able to reach. At a high level, these resources are as follows:

■ **Cisco Integrated Management Controller (CIMC):** To configure the basic features and settings on the Cisco UCS server itself, an administrator needs to be able to reach the CIMC. This is also how the Cisco DNA Center installation wizard is accessed initially.

■ **Internet:** Updates to the Cisco DNA Center application and packages come from the cloud, and as such, the appliance needs network reachability to the Internet. This connectivity can also be through an HTTP proxy.

- **Enterprise:** Network devices that need to be managed, such as routers, switches, and wireless LAN controllers (WLCs), must be reachable from Cisco DNA Center. Other common services' resources, such as Cisco Identity Services Engine (ISE) or IP address managers (IPAMs), must also be reachable.

- **Management:** To manage Cisco DNA Center, an administrator needs to be able to reach the GUI via HTTPS.

- **Peer Cisco DNA Center appliances (intra-cluster):** If Cisco DNA Center is configured in High Availability (HA) mode, it needs to be able to communicate with the other nodes in the cluster. HA and clustering in Cisco DNA Center is discussed later in this chapter.

The most common and recommended way to configure connectivity to these resources is via three physical interfaces on the Cisco DNA Center appliance used for the following roles:

- **CIMC:** Because the CIMC interface is technically managed by the Cisco UCS BIOS, this interface is isolated by itself in its own network and configuration plane. The interface is not visible or configured by Cisco DNA Center.

- **Intra-Cluster:** Although this interface is visible and configured in Cisco DNA Center using the initial installation wizard, it can also be isolated from the rest of the network, as the communication only takes place within the local subnet, and no routing decisions are required. This interface configuration cannot be changed post-install.

- **Enterprise/Internet/Management:** This interface should have connectivity to the enterprise network and reachability to the Internet. It also is used for GUI access and should be the only interface reachable by the rest of the network.

Figure 8-1 shows the most common connectivity configuration for a Cisco DNA Center appliance. In this configuration, the default route for Cisco DNA Center would be out of the interface labeled as Enterprise, Management, and Cloud.

For enterprises that already have dedicated and/or separate networks for management and Internet connectivity, extra physical interfaces on the Cisco DNA Center appliance can be configured and used for these functions. However, static routes are also required to ensure that traffic egresses the desired interface. The reason is that Cisco DNA Center runs on top of a customized Linux-based operating system, which, as shipped, has only one routing table/domain and, hence, allows only a single default route or gateway. Any traffic that needs to egress an interface other than the default route must be statically routed. In some larger enterprises, this might already be common practice on multihomed servers, but in general this configuration comes with a higher risk and workload, because static routes must be created and maintained on a regular basis as network changes are made. In this scenario, missing static routes can result in asymmetric traffic patterns or connectivity issues.

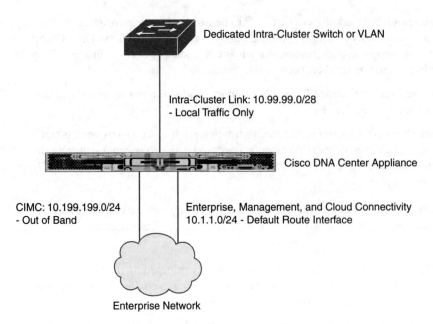

Dedicated Intra-Cluster Switch or VLAN

Intra-Cluster Link: 10.99.99.0/28
- Local Traffic Only

Cisco DNA Center Appliance

CIMC: 10.199.199.0/24
- Out of Band

Enterprise, Management, and Cloud Connectivity
10.1.1.0/24 - Default Route Interface

Enterprise Network

Figure 8-1 *Cisco DNA Center Appliance: Common Connectivity*

High Availability and Clustering with Cisco DNA Center

High Availability (HA) offers resiliency and failover for services in the event of a hardware or network failure. HA with Cisco DNA Center is accomplished with a cluster of three appliances. The high-level requirements for this cluster of appliances are as follows:

- All appliances in a cluster must be the same size (entry, midsize, or large).

- All appliances in a cluster must exist in the same geographic location.

- The appliances must have round-trip time (RTT) latency of 10 ms or less between them.

> **Note**   Cisco DNA Center HA requires three nodes in a cluster to avoid a "split-brain" scenario in which two single isolated nodes both think that they're active. Using three nodes eliminates this scenario by using a quorum of two nodes to determine which nodes remain active in the event of a failure. This is a common methodology in HA architectures and is used in many HA solutions, such as databases.

The Cisco DNA Center services and configuration exist on all nodes in a cluster; however, they respond only on the active node. During normal operation, all services and configurations are synchronized between the nodes in a cluster. When a failure or isolation occurs on the active node, one of the remaining two nodes becomes active and responds to the services.

During the initial Cisco DNA Center installation, a virtual IP (VIP) address is specified in the installation wizard. This VIP address is shared between all nodes in a cluster and is used for GUI access as well as data collection from the devices (Syslog, NetFlow, etc.). The VIP address responds on the active node in a cluster and moves to the new active node during a failure scenario.

Figure 8-2 shows a commonly used topology for a Cisco DNA Center cluster, with the intra-cluster connections being on a dedicated switch or VLAN, and the Enterprise, Management, and Cloud connections being shared on one interface connecting to a Cisco Data Center core switch.

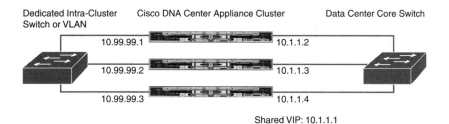

Figure 8-2   *Cisco DNA Center Appliance Cluster: Common Connectivity*

Note   It is important to remember that Cisco DNA Center is not responsible for any control or data plane traffic, and that any kind of failure does not disrupt traffic on the network. Only new configuration and orchestration tasks are affected.

Software Image Management

One of the most time-consuming tasks in network operations is software maintenance on network devices. A lot of effort is required not only for the actual upgrades themselves, but also for maintaining and tracking standard versions and images for each platform.

Software upgrade processes on network devices can be triggered by many requirements, including

- Security fixes

- Bug fixes

- Requirement for new features

- End of life (EoL) remediation

Due to change control or network availability requirements, software upgrades may be a never-ending process in some large enterprises.

Selection of the appropriate standard software version and image depends on a variety of factors, including

- Network device platforms and generations

- The amount of flash memory and RAM in the network devices

- Specific application or business requirements in the network environment, which might drive the need for unique features

- The function or role of the devices in the network

- Licensing limitations on network devices

For example, if a financial services company has a unique environment in its network that provides services for high-speed stock trades, specific features for low latency might determine the software versions running on the network devices in that environment. The version of software running on these devices might differ from the version running on other, identical devices in a different environment that needs to provide only stable connectivity for general users. As another example, switches in the core layer of a network might need to run a version of software with specific features for a routing protocol such as Open Shortest Path First (OSPF), which might differ from the software version running on switches in the distribution layer of the network that provide basic Layer 2 features such as Spanning Tree Protocol (STP). Software versions might also differ between network devices of the same platform that have more or less flash or RAM than other devices in that platform.

The tracking of the standard software versions in a large enterprise can also be a complex task with a lot of manual effort. Spreadsheets are often used to track software versions per platform or role. After the appropriate software standards are established for a network, the actual images themselves must be stored somewhere that is readily accessible by network operators to perform the actual upgrades.

Although upgrading software on a network device is a fairly routine task, it does require a time-consuming manual process, including

- Verifying that the network device has enough flash memory or RAM to run the new image

- Transferring the image from the storage location to the device itself using a protocol such as Secure Copy (SCP) or Trivial File Transfer Protocol (TFTP)

- Verifying that the image transfer was successful and that the new image on the device is intact

- Altering the boot statements on the device so that it loads the freshly transferred image properly on the next reload

- Reloading the device during a change window and verifying that it boots up properly

- Verifying that the device is running the new image and is in a stable state

There are a number of risks in this process that can cause a device to not reload properly and cause a network outage. In some cases, these risks can result in having to manually recover a device in person, which can cost a company time and money.

Cisco DNA Center solves many of these issues with a tool called Software Image Management (SWIM).

Image Repository

SWIM features a software image repository that allows network operators to store software images on the Cisco DNA Center appliance itself or on a remote Secure File Transfer Protocol (SFTP) server for distribution to remote environments.

Software images can be added to the SWIM Image Repository in three ways:

- Directly from Cisco.com with a valid Cisco Connection Online (CCO) ID

- Importing in the GUI from the local PC or remote URL

- Downloading a currently running image from a network device in the Cisco DNA Center Inventory

After an image is added to the SWIM Image Repository, it is verified against checksums downloaded from Cisco.com and then is available for use.

Figure 8-3 shows the Image Repository screen in Cisco DNA Center with various platforms in the Inventory.

Figure 8-3 *Image Repository Screen in Cisco DNA Center*

Golden Image

A Golden Image in SWIM is any software image that has been selected to be the "standard" image and can be selected based on any of the following criteria:

- Device platform or model

- Location in the network hierarchy, as discussed in Chapter 3, "Introduction to Cisco DNA Center"

- Device role or tag, also discussed in Chapter 3

These criteria allow for the flexibility to select a different Golden Image for identical devices based on the way that the site hierarchy or device role is customized in Cisco DNA Center.

For example, if access switches in a network require a specific feature that is only available in a version of code that might not be appropriate for switches in the distribution or core layer, then a Golden Image may be selected only for switches in the access role, while the other switches can have a different Golden Image.

Figure 8-4 demonstrates this concept, showing the Image Repository with Cisco IOS-XE version 16.12.2t being set as the Golden Image for access switches, and all other Cisco Catalyst 9300 switches having Cisco IOS-XE version 17.01.01 as their Golden Image.

Figure 8-4   *Different Golden Images Based on Device Role*

Upgrading Devices

Device upgrades are performed in the Provision tool of the Cisco DNA Center GUI. Cisco DNA Center displays an alert to the network operator when a device's current image does not match the Golden Image selected and requires an upgrade. This alert also contains the results of a pre-upgrade check that is automatically performed for each device that requires an upgrade. The pre-upgrade check verifies the following software upgrade requirements:

- A startup configuration exists on the network device.

- The configuration register on the network device is set to default boot mode.

- The device has enough free space on flash memory for the new image.

- The device is reachable via SCP or HTTPS for the image transfer.

- The device has appropriate licensing for the image and is eligible for the upgrade.

Figure 8-5 demonstrates the Software Images section of the Provision tool in Cisco DNA Center and shows devices in Inventory that require upgrades based on the Golden Image.

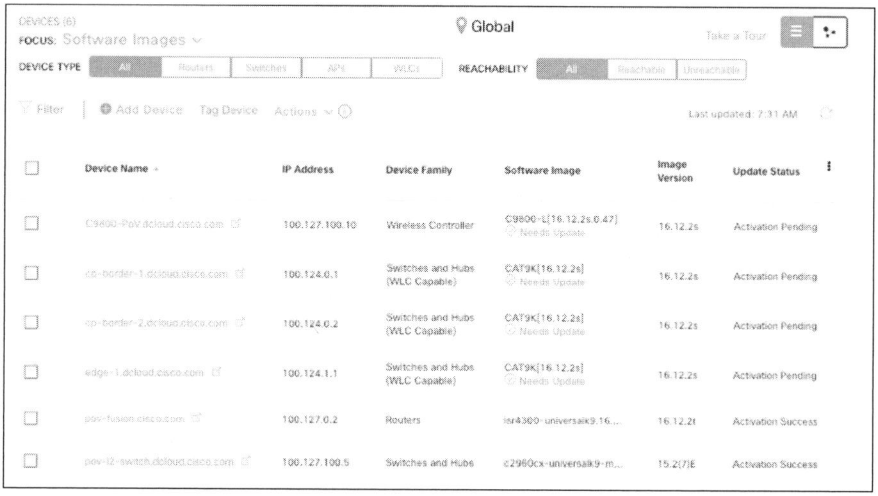

Figure 8-5 *Software Images Screen in the Provision Tool of Cisco DNA Center*

If a device fails the pre-upgrade check, the results show which test caused the failure. After resolving the issue, the network operator can rerun the pre-upgrade check and select the device for an upgrade from the Actions menu.

Figure 8-6 shows the list of pre-upgrade checks that SWIM performs on a device to validate its eligibility for an upgrade.

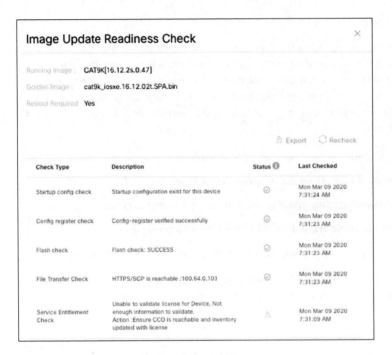

Figure 8-6   *Pre-upgrade Check for SWIM*

The device upgrade process is separated into two phases:

- **Image distribution:** This phase performs the actual distribution of the software image to the device using either SCP or HTTPs. SWIM also checks whether the software image already exists on the device and will allow the next phase to proceed. This can be useful when another method is used to distribute software images to network devices, such as local copying from a flash drive.

- **Image activation:** This phase configures the appropriate commands on the network device so that the new software image will be activated on the next reload. SWIM then reloads the device and performs a post-upgrade check to verify the upgrade and proper device operation.

Figure 8-7 shows the image activation screen of the SWIM process, enabling the network operator to schedule the image upgrade for a specific time and date.

These phases can be performed together immediately or scheduled separately. This is useful in the case where the network operator wants to distribute the new software images to network devices overnight, when network bandwidth is available, and then perform the image activation during a network maintenance window to avoid network disruptions.

Figure 8-8 shows further checks that SWIM performs on a device prior to the new software image being activated. These checks are also performed post-upgrade, as shown in Figure 8-9.

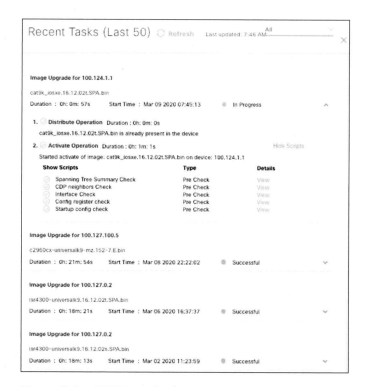

Figure 8-7 *SWIM Activation Configuration Screen*

Figure 8-8 *SWIM Precheck Scripts During Activation*

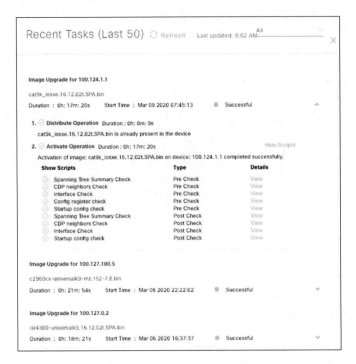

Recent Tasks (Last 50) ⟳ Refresh   Last updated: 8:02 AM ̶A̶l̶l̶ ˅   ✕

Image Upgrade for 100.124.1.1

cat9k_iosxe.16.12.02t.SPA.bin

Duration : 0h: 17m: 20s   Start Time : Mar 09 2020 07:45:13   ● Successful   ⌃

1. ⊘ Distribute Operation Duration : 0h: 0m: 0s

   cat9k_iosxe.16.12.02t.SPA.bin is already present in the device

2. ⊘ Activate Operation Duration : 0h: 17m: 20s   Hide Scripts

   Activation of image: cat9k_iosxe.16.12.02t.SPA.bin on device: 100.124.1.1 completed successfully.

Show Scripts	Type	Details
⊘ Spanning Tree Summary Check	Pre Check	View
⊘ CDP neighbors Check	Pre Check	View
⊘ Interface Check	Pre Check	View
⊘ Config register check	Pre Check	View
⊘ Startup config check	Pre Check	View
⊘ Spanning Tree Summary Check	Post Check	View
⊘ CDP neighbors Check	Post Check	View
⊘ Interface Check	Post Check	View
⊘ Startup config check	Post Check	View

Image Upgrade for 100.127.100.5

c2960cx-universalk9-mz.152-7.E.bin

Duration : 0h: 21m: 54s   Start Time : Mar 08 2020 22:22:02   ● Successful   ˅

Image Upgrade for 100.127.0.2

isr4300-universalk9.16.12.02t.SPA.bin

Duration : 0h: 18m: 21s   Start Time : Mar 06 2020 16:37:37   ● Successful   ˅

Figure 8-9 *SWIM Post-Check Scripts Following Image Activation*

Cisco DNA Center Templates

Rolling out configuration changes network-wide can be a daunting task for any network operations team. In addition to designing and creating the actual configuration changes, the team must create and maintain lists to keep track of which network devices require these changes. The team then needs to track device configurations to make sure that every device has been updated with the change.

Mass configuration changes are typically required when a company or security standard is updated, such as:

- Changes to access control lists (ACLs) that protect the network infrastructure

- Changes to Simple Network Management Protocol (SNMP) strings

- Banner changes

- Hostname changes

- Network Time Protocol (NTP)/Domain Name System (DNS) server changes

- Syslog server changes

In many of these cases, the configuration changes are identical across all network devices and just need to be pushed to each device. In some cases, such as a syslog or NTP change, the configuration might need to be customized for each region. In other cases, such as a hostname change, the change is unique to each device. This adds an extra layer of complexity to these types of changes, as the network operator needs to track these customizations and enter them during the change deployment.

Cisco DNA Center features the Template Editor tool to deploy network-wide changes at scale, but with the added flexibility to customize these templates to suit the network environment.

Template Creation

The Template Editor stores individual templates in Projects, which behave like folders, for easy organization and management. Projects can be created based on any structure that suits the company.

Figure 8-10 shows the Template Editor in Cisco DNA Center and demonstrates template projects with templates inside them.

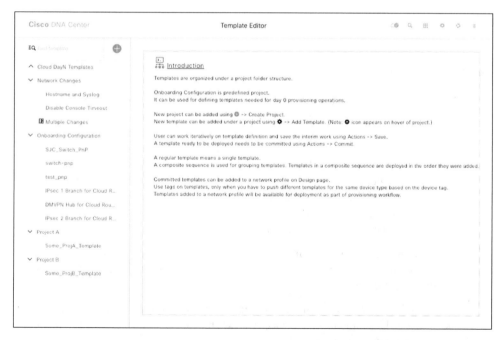

Figure 8-10 *Template Editor with Projects and Templates*

Note The Onboarding Configuration project is a special template in Cisco DNA Center that is used for Plug and Play (PnP) deployments. PnP and the Onboarding Configuration project are discussed later in this chapter.

The Template Editor also features composite templates, which are special templates that allow the execution of a sequence of multiple individual templates. This feature is useful for where the requirement is to have a certain set of changes that can be pushed to a large set of devices, followed by changes that are for a smaller set. This enables the network operator to efficiently create shared templates and still allow for flexibility. Templates can also be created for specific configuration sections and then combined into a composite template to be executed in a specific order.

Figure 8-11 shows a composite template named Multiple Changes that contains two templates to be executed in sequence.

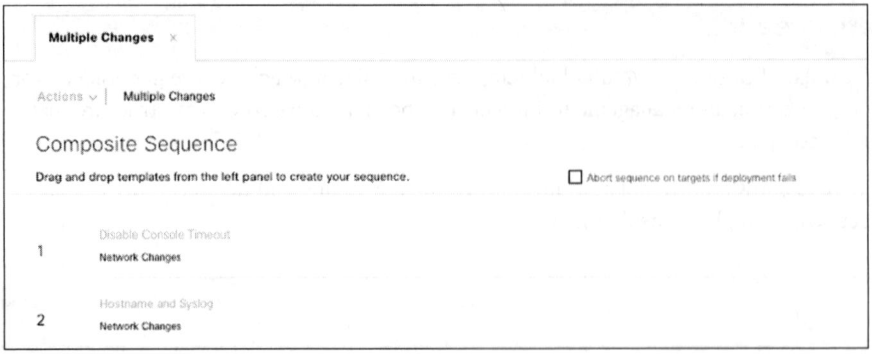

Figure 8-11   *Sample Composite Template*

Templates in Cisco DNA Center can be assigned to network devices based on location, hardware platform, software version, or custom tag. Templates can also contain variables for per-device customization and can be written in either the native command-line interface (CLI) syntax of the target network platform (for instance, Cisco IOS-XE) or the Apache Software Foundation's Velocity Template Language (VTL) for more increased flexibility and logic within them. Templates written in VTL can be combined with traditional templates in composite templates to create very structured and complex configuration deployments. Future versions of Cisco DNA Center will also feature support for composing templates using the Jinja2 templating engine.

Figure 8-12 shows the Add New Template dialog box in the Template Editor with Device Type and Software Type options that can be used to define which platform(s) a template should be executed on.

Figure 8-13 displays a sample template named Hostname and Syslog that contains commands that set the hostname on a device to a variable ($devicename) that will be defined during the template provisioning. The template also changes the syslog server on the device.

Figure 8-12 *Add New Template Dialog Box*

Figure 8-13 *Sample Template That Changes the Hostname and Syslog Server*

The Template Editor also tracks changes to templates and supports versioning via a commit process, enabling the network operator to go back through the template's commit history to see what has been changed between versions.

Template Assignment and Network Profiles

Templates can be associated with devices in geographical areas, buildings, or floors via network profiles in the Design section of Cisco DNA Center. Network profiles are created specifically for the type of devices that they'll be applied to, such as routers, switches, wireless, or firewalls. Templates can then be added to these network profiles, followed by assigning the profiles to the sites to which the templates should be applied.

Figure 8-14 shows the assignment of a template named Multiple Changes to a network profile under the Day-N Template(s) tab. The network profile is then associated to all sites in San Jose in Figure 8-15.

Figure 8-14   *Assigning a Template to a Network Profile*

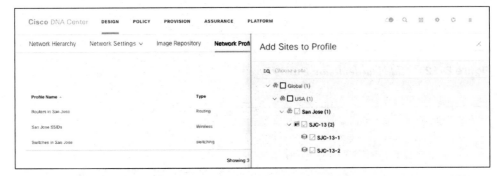

Figure 8-15   *Associating Sites from the Design Hierarchy to a Network Profile*

This allows network operators to create templates that can be assigned to multiple sites via network profiles for greater scalability and efficiency.

Note   Network profiles are also used to assign wireless service set identifiers (SSIDs) to sites, as discussed in Chapter 3.

Deploying Templates

Templates are deployed using the Provision tool in Cisco DNA Center. This tool allows network operators to select multiple or individual devices at any level in the design hierarchy for provisioning, and the workflow provides the ability to fill in any information required for templates that contain variables. Variable values for templates can also be imported from a comma-separated values (CSV) file, making it easier to add custom information for many devices at once.

Figure 8-16 shows a template being deployed during the Provision process and demonstrates assigning a value to a variable in a template. In this case, the $devicename variable is set to new-cp-border-1-name.

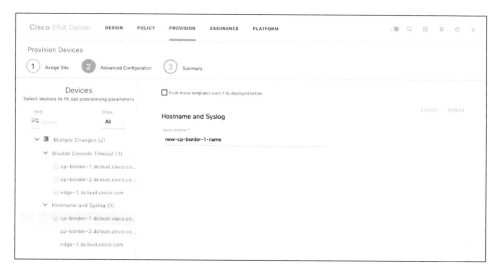

Figure 8-16 *Provisioning a Template to a Device and Filling in Template Variables*

As discussed in Chapter 3, provisioning of devices can be pushed immediately or scheduled for a later date and time, such as during a network maintenance window. This allows for staging and configuration of templates ahead of time and a more efficient change process during the actual maintenance window.

Note Due to their structure, templates pushed by Cisco DNA Center result in the raw CLI commands being input into the device configuration as if they were entered manually. As such, there is no automation currently available to roll back a template's change. To remove the configuration, a new template would have to be created to undo the commands on the device.

Figure 8-17 shows the final screen of the Provision process demonstrating the ability to schedule the provisioning for a future date and time.

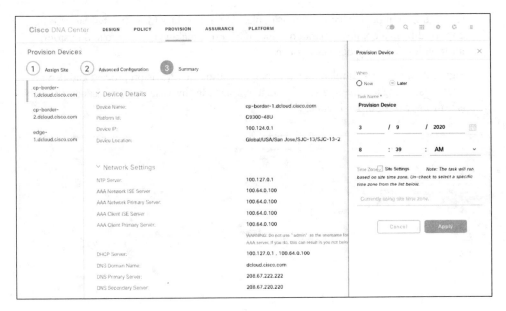

Figure 8-17 *Provisioning Schedule Example*

Plug and Play

As enterprises grow and expand to meet business requirements, network device refreshes and new deployments are required for the infrastructure to accommodate this growth. Deployments of new network devices are usually accomplished in two ways:

- The devices are configured and upgraded in a staging environment prior to being shipped to a remote site for facilities staff to physically install.

- Networking expertise is contracted and dispatched to sites with the new devices and perform onsite installation, configuration, and any required software upgrades.

Both of these methods require that a configuration with the various connection settings be prepared ahead of time. If the configuration isn't accurate or up to date when the device arrives onsite, local resources may be required to troubleshoot the problem in order to bring the connection up. Any software upgrades on new devices also have to be done manually by connecting to the new network device's console port. These tasks can be costly in both time and productivity, but using automation can make them more efficient and less risky. Cisco DNA Center features the Plug and Play (PnP) application to address this problem.

PnP allows network operators to onboard new devices in an automatic and seamless process when they are in either factory or out-of-the-box state. Originally introduced in Cisco Application Policy Infrastructure Controller Enterprise Module (APIC-EM), PnP is a secure and integrated solution that provides enterprises with a workflow-based approach for deploying and provisioning network devices to sites in an automated fashion with almost no interaction on the device itself. The PnP workflow in Cisco DNA Center can also automatically upgrade the image software on new network devices based on the SWIM Golden Image discussed earlier in this chapter.

Onboarding Templates

Onboarding templates for PnP in Cisco DNA Center are created using the Template Editor described earlier in this chapter and are stored in the Onboarding Configuration project. Templates in the Onboarding Configuration project differ from other templates in that they cannot be written in VTL or be composite templates, and as a result, can contain only platform/software-specific configuration commands. As such, an onboarding template should be used to provide a "Day-0" configuration to the new network devices containing the basic configuration required to establish connectivity to the rest of the network. After onboarding, further configuration can be applied using "Day-N" templates, as described earlier in this chapter, if more advanced logic is required.

As with traditional templates, onboarding templates can contain variables that can be filled out during the PnP claim process, described later in this section. This provides the capability to have a standard onboarding template for an area of the network and yet still be able to provide site-specific configuration parameters such as hostnames, interface descriptions, and IP addresses for each device.

Figure 8-18 shows a sample onboarding template to be pushed to a new PnP device. The template contains the basic configuration for a device, including variables that can be filled in during the claim process. Figure 8-19 shows a more advanced onboarding template demonstrating other configuration commands and variables that can be pushed during onboarding.

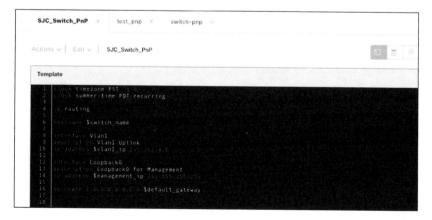

Figure 8-18 *Sample Onboarding Template*

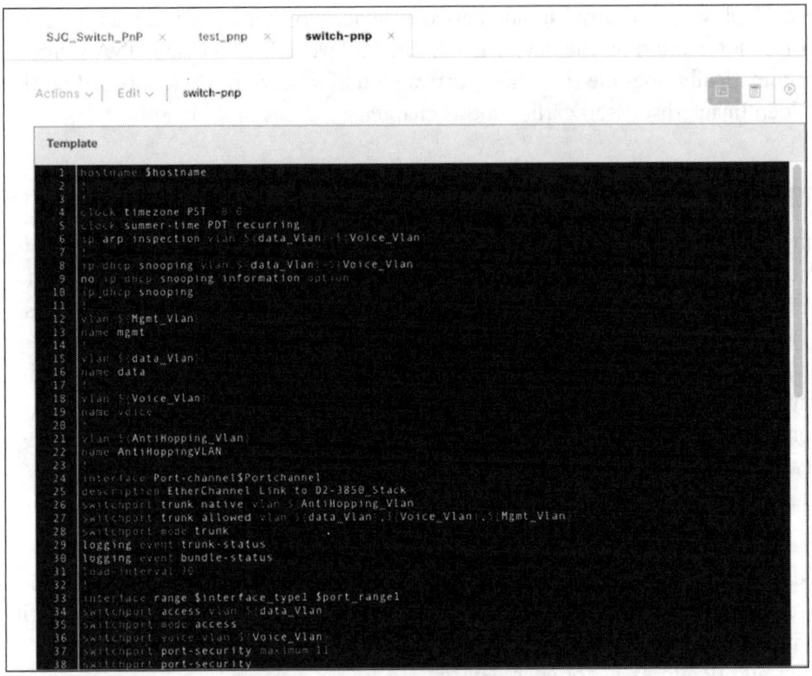

Figure 8-19 *Sample Advanced Onboarding Template*

As with the conventional templates described in the prior section, onboarding templates are added to network profiles using the Design tool in Cisco DNA Center. This workflow associates the onboarding templates with any network devices that are onboarded and assigned to sites associated with the network profiles.

Figure 8-20 shows the assignment of an onboarding template to the network profile defined previously.

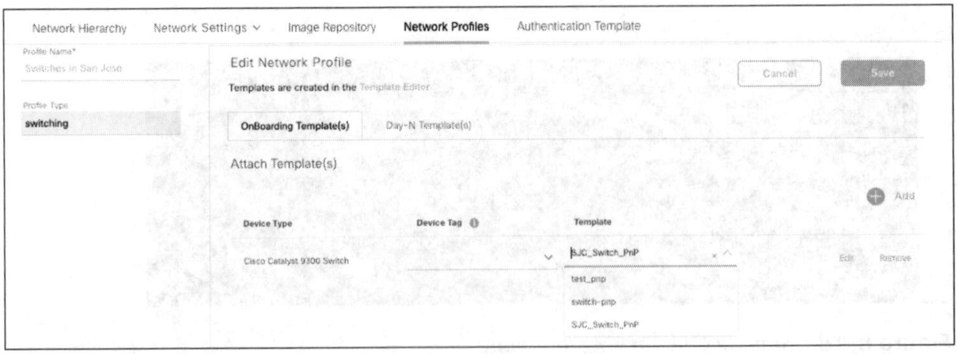

Figure 8-20 *Assigning an Onboarding Template to a Network Profile*

PnP Agent

Most current Cisco devices in a factory or out-of-the-box state boot with an active PnP Agent that automatically tries to discover a PnP controller for its onboarding configuration. The two most common methods that are used to advertise the IP address of the PnP controller to new devices are

- Option 43 in Dynamic Host Configuration Protocol (DHCP)

- A DNS lookup of pnpserver.domain.com, where domain.com is the DNS domain of the organization

Example 8-1 shows a sample DHCP scope configured on a Cisco IOS-XE device that sends DHCP Option 43 to clients with an IP address of 100.64.0.103.

Example 8-1   *Sample DHCP Scope with DHCP Option 43 Set to 100.64.0.103*

```
ip dhcp pool pool-100.101
 network 100.101.0.0 255.255.0.0
 default-router 100.101.0.1
 domain-name dcloud.cisco.com
 option 42 ip 100.127.0.1
 option 43 ascii "5A1N;B2;K4;I100.64.0.103;J80"
 dns-server 100.64.0.102
```

On a new or factory-defaulted Cisco Catalyst switch, the PnP Agent automatically enables the switch virtual interface (SVI) for VLAN 1 with DHCP, which triggers the switch to search for a DHCP server on all ports. After the switch receives the response from the DHCP server with its IP address and default gateway, the switch uses the two methods to attempt to discover the PnP controller's IP addresses. If the switch successfully discovers the PnP controller's IP address, it establishes a secure connection with the controller for onboarding. Cisco DNA Center acts as the PnP controller in this process if its IP address or VIP address is sent to the new device.

Example 8-2 shows the output from a new Cisco Catalyst switch as it discovers the IP address of the Cisco DNA Center PnP controller and establishes its connection.

Example 8-2   *Console Output from a New Switch Discovering a PnP Controller*

```
        --- System Configuration Dialog ---

Would you like to enter the initial configuration dialog? [yes/no]:


Press RETURN to get started!


*Mar  8 16:56:32.206: %PNP-6-PROFILE_CONFIG: PnP Discovery profile pnp-zero-touch
  configured
```

```
*Mar  8 16:56:33.172: %CRYPTO_ENGINE-5-KEY_ADDITION: A key named TP-self-
  signed-3356507413 has been generated or imported by crypto-engine
*Mar  8 16:56:33.174: %SSH-5-ENABLED: SSH 1.99 has been enabled
*Mar  8 16:56:33.218: %PKI-4-NOCONFIGAUTOSAVE: Configuration was modified.  Issue
  "write memory" to save new IOS PKI configuration
*Mar  8 16:56:33.219: %SYS-5-CONFIG_P: Configured programmatically by process PnP
  Agent Discovery from console as vty0
*Mar  8 16:56:33.284: %CRYPTO_ENGINE-5-KEY_ADDITION: A key named TP-self-
  signed-3356507413.server has been generated or imported by crypto-engine
*Mar  8 16:56:35.221: %SYS-5-CONFIG_P: Configured programmatically by process PnP
  Agent Discovery from console as vty0
*Mar  8 16:56:37.225: %PNP-6-PNP_SAVING_TECH_SUMMARY: Saving PnP tech summary
  (pnp-tech-discovery-summary)... Please wait. Do not interrupt.
*Mar  8 16:56:46.988: %SYS-5-CONFIG_P: Configured programmatically by process PnP
  Agent Discovery from console as vty0
*Mar  8 16:56:42.000: %SYS-6-CLOCKUPDATE: System clock has been updated from
  16:56:47 UTC Sun Mar 8 2020 to 16:56:42 UTC Sun Mar 8 2020, configured from
  console by vty0.
Mar  8 16:56:42.000: %PKI-6-AUTHORITATIVE_CLOCK: The system clock has been set.
Mar  8 16:56:42.004: %SYS-5-CONFIG_P: Configured programmatically by process
  XEP_pnp-zero-touch from console as vty0
Mar  8 16:56:42.005: %SMART_LIC-5-SYSTEM_CLOCK_CHANGED: Smart Agent for Licensing
  System clock has been changed
Mar  8 16:56:42.573: %PNP-6-PNP_TECH_SUMMARY_SAVED_OK: PnP tech summary
  (pnp-tech-discovery-summary) saved successfully.
Mar  8 16:56:42.573: %PNP-6-PNP_DISCOVERY_DONE: PnP Discovery done successfully
  (PnP-DHCP-IPv4)
Mar  8 16:56:48.087: %PKI-4-NOCONFIGAUTOSAVE: Configuration was modified.  Issue
  "write memory" to save new IOS PKI configuration
Mar  8 16:56:49.708: %SYS-5-CONFIG_P: Configured programmatically by process
  XEP_pnp-zero-touch from console as vty0
```

Claiming a Device

After the new device has established its connection with Cisco DNA Center, it appears in the Provision > Devices > Plug and Play Devices section in an Unclaimed state, ready for claiming. Figure 8-21 shows a new PnP device with an Unclaimed status that has established a connection with Cisco DNA Center.

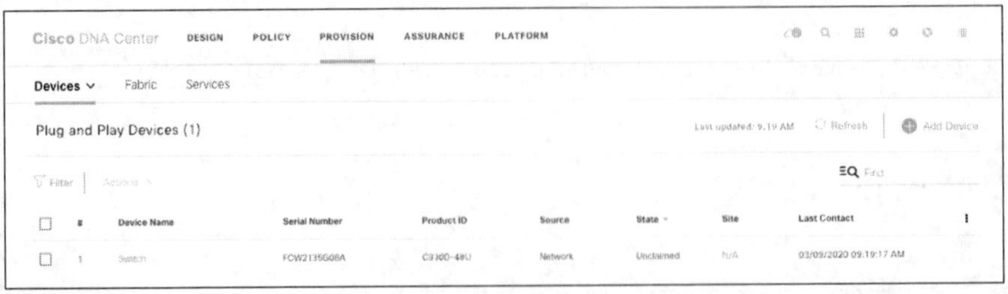

Figure 8-21 *PnP Device in Unclaimed State*

The claim process for each new device allows for the configuration of the following parameters:

- Area, building, or floor to which the switch will be assigned
- Selection of onboarding template from the network profile associated with the chosen site
- Selection of target software image based on the Golden Image selected for the site Image Repository
- Configuration of any variables contained in the onboarding template

Figures 8-22 through 8-25 show each stage of the PnP claim process and demonstrate the selection of site, onboarding template, Golden Image, and variable assignments.

Figure 8-22   *PnP Claim Step Showing Site Assignment*

Figure 8-23   *PnP Claim Step Showing Site Onboarding Template and Golden Image Selections*

Figure 8-24 *PnP Claim Step Showing the Variable Values from the Onboarding Template That Should Be Configured*

Figure 8-25 *Summary Screen of PnP Claim Process That Shows All the Configured Parameters*

After the claim process is complete, Cisco DNA Center pushes the onboarding template to the device and copies it into the running configuration. This process, as opposed to entering the configuration manually into the device line by line, allows for the device to be configured over its uplink connection without relying on a stable connection back to Cisco DNA Center. Cisco DNA Center also performs a software upgrade on the device if the current image does not match the Golden Image. Following this process, the device appears in the Cisco DNA Center Inventory for further provisioning of standard settings and Day-N templates if required.

Network devices can be added and pre-claimed in Cisco DNA Center PnP prior to establishing a PnP connection, using one of three methods:

- **Single device:** Each device can be added manually in the PnP tool using the serial and product ID numbers of the device.

- **Bulk devices:** Bulk additions can be made by importing a CSV file containing the serial numbers, product IDs, and site names of the new devices.

- **Smart Account devices:** Newly purchased and licensed devices can be added to the PnP inventory directly from Cisco Smart Licensing accounts.

Using any of the three methods makes for a much more efficient onboarding process, as devices can be added and claimed in advance and are automatically onboarded once they are connected to the network and establish a session with Cisco DNA Center.

Figure 8-26 shows the Add Devices dialog box for the PnP process and demonstrates the settings required to pre-claim a device.

Figure 8-26   *PnP Add Devices Dialog Box*

Cisco DNA Center Tools

Aside from the main automation workflows discussed in this chapter, Cisco DNA Center features other tools that can help network operators in a variety of ways. Three of the most commonly used tools are

- **Topology:** Helps visualize the network topology and shows information about each device and link in the network

- **Command Runner:** Provides the ability to run CLI commands on multiple devices simultaneously to quickly gather output during troubleshooting or inventory operations

- **Security Advisories:** Compares the network device inventory against published Cisco security advisories and produces a report of which devices might be vulnerable

Topology

The Topology tool in Cisco DNA Center allows a network operator to take advantage of the defined site hierarchy and visualize the network at every level of the hierarchy. The visualization in the Topology tool shows basic information about each device, including the name and health score, along with links between devices. Clicking any device or link provides more detailed information about the element and allows the user to quickly run commands on the device or jump to the Device 360 page in Cisco Assurance.

Figure 8-27 demonstrates the visualization of the network topology using the Topology tool, with one of the devices selected showing more detailed information of the device.

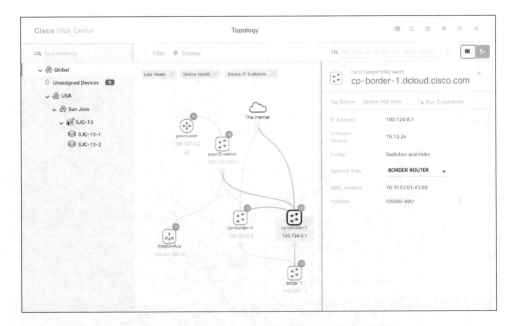

Figure 8-27 *Sample Topology View with Detailed Device Information*

Although the view is presented in a hierarchical format by default, devices in Topology can be dragged around freely to provide a custom layout, which can then be saved and loaded at a later time. View filters can also be applied to limit the number of devices shown in the Topology view based on features that are enabled on the devices.

Command Runner

During troubleshooting or inventory operations, network operators sometimes need to gather information from network devices using the CLI. This process typically involves using a terminal client to connect to the device, executing the command(s), and then copying and pasting the output to a spreadsheet or a text file. This repetitive task can be very time consuming when multiple devices or commands are required.

The Command Runner tool in Cisco DNA Center makes this task easier by allowing network operators to select up to 20 devices on which to run up to five commands simultaneously. The output of the command(s) is then displayed in a dynamic report that allows the user to select each command and device to view the output. The output from each command can also be easily exported to a text file.

Figure 8-28 shows Command Runner with multiple devices selected, followed by the commands that are selected to run on each device.

Figure 8-28   *Command Runner with Multiple Devices Selected and Multiple Commands to Be Entered on Each Device*

Figure 8-29 shows the results of the commands run on each device from Command Runner. The output of one of the commands on a device is highlighted.

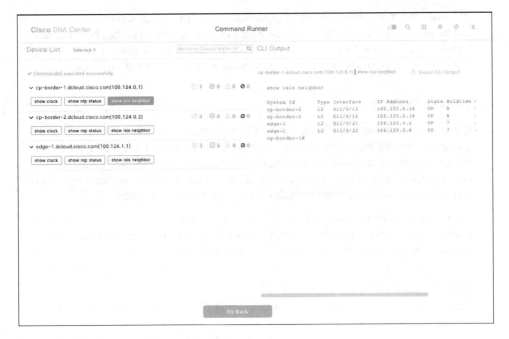

Figure 8-29   *Command Runner Results*

A compact version of Command Runner can also be displayed at any time in the Cisco DNA Center GUI by pressing Q and T at the same time on any screen. This compact version can be used to quickly issue most CLI commands on a single device right from the GUI window itself.

Figure 8-30 shows the compact version of Command Runner that is triggered by the Q and T keystroke. The device edge-1 is selected, and the output of an IS-IS command is displayed.

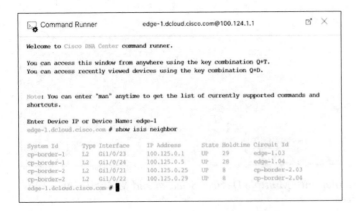

Figure 8-30   *Compact Command Runner Sample*

Security Advisories

Network security is a major concern to all enterprises. They not only need to protect the network infrastructure from outside intruders and unwanted traffic, but also need to protect the network devices themselves from compromise. Security vulnerabilities are an unfortunate reality for all connected devices, and given the importance of the network infrastructure to the business, enterprises must pay extra attention to making sure that the network devices are protected and updated to versions of software or configurations that are not vulnerable. In some companies, entire teams are dedicated to track and remediate software vulnerabilities on the network. Security advisories are usually released via mailing lists or on websites along with workarounds or "fixed-in" versions, and the team must then audit the network inventory to figure out which devices may be vulnerable and would require remediation. This can be a time-consuming, manual process, and vulnerabilities can sometimes exist in network devices for months before they're remediated.

Cisco DNA Center makes the auditing process simpler and more efficient with the Security Advisories tool. Security Advisories compares the platforms and software versions in the Cisco DNA Center Inventory with any vulnerabilities published by Cisco and produces a report showing which vulnerabilities exist, their potential impact, and the devices that may be impacted by them. The potential vulnerabilities are linked to the published advisory, which contains additional details about the vulnerability, workarounds, or patched software. Network operators can then take that information and use the SWIM tool to download and schedule upgrades to nonimpacted software.

Figure 8-31 shows the output of the Security Advisories tool after performing a scan. The output shows any security advisories that may affect devices in the Cisco DNA Center Inventory.

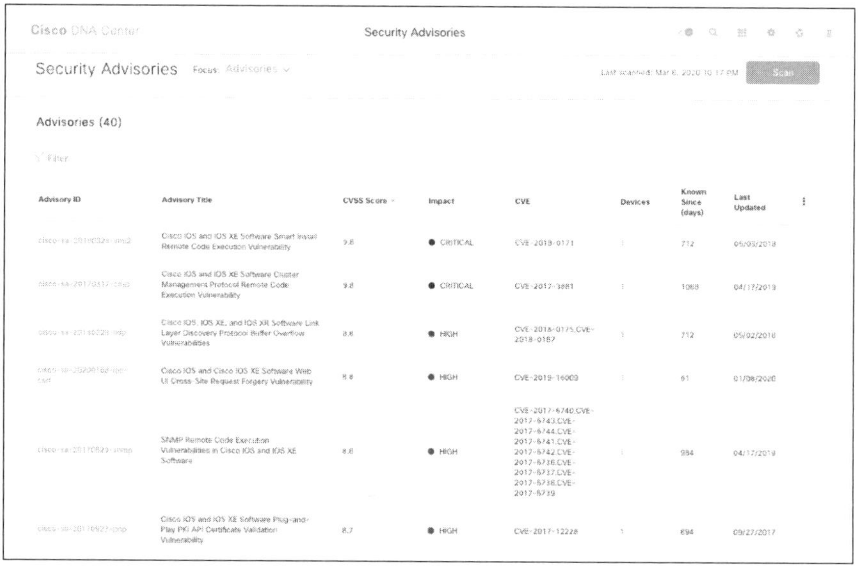

Figure 8-31 *Security Advisories Output*

Summary

This chapter covered some of the workflows and tools in Cisco DNA Center that can be used alongside Cisco Software-Defined Access to provide more efficient deployment and day-to-day operations of the network. Some of the workflows discussed were Software Image Management (SWIM), templates, and Plug and Play (PnP), which can be used for upgrades, mass configuration changes, and automated device onboarding, respectively. It also discussed the Cisco DNA Center appliance and connectivity options along with High Availability for the Cisco DNA Center solution.

References in This Chapter

Apache Software Foundation, Apache Velocity Project: https://velocity.apache.org/

Cisco Digital Network Architecture Center Administrator Guide: https://www.cisco.com/c/en/us/support/cloud-systems-management/ dna-center/products-maintenance-guides-list.html

Cisco DNA Center 3-Node Cluster High Availability Scenarios and Network Connectivity Details (Document ID 214471): https://www.cisco.com/c/en/us/ support/docs/cloud-systems-management/dna-center/214471-cisco-dna-center-3-node-cluster-high-ava.html

Cisco DNA Center Platform Overview: https://developer.cisco.com/docs/dna-center/

Cisco DNA Center User Guide: https://www.cisco.com/c/en/us/support/ cloud-systems-management/dna-center/products-user-guide-list.html

Network Device Onboarding for Cisco DNA Center Deployment Guide: https://www.cisco.com/c/dam/en/us/td/docs/solutions/CVD/ Campus/dnac-network-device-onboarding-deployment-guide-2019nov.pdf

Chapter 9

Cisco DNA Assurance

This chapter covers the following topics:

- **Assurance Benefits:** This section covers the need for assurance in modern and dynamic IT and OT networks.

- **Cisco DNA Assurance Architecture:** This section covers the components that make up Cisco DNA Assurance for wired and wireless networks. This section examines the health score capabilities offered by Cisco DNA Assurance.

- **Cisco DNA Assurance Tools:** This section highlights various tools available with Cisco DNA Assurance. These tools are helpful for the operations team in troubleshooting issues seen in a network.

Assurance Benefits

An enterprise network consists of users, endpoints, network infrastructure devices, and business-critical applications—email, web-based applications, and business-relevant applications. More and more devices such as Internet of Things (IoT) devices are being connected to the network every day, and these components are heavily dependent on the network infrastructure. The success of the services, user experience, and business efficiency depends on the enterprise infrastructure. Because the network has become critical to business operations, continuous monitoring of the network is needed as the network extends further to branch locations, complexity increases with many applications running simultaneously, and the threat surface increases.

Challenges of Traditional Implementations

A traditional network is implemented by network architects and operated by network operators who are command-line interface (CLI) driven. This method has been in place for a while and has been working well. When changes need to be made to the network, for example, a new business-critical application needs to be prioritized for an improved level of service. This application prioritization involves changing the Quality of Service (QoS) policies and applying the new traffic policies to the devices in the network. Although this task might sound simple, the change needs to involve several syntaxes depending on the type of Interoperating System (IOS) running on the network devices. If any configuration error or miscalculation of the policies happens, it is difficult to narrow down the device on which the misconfiguration was made. Similarly, if an end user reports an issue regarding access to a business application, there might be more than 100 points of failure between the user and the application. Understanding the context of what, where the problem lies is the key for quicker resolution.

Based on a Cisco McKinsey study in 2016, enterprises spend around $60 billion on network operations, labor, and tools, out of which 75 percent of the operational expenses is on changes and troubleshooting. One of the main challenges is that too many tools give only fragmented visibility and limited insights into the network. Most networks use reactive systems that can only play catchup analysis after the problem is reported instead of proactively probing the network. Legacy approaches such as Simple Network Management Protocol (SNMP)-based polls are very common but do not provide real-time visibility, and they result in slow resolution times for any reported issues. Replication of the reported issue(s) is another challenge for the operations team, because some issues are intermittent or are not easily reproducible.

To address these tasks, Cisco has developed intent-based networking (IBN). As discussed in previous chapters, IBN inputs the business intent to a unified tool that has visibility and control to the whole network. Apart from the automation capabilities and policy-based Campus Fabric, Cisco has added another pillar called Cisco DNA Assurance to Cisco DNA Center. As an example of how IBN is applied, suppose the intent of the network administrator is to prioritize an application through QoS policy. Cisco DNA Center automation implements the network intent change by configuring the needed change on all the network devices based on their Cisco IOS version. The assurance feature of Cisco DNA Center provides monitoring of the network to ensure that the change is applied correctly and that the application health is prioritized as it should be as per the changes implemented. This chapter focuses on the key features Cisco DNA Assurance offers, such as visibility into the network devices, clients, and application traffic in an enterprise network. These features are helpful in day-to-day operations for troubleshooting issues and maintenance of the network.

Cisco DNA Analytics

With the new paradigm of intent-based networking, Cisco DNA Assurance gathers data from the network devices, users, endpoints, and applications to provide end-to-end visibility of network performance and client experience. The data received from the network uses smart algorithms to correlate the trends, issues, Cisco best practices, Cisco-validated configuration databases, and Cisco Technical Assistance Center (TAC) databases to give meaningful insights into and root causes for the issues. Cisco DNA Assurance also provides guided remediation steps to resolve the issues. As shown in Figure 9-1, context is the key for IBN infrastructure.

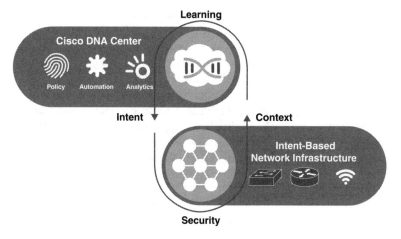

Figure 9-1 *Cisco DNA Center Intent-Based Networking*

Cisco DNA Center creates a context and learns from the information collected by continuous data collection from the network. The network administrator has a holistic view of the network from both a configuration standpoint and a troubleshooting standpoint. Security cannot be compromised when Cisco DNA Center pushes the intent deployed in the network. Cisco DNA Center leverages an application programming interface (API) for northbound management tasks and southbound tasks to the network devices. For the southbound operations to the network, the infrastructure needs to be programmable, such as the Cisco Catalyst 9000 Series switches that leverage the Unified Access Data Plane (UADP) application-specific integrated circuit (ASIC). UADP is flexible and can adapt to new protocols and encapsulations over a period of time using a simple switch code upgrade.

Cisco DNA Assurance Architecture

Cisco DNA Assurance uses "everything as a sensor," meaning it pulls network data from all different types of sources using networking telemetry—and it is expected to be able to collect data from more sources as the solution grows with each new release. This extensive and granular data collection gives greater breadth and depth to produce a clearer picture of the state of the network devices and the overall network performance, clients, and applications. The data received by the Assurance engine on Cisco DNA Center goes to the powerful correlation engine, which correlates and analyzes the data and provides only the information the network operator needs, such as issue insights for the network devices, applications, and clients. Cisco DNA Center also baselines this information to enable network managers to start seeing trends. The network managers get a 360-degree view of the state of the network. Instead of receiving multiple data points, the network operator receives a baseline of the network and easy correlation metrics from the network devices and applications in the form of color-coded "health scores." Simplifying the view helps network operators to focus on areas of business impact and, at the same time, to have the flexibility to troubleshoot at the packet level if needed.

Cisco DNA Assurance is a Cisco DNA Center application that needs to be installed for Cisco DNA Center to start consuming the network telemetry. In addition to providing user and application experience, Cisco DNA Assurance provides device-level visibility for Apple devices using iOS Analytics and Samsung client device analytics. Figure 9-2 shows the flow between various applications of Cisco DNA Center and the infrastructure devices. The Automation aspect drives the configuration and business intent to the network infrastructure in a simple, scalable method. The Assurance aspect extracts data from the network to understand the health of the clients, applications, and devices. Cisco DNA Assurance consumes information from wired networks, wireless networks, traditional network topologies, and new options such as Cisco SD-Access fabrics.

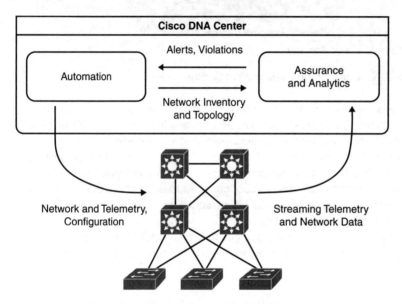

Figure 9-2 *Cisco DNA Center Automation and Assurance Loop*

Figure 9-3 shows the underlying architecture of Cisco DNA Assurance. Assurance and Automation are two applications running on Cisco DNA Center that have continuous flow of information.

Figure 9-3 depicts Cisco DNA Assurance receiving data from customer ACME network devices via protocols such as syslog, streaming telemetry, NetFlow, pxGrid from Cisco ISE, SNMP, DHCP, and so on. This information is received by Cisco DNA Assurance (also known as the Network Data Platform), where the data is sent through the correlation engine as well as the Cisco AI Network Analytics engine on the Cisco AI cloud. The correlation and insights are provided to Cisco DNA Assurance in the form of health scores, top issues, and guided remediations. The guided remediations or best practices can be implemented on the network through Cisco DNA Automation (also known as the Network Control Platform), which uses secure protocols such as Secure Shell (SSH) and Network Configuration Protocol (NETCONF) to implement the changes on the network devices.

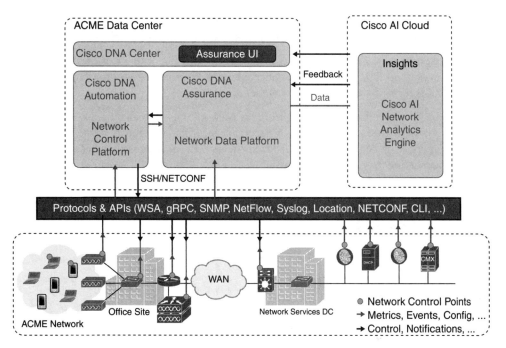

Figure 9-3 *Cisco DNA Center Architecture*

Cisco DNA Assurance Data Collection Points

Cisco DNA Center uses several data collection sources to understand the context of the traffic. The following list describes some of the information retrieved from the network for a user who reported an application experience issue:

- Cisco ISE integration with Cisco DNA Assurance provides the username, device information, and user group (Scalable Group Tag) assigned to the user. Cisco ISE reported the username as Jane Smith, assigned to the HR scalable group and connected using two devices—a workstation and a mobile phone—as shown in Figure 9-4. Cisco ISE uses pxGrid to push this information to the Cisco DNA Assurance engine.

- IP Address Management (IPAM) integration to Cisco DNA Assurance provides details of the IP address assigned to user Jane Smith. IPAM integration with Cisco DNA Center uses APIs.

- Using NetFlow information received from the network, Cisco DNA Center filters based on the source IP address (10.10.10.6, as shown in Figure 9-4) to identify the traffic flow. The destination IP addresses of the applications trying to access are 8.4.2.2 and 4.4.4.4.

- Cisco Application Visibility and Control (AVC) identifies that the flow records are for Cisco Webex traffic.

- Cisco DNA Assurance contextually correlates where the user device "Jane Smith" attaches to the network and which network devices the flow traverses.

- Location services contextually correlate the geographic locations of the user/ network devices. Jane Smith is connected to the Building 10, third floor access point and is trying to access the Cisco Webex application.

- The network telemetry received from the network is used to identify, isolate, and root-cause the issues. Cisco DNA Assurance identified that the user Jane Smith is experiencing degraded Cisco Webex application traffic because there is no QoS traffic marking for Cisco Webex traffic.

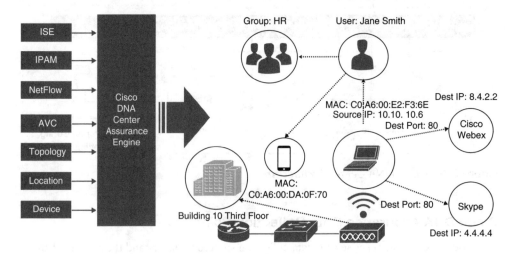

Figure 9-4   *Cisco DNA Assurance Contextual Data*

Once the issue is identified, easy QoS policies available on Cisco DNA Center Automation are available to push the relevant QoS configurations.

Figure 9-5 shows various collectors available in Cisco DNA Center 1.3.3.x. With upcoming releases, more collectors are expected to be added to the list.

Streaming Telemetry

Legacy protocols such as SNMP, syslog, and NetFlow are the most common ways of conducting telemetry in traditional networks. However, some of these protocols, such as SNMP, have serious shortcomings because they use a poll-based mechanism. If a critical key performance indicator (KPI) was measured on a device, the collector wouldn't know about it until the next polling interval. SNMP also uses management information base (MIB) to get data points about the network device performance, and the entire MIB would need to be read into the collector, even if only a single data point was required. If multiple collectors needed this information, SNMP information would have to be unicast to each receiver, using a lot of the network bandwidth for operational purposes. Some of these restrictions make SNMP slow and inefficient for programmable infrastructures.

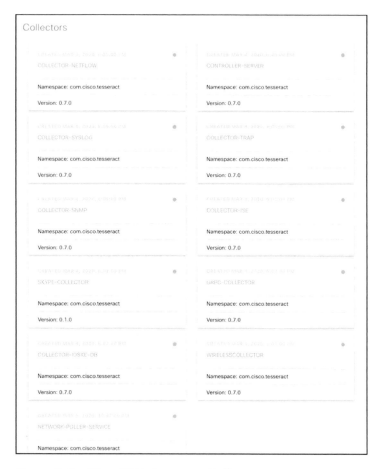

Figure 9-5 *Cisco DNA Assurance Collectors*

A model-based streaming telemetry provides significant improvements in extracting data from a device. In this model, devices export enriched, consistent, and concise data with context from network devices for a better user experience and operator experience. The data can be "pushed" off a device at any time, unlike the "pulled" method, and when a KPI is met, the device can immediately push the data to the collector (Cisco DNA Assurance). Individual metrics can be streamed (rather than entire MIBs). For example, the network operator can configure the router to push an alert whenever a drop for a specific application is counted, instead of polling the whole MIB database. Furthermore, information can be streamed on a message bus, so that any authorized parties interested in the data can receive it immediately and efficiently. Table 9-1 summarizes the advantages of the streaming telemetry model over legacy polling methods.

Table 9-1 *Key Differences Between Traditional and Streaming Telemetry*

Traditional Telemetry	Streaming Telemetry
Pull-based data import (e.g., SNMP)	Push-based data export
High CPU overhead with data crawlers	Low CPU overhead
Data intensive without optimizations	Optimized for data export (only Key Performance Indicators, Events are exported)
No real-time notification; false alarms	Notification sent seconds after change
Minimum polling has too many black holes	Reduced delay in management data

Network Time Travel

The Cisco DNA Assurance database collects data from the network devices, clients, and applications, and it correlates it in a time series. The network operator has the flexibility to "time travel" to check the state of a network device, a client, or an application at a specific time. One of the challenges of not being able to replicate the issue could be addressed through network time travel. Because of the vast amount of data collected, Cisco DNA Assurance retains only the past 14 days of data from the network. Cisco DNA Assurance is designed to provide visibility, actionable insights, and trends, but it is not intended to be a syslog server to collect data for audit logs. Customers are recommended to use syslog servers for audit log purposes and to leverage Cisco DNA Center for monitoring and troubleshooting purposes.

Health Dashboards

One of the challenges of traditional networks is the amount of raw data the operator needs to go through to make a meaningful connection to the network or the issue. To simplify the Cisco DNA Assurance data consumption, Cisco DNA Assurance introduced *health scores*, which are assigned to network devices, clients, and applications based on several KPIs received from the network. Health scores are colored coded to reflect the alert level so that the network operator can easily see which items warrant immediate attention. Figure 9-6 provides an example of the health score range offered by Cisco DNA Assurance.

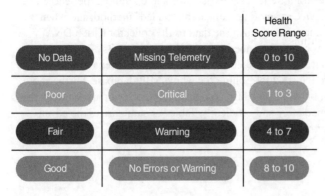

Figure 9-6   *Cisco DNA Assurance Health Score Range*

Note The network operator has the option to change the health score KPIs to make them relevant to their infrastructure. For example, the default KPI for CPU utilization is Good if the CPU utilization is less than 95 percent. The network operator can change this KPI if the network infrastructure requirement is to be within 80 percent CPU utilization.

Overall Health Dashboard

A high-level view of the health of the network is shown in the Overall Heath dashboard of Cisco DNA Assurance. The Overall Health dashboard provides a summary of the network health and the client health (wired and wireless clients). The dashboard has a Top Ten Issue Types section for the network operator to quickly glance through. Figure 9-7 shows an example of the Overall Health dashboard from a lab network.

Figure 9-7 *Cisco DNA Assurance Overall Health Dashboard*

In Figure 9-7, the network health is shown as 77 percent healthy with a total of 31 devices discovered by Cisco DNA Center. The drop-down box in the top-right area of the dashboard can be used to select a different time period to evaluate, going all the way back to 7 days to understand the overall health for the past 7 days. There is also a site view available on the dashboard next to the Last 7 Days dropdown if the network operator intends to sort the health based on the site location. The Top 10 Issue Types section indicates the issues that need attention from the network operator. From this dashboard, the operator can drill down to the network device health or client health.

Network Health Dashboard

The Network Health dashboard provides the overall network infrastructure health summary. The network device health scores are calculated based on the system health, data plane health, and control plane health. System health includes memory and CPU utilization. Data plane health consists of link errors and link status on routers and switches. In the case of access points, the data plane health consists of the link errors, radio utilization, noise, signal to noise ratio (SNR), interference, and so forth. Control plane health mainly covers the reachability of the control plane node for fabric devices. Figure 9-8 provides an example of the Network Health dashboard viewed from Cisco DNA Assurance. Overall, 68 percent of the devices are healthy, which is calculated based on the number of healthy devices divided by the total number of devices monitored by Cisco DNA Center.

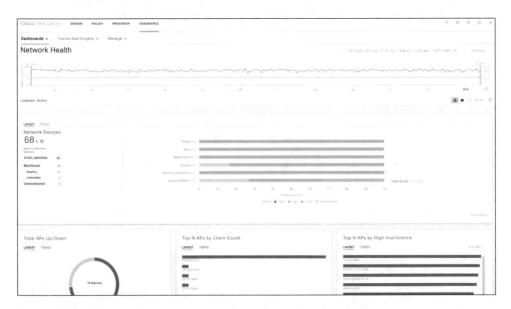

Figure 9-8 *Cisco DNA Assurance Network Health Dashboard*

From the Network Health dashboard, the network operator can drill down to a particular device's health history based on the role or the type of the device. Figure 9-9 provides a Device 360 view of an access point with a low health score. The time graph gives an indication of the AP system health during a specific range of time.

The Device 360 page of a network device also contains the physical neighbor topology of the device in focus. Figure 9-10 shows the physical topology of the access point selected in Figure 9-9. The access point has eight clients connected to it, and it is connected to a 5520 model Wireless LAN Controller (WLC). You can easily view the device health of a device by clicking the device icon when you see it on any DNA Assurance page.

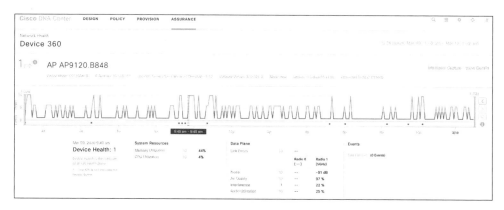

Figure 9-9 *Cisco DNA Assurance Device 360 View*

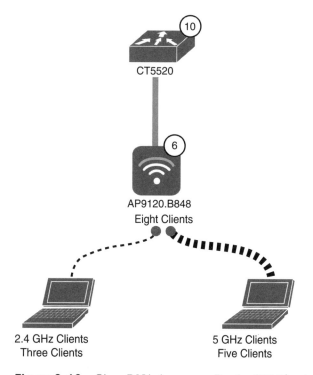

Figure 9-10 *Cisco DNA Assurance Device 360 Physical Neighbor Topology*

The Device 360 page contains additional details, such as the Top 10 issues associated with that device. In the case of an access point, the page shows the radio frequency (RF) details and connectivity information in addition to the device system health. Figure 9-11 shows the RF graph of the access point 9120.

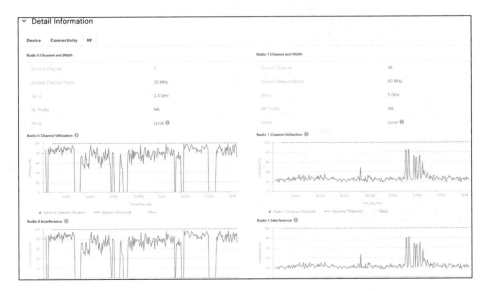

Figure 9-11   *Cisco DNA Assurance Device 360 RF Detail*

Cisco SD-Access Fabric Network Health

The Cisco DNA Assurance Network Health dashboard offers health state visibility of a Cisco SD-Access fabric site and a domain. The health state of the fabric domain is the aggregation of individual fabric sites. Figure 9-12 shows a dashlet of the fabric domain named SanJose Fabric. The dashboard provides a summary of the health of the fabric control nodes, border, edges, and fabric wireless controller.

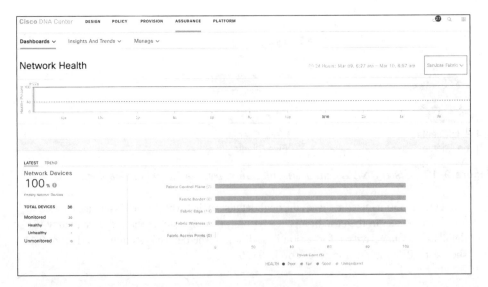

Figure 9-12   *Cisco DNA Assurance Device Fabric Health*

Client Health Dashboard

The Cisco DNA Assurance Client Health dashboard provides a health summary of all the clients. It breaks down the client health scores into categories for wired clients and wireless clients. In Figure 9-13, the Client Health dashboard shows several client analytics, such as Client Onboarding Times, Client Data Rate, and Connectivity SNR, and the trends for these various attributes. The trendline health summary chart at the top of Figure 9-13 shows the client health for the last 24 hours. The timeline can be customized to view the health state up to the last 7 days.

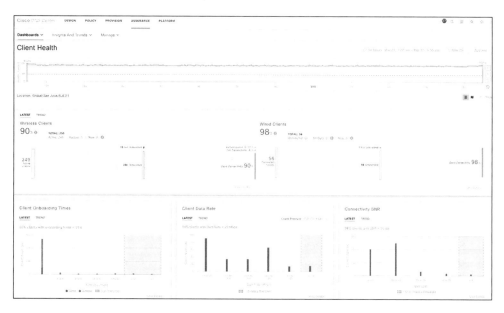

Figure 9-13 *Cisco DNA Assurance Device Client Health Dashboard*

A network operator can use the Client Health dashboard to navigate to an individual site-specific client summary page, which is beneficial for viewing and comparing the per-site client health. The client health score is calculated based on the client onboarding time, authentication success, connection status, RF quality, SNR, and received signal strength indicator (RSSI) from the WLC.

The network operator can drill down to the client onboarding times, as shown in Figure 9-14, to view the overall onboarding times, association times, authentication times, and DHCP times. In the figure, the average response time details are listed for the two authentication servers (AAA).

The network operator can drill down to the client roaming times from the dashboard, as shown in Figure 9-15, to view the overall roaming times, fast roaming times, and so forth. The right side of the figure shows the overall trend of the roaming times at a given point in time. The network operator can go back to view the data up to the last 14 days.

Figure 9-14 *Cisco DNA Assurance Device Client Onboarding Time*

Figure 9-15 *Cisco DNA Assurance Device Client Roaming Time*

Similar to the Network 360 view in the Network Health dashboard, the Client Health dashboard can show a Client 360 view of a specific client (user or endpoint). Figure 9-16 illustrates a Client 360 page for the username matt, showing that user matt logged in from two different devices with MAC addresses 8C:3A:E3:6C:11:2E and 8C:3A:E3:4E:CB:A1.

Here is a summary of some of the useful data displayed in Client 360 view:

- Timeseries chart of the client health score

- Individual client issues

- Onboarding state analytics

- Event Viewer: onboarding events, authentication events, DHCP events

- Application Experience

- Path trace tool, which will be discussed later

- RF and usage details

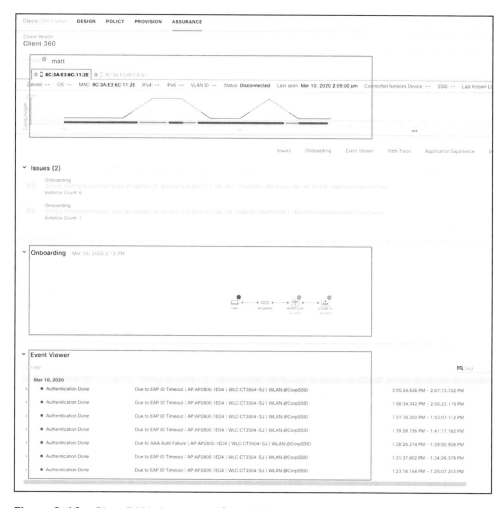

Figure 9-16 *Cisco DNA Assurance Client 360*

Application Health Dashboard

The Application Health dashboard of Cisco DNA Assurance allows the network operator to monitor the health of applications accessed in the network. Application health is based on the NetFlow records received from the routers in the infrastructure, such as Cisco Aggregation Services Routers (ASRs), Integrated Services Routers (ISRs), and Cloud Services Routers (CSRs). The applications are classified as Business Relevant, Business Irrelevant, or Default based on the Network Based Application Recognition (NBAR2) feature on the routers. The application health score is based on the application response time from the client and the servers. Figure 9-17 displays an example of the Application Health dashboard. The health score is the percentage of the number of healthy business-relevant applications divided by the total number of business-relevant applications. The health score is calculated every 15 minutes.

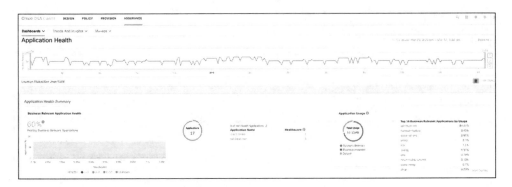

Figure 9-17   *Cisco DNA Assurance Application Health Dashboard*

Cisco DNA Assurance Tools

Cisco DNA Assurance offers various tools to proactively monitor the network to help troubleshoot the network, network devices, clients, applications, and services. This section focuses on the capabilities offered by Cisco DNA Assurance that network operators can use to troubleshoot issues faster and more efficiently.

Intelligent Capture

Traditionally, Cisco DNA Center receives information about device and client health from Cisco wireless LAN Controllers. The Intelligent Capture feature provides support for a direct communication link between Cisco DNA Center and the access points, so each of the APs can communicate with Cisco DNA Center directly. Using this channel, Cisco DNA Center receives packet capture data, AP and client statistics, and spectrum data. This gives visibility into data from APs that is usually not available from wireless LAN controllers. The network operator can use this tool to proactively find and resolve wireless problems with onboarding, interference, poor performance, and spectrum analysis. Please refer to the Cisco DNA Center Supported Devices to view the list of the supported hardware and software supporting the Intelligent Capture feature.

Figure 9-18 shows the communication flow between the AP and Cisco DNA Center. To achieve real-time telemetry, the AP establishes a new direct communication channel to Cisco DNA Center on TCP port 32656. The AP sends real-time telemetry information such as RF stats and anomaly events and can send packet capture and spectrum data. The real-time nature of Intelligent Capture accelerates data transmission up to 2 to 5 seconds, enabling real-time analysis of the wireless network. Cisco DNA Center integrates with Cisco Connected Mobile Experience (CMX), which uses location and other intelligence from the wireless infrastructure to generate analytics and location updates.

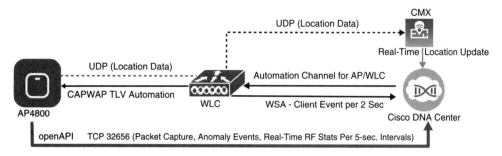

Figure 9-18 *Cisco DNA Assurance Intelligent Capture Data Flow*

Intelligent Capture offers anomaly-triggered packet captures (PCAPs) to allow network operators to overcome the challenge of replicating wireless issues. Capturing packets over wireless networks is difficult, and Cisco DNA Assurance simplifies the collection of PCAPs across multiple access points with zero packet loss during client roaming. The goal of Intelligent Capture is to reduce the average resolution time. Figure 9-19 represents an example of the automated stitching of multiple PCAPs performed by Cisco DNA Center.

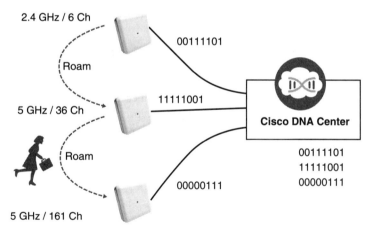

Figure 9-19 *Cisco DNA Assurance Multiple PCAP Stitching*

When a wireless client roams across the network, the access points capable of Intelligent Capture track the client roaming and provide individual packet capture files to Cisco DNA Center. Cisco DNA Assurance automatically stitches multiple PCAPs into a single PCAP file. With this stitching, there is zero packet loss during client roaming. The packet capture can be collected across access points and across floors.

Anomaly Capture

WLC generates the client event and shares with Cisco DNA Assurance through streaming telemetry whenever a wireless client connects. The access point has visibility into client onboarding events and can collect captures in case of a client anomaly event. Figure 9-20 depicts the packet flow that occurs in an anomaly event.

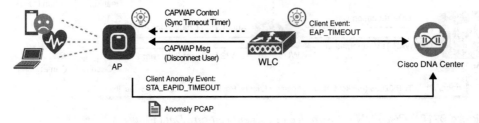

Figure 9-20   *Cisco DNA Assurance Anomaly Capture Flow*

In this case, the client was disconnected because of the event EAP_TIMEOUT. The access point is configured to collect the packet capture in an anomaly event. Here are some of the client anomaly events:

- DHCP failure

- 802.1X failure

- Extensible Authentication Protocol (EAP) Key Exchange failure (4-way, GTK Failure, Invalid EAPOL Key MIC, EAP timeout, etc.)

- Protocol Mismatch (Invalid RSN IE, Supported Rate Mismatch, Mismatching Replay Counter, etc.)

The access point monitors the client onboarding activity and, in case of any of the preceding events, collects packet captures. Enabling anomaly capture ensures that all anomaly onboarding events (globally or for all clients associated with the selected access points) are captured for download and display. Figure 9-21 shows the anomaly packet capture for a client in Client 360 view.

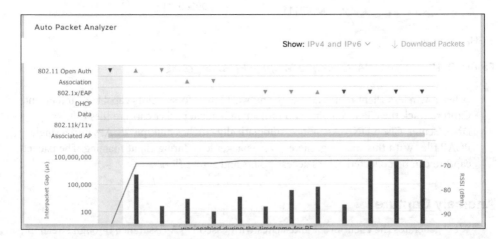

Figure 9-21   *Cisco DNA Assurance Anomaly Capture Example*

Path Trace

Path Trace is a useful Cisco DNA Assurance tool that lets the operator see the application or service path that traffic takes from a source to a destination. It provides the visibility at the hop level, similar to a traceroute, because it uses traceroute to identify the traffic path. The source and the destination for a path trace can be a combination of wired or wireless clients or the device interface IP addresses.

A common and critical troubleshooting task that normally requires 6 to 10 minutes of research is displayed instantly when you click on a client or an application. In addition to providing the traffic path at a hop level, Path Trace provides interface details such as the port number, interface statistics, the QoS policy applied, and the access list (ACL) applied to the interfaces along the traffic path.

For example, the Company ACME operations team received a ticket from the user Grace Smith saying she is unable to reach a server with an IP address 10.20.101.2. The operator goes to the Client 360 view of Grace Smith and runs a path trace to the destination address 10.20.101.2. Figure 9-22 shows the output of the path trace.

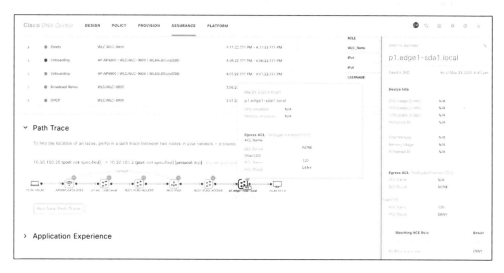

Figure 9-22   *Cisco DNA Assurance Path Trace Example*

The path trace for Grace Smith indicates that the issue is an interface ACL applied on the p1.edge1-sda1.local device along the traffic path. Path Trace essentially helps the operator resolve issues faster without logging in to multiple devices.

Sensor Tests

Let's consider a hypothetical use case where Company ACME has an executive leadership event scheduled in a week and the network operations manager has been told to make sure the wireless environment is ready for the event. The CIO would like to make sure the wireless environment in that area is performing as expected, and if there are any reported issues, they need to be reported proactively. Company ACME is looking for a solution that can proactively check the system and replicate client behavior without the network team doing on-premise testing. Cisco introduced Cisco Aironet 1800s Active Sensor, a dedicated compact wireless network sensor designed to be placed anywhere in the network to monitor the wireless network. It simulates real-world client experiences by running periodic wireless connection tests to validate wireless performance and to make sure the network is adhering to the committed SLAs. Deployment of the 1800s sensors is beneficial in proactively monitoring the network for critical venues and high-value loca-tions, such as conference halls and meeting rooms.

Cisco Aironet 1800's Active Sensor can be onboarded using the Cisco DNA Center plug-and-play feature. Cisco DNA Center can perform various sensor tests periodically. The sensor can simulate a real client and perform onboarding tests such as 802.11 onboard-ing, DHCP, 802.1X authentication using EAP-TLS or PEAP, as well as guest access. Active Sensor can also perform periodic tests to check network services such as DNS and RADIUS and do speed tests from the network to the cloud. Application experiences, such as packet loss, jitter, and latency streaming applications, are possible with the sensor proactive testing. Sensors can also perform connectivity tests for web traffic, email, file transfer, and host reachability. Figure 9-23 provides the sensor test results for the sensor named AP1800S_Sensor_04 seen on Cisco DNA Assurance. The green boxes in the test results indicate the results for different types of sensor tests.

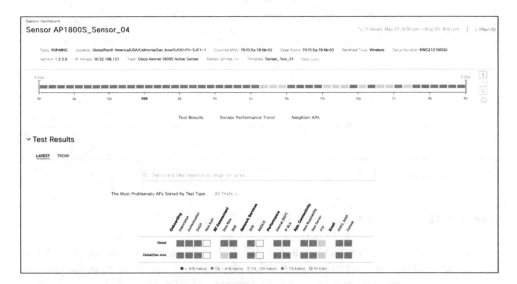

Figure 9-23   *Cisco DNA Assurance Sensor Test*

Cisco AI Network Analytics

In today's business climate, network outages adversely affect end-user experiences and application performance and can possibly affect the enterprise's revenue and reputation.

Network operations often see themselves in a state where the issues are discovered after the fact, which then call for root cause analysis. Cisco AI Network Analytics addresses this problem by leveraging secure cloud, identifying patterns from complex volumes of data from numerous networks, cross learning, building sophisticated machine learning models, and using these models to anticipate and notify the occurrence of critical problems before they happen. Cisco AI Network Analytics uses machine learning and machine reasoning to provide accurate insights that are specific to their network deployment and helpful in quickly troubleshooting issues.

Figure 9-24 shows the features Cisco AI Network Analytics brings to enrich Cisco DNA Assurance.

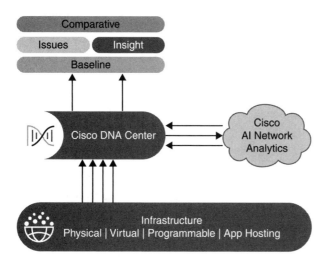

Figure 9-24   *Cisco AI Network Analytics Features*

Cisco AI Network Analytics is an application running on Cisco DNA Center. Enabling Cisco AI Network Analytics on Cisco DNA Center enables Cisco DNA Assurance to anonymize these complex volumes of the network telemetry data before sending them securely to the Cisco AI Network Analytics cloud. The Cisco AI Network Analytics cloud runs the machine learning model against the received anonymized event data and brings the issues and overall insights back to Cisco DNA Center. Cisco AI Networks Analytics drives intelligence in the network, empowering administrators to accurately and effectively improve performance and issue resolutions. It increases visibility by defining an appropriate baseline for alerts. Every network is distinctive, and one size does not fit all. Machine learning (with complex machine learning and data regression baselining) can accurately define what levels of performance are required for the optimal user experience for the specific network. This provides a realistic visibility into the network performance. Dynamic baselining allows normal operations profiling, anomaly detection, and adaptive thresholds based on a customer's environment instead of the static model with a predefined threshold.

Cisco AI Network Analytics provides better insights by reducing noise and false positives while accurately identifying issues that have the greatest impact on the network. Along with identifying issues, Cisco AI Network Analytics makes taking action easier and faster through accelerated and guided remediation. It offers comparative insights to determine how one site compares against another site for a selected key performance indicator (KPI). Cisco DNA Center offers an extensive API support to share the events, issues, insights, and trends learned from Cisco DNA Assurance and Cisco AI Network Analytics with the IT Service Management (ITSM) tools. The Cisco DNA Center platform application must be installed to enable the API support. The Cisco DNA Center platform natively supports integration with Service Now. The platform provides the capability to dynamically open a service request on a Service Now system when a configured event or an issue is triggered. The operations team can start working on the Service Now ticket even before the impacted user calls in, thereby improving the resolution time and reducing user impact.

Summary

The Cisco DNA Assurance solution provides new capabilities that enable network operators to monitor and troubleshoot the network more easily. This chapter introduced some highlights of the Cisco DNA Assurance capabilities, such as streaming telemetry, intelligent capture for real-time wireless client troubleshooting, proactive monitoring using sensors, path trace features to visualize the packet flow with every hop in detail, network time travel, and 360 views of clients, network devices, and applications. The new machine learning algorithms along with guided remediations based on the Cisco knowledge database provide valuable insights for maintaining the network. Intent-based networking has taken network operations a step further with Cisco DNA Assurance.

References in This Chapter

Cisco AI Network Analytics Overview: https://www.cisco.com/c/en/us/td/docs/cloud-systems-management/network-automation-and-management/dna-center-assurance/1-3-3-0/b_cisco_dna_assurance_1_3_3_0_ug/b_cisco_dna_assurance_1_3_2_0_chapter_010.html

Cisco DNA Assurance Solution Overview: https://www.cisco.com/c/en/us/solutions/collateral/enterprise-networks/digital-network-architecture/nb-06-dna-assurance-cte-en.html

Cisco DNA Assurance: Unlocking the Power of Data: https://www.cisco.com/c/dam/en/us/solutions/collateral/enterprise-networks/digital-network-architecture/nb-06-cisco-dna-assurance-technical-ebook-cte-en.pdf

Cisco DNA Assurance User Guide: https://www.cisco.com/c/en/us/td/docs/cloud-systems-management/network-automation-and-management/dna-center-assurance/1-3-3-0/b_cisco_dna_assurance_1_3_3_0_ug.html

Glossary

A

access control list (ACL)   A set of rules based on IP addresses that is used to permit or deny network traffic passing through network devices.

access point (AP)   A network device used with wireless networks that transmits and receives wireless signals from wireless-enabled endpoints.

AireOS   The operating system in use on many Cisco Wireless LAN Controllers.

Anycast   An addressing protocol that allows for the same IP address to exist on multiple physical devices, providing for more efficient and redundant network reachability.

Application 360   In Cisco Assurance, a complete view of a specific application on the network, including performance statistics such as latency, jitter, and reachability.

Application Policy Infrastructure Controller – Enterprise Module (APIC-EM)   A Cisco network controller solution that is the predecessor to Cisco DNA Center.

application programming interface (API)   A flexible interface beyond the traditional user interface that can be used programmatically to manage and monitor an application, device, or operating system.

artificial intelligence (AI)   The use of compute power to make human-like and informed decisions based on real-time data in the environment.

Autoconf   A Cisco proprietary solution that can automatically configure connection parameters on a switch interface based on its downstream connection and device type.

B

Bidirectional Forwarding Detection (BFD)   A standards-based protocol that detects the connectivity state between network devices and alerts higher-layer protocols to state changes.

Border Gateway Protocol (BGP)   A standards-based routing protocol that is used to exchange routing and reachability information between routers.

bring your own device (BYOD)   A common enterprise administrative policy that allows employees to connect to enterprise networks or the Internet with their personal devices such as phones and tablets.

C

Cisco Application Centric Infrastructure (Cisco ACI) A software controller–based solution that uses software-defined networking (SDN) to deploy, monitor, and manage enterprise data centers and clouds.

Cisco Application Policy Infrastructure Controller (Cisco APIC) The software controller used by Cisco ACI.

Cisco Connected Mobile Experience (Cisco CMX) A Cisco solution that is used to monitor large enterprise wireless networks and provide contextual data for endpoints on the network, including location and roaming patterns.

Cisco Digital Network Architecture (Cisco DNA) The Cisco suite of solutions to modern network challenges featuring automation, cloud, multi-domain, and security approaches.

Cisco Discovery Protocol (CDP) A Layer 2–based protocol that is used between directly connected Cisco devices to share connection and platform details.

Cisco DNA Center The software controller used by Cisco SD-Access.

Cisco Express Forwarding (CEF) A forwarding solution used on Cisco routers and switches that supports faster processing and forwarding of Layer 3 packets than is supported by traditional centralized routing mechanisms.

Cisco Identity-Based Networking Services 2.0 (IBNS) A flexible identity framework that uses a traditional configuration based on class map and policy map similar to QoS.

Cisco Identity Services Engine (Cisco ISE) An application that provides centralized security services such as network access control (NAC), profiling, compliance, asset visibility, authentication, and authorization. Cisco ISE is used as the policy engine for Cisco SD-Access.

Cisco Internetworking Operating System (Cisco IOS-XE) A Linux-based operating system that runs on many Cisco switching and routing platforms.

Cisco Network Plug-and-Play (PnP) A mechanism that can be used by Cisco devices to automatically onboard and configure the devices from a factory out-of-the-box state.

Cisco Platform Exchange Grid (Cisco pxGrid) An open, scalable, and IETF standards-driven platform that supports bidirectional, any-to-any partner platform integrations.

Cisco Prime Infrastructure A Cisco network management system (NMS) solution that can be used to monitor, manage, and deploy enterprise network devices.

Cisco Software-Defined Access (Cisco SD-Access) A software controller–based solution that uses SDN to deploy, monitor, and manage local-area networks in enterprise branches and campuses.

Cisco Software-Defined WAN (Cisco SD-WAN) A software controller–based solution that uses SDN to deploy, monitor, and manage wide-area networks.

Cisco TrustSec (CTS) A solution to classify and deploy network segmentation based on Scalable Group Tag (SGT) and Security Group Access Control List (SGACL).

Cisco vManage The software controller used by Cisco SD-WAN.

cloud Shared compute and application resources that exist in a domain away from the physical enterprise network, such as the

Internet or a shared data center. Examples of cloud service providers include Amazon Web Services (AWS) and Microsoft Azure.

comma-separated values (CSV)   A file format that is typically used to import or export a series of data in bulk. The data fields inside the file are separated by commas.

command-line interface (CLI)   Method of configuring network devices individually by inputting configuration commands.

Control and Provisioning of Wireless Access Points (CAPWAP)   A virtual tunneling protocol that is established between APs and WLCs.

D

Device 360   In Cisco Assurance, a complete view of a particular network device's information and location on a network.

downloadable access control list (dACL)   An ACL that is dynamically pushed by Cisco ISE to a network switch after a client authenticates.

E

EtherChannel   Grouping of multiple physical links between devices into a single virtual link to optimize bandwidth usage and provide failover.

Extensible Authentication Protocol (EAP)   A Layer 2 authentication protocol that is used between an endpoint and a network device.

External RESTful Services (ERS) API   *See* Representational State Transfer (REST or RESTful) API.

F–K

fabric border node   A node in the Cisco Software-Defined Access fabric that facilitates traffic entering and exiting the fabric domain.

fabric control plane node   A node in the Cisco Software-Defined Access fabric that tracks all endpoints in the fabric traffic along with their locations. Other nodes in the fabric will query the fabric control plane for these locations.

fabric edge node   A node in a Cisco Software-Defined Access fabric to which endpoints are connected. Similar to an access switch in traditional networking.

Infrastructure as a Service (IaaS)   Virtualized hardware that is outsourced to providers and that typically runs in the cloud.

Intelligent Capture (ICAP)   A packet capture view of the transactions between wireless clients and wireless APs.

Interior Gateway Protocol (IGP)   A protocol that is commonly used by routers in a network to exchange route information and location.

intermediate node   A node in the Cisco Software-Defined Access fabric that serves as an intermediate connection point between other fabric roles. The intermediate node is not technically part of the Cisco Software-Defined Access process except to route packets between other nodes in the fabric.

Internet of Things (IoT)   A collection of nontraditional network-connected devices that are typically unmanned, such as manufacturing equipment, lighting, security cameras, and door locks.

IP address manager (IPAM)   A centralized database used to track IP addresses and pools in use across an enterprise network.

IP Device Tracking (IPDT)   A feature that a Cisco switch uses to track endpoints that are connected to it.

L

Link Layer Discovery Protocol (LLDP)   A Layer 2–based protocol that functions similarly to Cisco Discovery Protocol(CDP) but can also be used between non-Cisco devices.

Locator/ID Separation Protocol (LISP) An industry-standard protocol that separates reachability information into routing locator (RLOC) and endpoint identifier (EID).

M

machine learning   A subset of artificial intelligence used to gather data and information from the network environment to constantly learn, adapt, and improve the accuracy of the AI.

maximum transmission unit (MTU) The maximum packet (Layer 3) or frame (Layer 2) size that can pass through an interface without requiring fragmentation.

multidomain   An end-to-end network architecture that comprises different types of solutions to fit the requirements of each environment, such as campus, WAN, data center, and cloud.

N–O

NetFlow   A standards-based protocol that contains explicit application data and is used by many network management systems to monitor network devices and flows.

network access control (NAC)   A secure process that a user or endpoint uses to negotiate access to a network.

network access device (NAD)   An element that is used in Cisco ISE to identify any network devices that will interact with Cisco ISE for authentication or authorization purposes.

Network-Based Application Recognition (NBAR)   A Cisco proprietary classification system that is used to identify applications present on a network for reporting and QoS purposes.

Network Configuration Protocol (NETCONF)   A standards-based protocol used to install, manipulate, and delete the configuration of network devices.

network management system (NMS) An application specifically developed to manage and monitor enterprise network elements and architectures.

P

Port Aggregation Protocol (PAgP)   A protocol that is used for EtherChannel. *See also* EtherChannel.

Power over Ethernet (PoE)   An IEEE standard (802.3af) that allows endpoints to obtain operational power directly inline over their Ethernet connection.

Q

quality of service (QoS)   The categorizing and prioritization of traffic in a network, typically based on application type and requirements.

R

received signal strength indicator (RSSI)   The signal strength that a wireless device receives from a wireless transmitter.

Remote Authentication Dial-In User Service (RADIUS)   A networking protocol that is used for user or device authentication, authorization, and accounting.

Representational State Transfer (REST or RESTful) API   An API that uses Hypertext Transfer Protocol (HTTP) to communicate between a controller and a device or operating system.

routing locator (RLOC)   Used in Cisco SD-Access to define the network device where a connected endpoint is located. In Cisco SD-Access, this is defined by the address on the Loopback0 interface.

S

Scalable Group Tag (SGT)   A unique identification assigned to an endpoint or group of endpoints for use in segmentation. Also known as Security Group Tag.

Security Group Access Control List (SGACL)   A set of rules based on SGT that is used to permit or deny network traffic passing through network devices.

service-level agreement (SLA)   A commitment made by a service or application provider to provide to customers no less than a minimum level of service or uptime.

service set identifier (SSID)   A unique name assigned to a wireless network for wireless endpoints to connect.

SGT Exchange Protocol (SXP)   A TCP-based protocol that is used to exchange SGT mapping information between network devices and Cisco ISE.

signal-to-noise ratio (SNR)   On wireless devices, the ratio of wireless signal power to the amount of noise power or interference.

Simple Network Management Protocol (SNMP)   A standards-based protocol that is used by many NMSs to manage and monitor network devices.

Software as a Service (SaaS)   Software applications that are outsourced to providers (called SaaS providers) that typically run in the cloud, providing application resiliency and high availability without having to host them locally.

software-defined networking (SDN)   A process by which network flows, rules, and operations are defined and deployed from a centralized controller rather than on each network device.

Spanning-Tree Protocol (STP)   A technology that is used between LAN switches to ensure loop-free topologies.

StackWise   A Cisco proprietary protocol that is used to group a series of like-modeled physical switches, such as Cisco Catalyst 9200 or 9300 switches, into one larger virtual switch providing redundancy to uplink and downlink connections.

StackWise Virtual (SVL)   A Cisco proprietary protocol that is used to group a pair of like-modeled physical switches, such as Cisco Catalyst 9500 or 9600 switches, into a virtual pair providing redundancy to uplink and downlink connections.

switch virtual interface (SVI)   A virtual interface on a switch or a router that terminates a Layer 3 boundary and can act as a default gateway.

Switched Port Analyzer (SPAN)   A process that is used to export traffic that crosses a switch for later analysis and troubleshooting.

Syslog   A standards-based logging protocol that is used by many NMSs to monitor network devices to collect information.

T

Terminal Access Controller Access-Control System Plus (TACACS+)   A networking protocol that is used primarily for device authentication, authorization, and accounting.

Ternary Content-Addressable Memory (TCAM)   A type of memory typically found on switches that stores address tables in a decentralized location, allowing for faster and more efficient packet forwarding.

U

User 360   In Cisco Assurance, a complete view of a particular user's devices and activities on a network.

V

Virtual Extensible LAN (VXLAN)   A network encapsulation protocol that allows for the transport of Layer 2 Ethernet frames over a Layer 3 infrastructure.

virtual network (VN)   As used in Cisco SD-Access, the same as a VRF instance.

virtual routing and forwarding (VRF)   A virtualization technology used by routers to provide multiple dedicated Layer 3 routing domains, paths, and tables that are segmented from each other. These domains are known as VRF instances.

virtualization   Abstracting applications and software from the underlying physical hardware resources and running them as virtual instances.

VXLAN Tunnel Endpoint (VTEP)   This is used interchangeably with RLOC in Cisco SD-Access.

W–X

Wireless LAN Controller (WLC)   A hardware or software-based network device that provides management and controller functions for APs.

Yet Another Markup Language (YAML)   A data format that is commonly used to provide settings and instructions to automation tools such as Ansible.

Zero-Touch Provisioning (ZTP)   An alternative to Cisco PnP based on open-sourced tools and protocols that can be used to provision both Cisco and non-Cisco devices from a factory-state without direct interaction on the device itself.

zero trust model   A security model based on the principle of maintaining strict access controls and not trusting anyone by default, even those already inside the network perimeter.

Index

A

AAA (authentication, authorization, and accounting), 33

access contracts, 123–124

access points, Cisco SD-Access, 89

access tunnels, displaying, 185–186

accounting, 33, 34

ACI (Cisco Application Centric Infrastructure), 16–17

analytics, 9
  ETA, 12

ANC (Adaptive Network Control), 49

Anomaly Capture, 301–302

Ansible Playbook, 61

APIC-EM (Application Policy Infrastructure Controller Enterprise Module),
  core applications, 62–63

APIs (application programming interfaces), 9

Application Health dashboard, Cisco DNA Assurance, 299–300

architecture, 50
  Cisco DNA Assurance, 287–288
  Cisco DNA Center, 256

ARP flooding, 218–219. *See also* Layer 2 networks

assigning, templates, 269–270

assurance, 285

authentication, 31, 33, 35
  Cisco ISE Compliance, 46–48
  IEEE 802.1X, 35–37
  troubleshooting in Cisco SD-Access, 188–190

authentication templates
  Cisco SD-Access, 105–106
  Closed Authentication, 140–141
  Easy Connect, 141–144
  editing, 142–144
  No Authentication, 137–138
  Open Authentication, 138–140

authenticators, 35

authorization, 33, 35

automation, 2, 7

Ansible Playbook, 61

border, 98–99

Cisco DNA Center, 25–26

copying configuration files, 60

GUIs, 62

LAN, 84–86

configuration, 87–88

first phase, 86

second phase, 87

and manually configured networks, 2–3

tools, history of, 60–62

B

bandwidth, in WAN environments, 19

bidirectional PIM, 210

border nodes, 96–98

automation, 98–99

control plane collocation, 99–100

BYOD (bring your own device), 4, 5, 45–46, 128

security, 31

C

campus networks

corporate network access use case, 149–159

desired benefits, 5–6

fabrics, 24–25

guest access use case, 159–164

Layer 2 intersite, 224

design and traffic flow, 224–227

multidomain, 16–18

three-tier, 14

CAs (certificate authorities), 114–115

certificates

Cisco ISE, 115–116

self-signed, 113

Cisco ACI (Application Centric Infrastructure), 252–253

Cisco AI Network Analytics, 304–306

Cisco Campus Fabric, 25–28

LISP, 26, 27

traffic flow for wired clients, 30

Cisco Catalyst 9000 Series switches, 11

Cisco DNA Assurance, 9, 286

architecture, 287–288

data collection points, 289–291

health dashboards, 292–293

Application Health, 299–300

Cisco SD-Access Fabric Network, 296

Client Health, 297–298

Network Health, 294–296

Overall Health, 293

network time travel, 292

streaming telemetry, 290–292

tools

Anomaly Capture, 301–302

Cisco AI Network Analytics, 304–306

Intelligent Capture, 300–301

Path Trace, 303

sensor tests, 303–304

Cisco DNA Center, 28–29, 63, 112, 197

access contracts, 123–124

APIC-EM, core applications, 62–63

architecture, 256

authentication templates
editing, 142–144
No Authentication, 137–138
Open Authentication, 138–140
automation, 25–26
Cisco Campus Fabric, 25–28
Cisco ISE integration, 116–122
certificates in Cisco DNA Center, 113–115
certificates on Cisco ISE, 115–116
Cisco SD-Access, 23–24
claiming devices, 276–279
CLI (command-line interface), 115
clustering, 258–259
communication flow with Cisco ISE, 120–121
corporate network access use case, 149–159
Design tool, 64–68
Network Hierarchy, 64–68
Network Settings, 69
wireless deployments, 70–72
Discovery tool, 72–75
fabrics, 24–25
group-based access control, 122–126
guest access use case, 159–164
HA, 258
home screen, 63–64
host onboarding, 128, 136–137
IBN (intent-based networking), 286–287
import file support, 115
Inventory tool, 74–77
network connectivity, 256–257
PKI Certificate Management feature, 114–115
PnP, 272–273

PnP Agent, 275–276
policies, 124
segmentation, 124–126
Provision tool, 77–78
resources, 256–257
roles, 75
scale numbers, 256
software image management, 259–261
Start Migration link, 123–124
SWIM
Golden Image, 262
image repository, 261
upgrading devices, 263–266
switchport override, 109
sync process, 74
templates, 266–267
assigning, 269–270
creating, 267–269
deploying, 270–272
onboarding, 273–274
third-party RADIUS server, 126–127
tools
Command Runner, 281–282
Security Advisories, 283
Topology, 280–281
verifying integration with Cisco ISE, 121–122
Cisco DNA (Digital Network Architecture), 10, 12
Cisco ISE (Identity Services Engine), 29, 31, 32, 33, 112, 196
architecture, 50
BYOD, 45–46
certificates, 115
Cisco DNA Center integration, 116–122

certificates in Cisco DNA Center, 113–115

certificates on Cisco ISE, 115–116

communication flow with Cisco DNA Center, 120–121

Compliance, 46–48

deployment options

dedicated distributed, 52

distributed, 51–52

standalone, 51

design considerations, 50

device administration, 37

differences between RADIUS and TACACS+ protocols, 33

group-based access control, 122–126

guest access, 38–40

integrations with pxGrid, 48–49

policy sets, 146–148

posture checks, 45–48

probes, 41, 42–43

profiling, 40–41, 43–45

role-based access control, 37

secure access, 34–37

TACACS+, 37–38

verifying integration with Cisco DNA Center, 121–122

Cisco Network Visibility Application, 63

Cisco Rapid Threat Containment, 49

Cisco SD-Access, 23–24, 112

access points, 89

authentication templates, 105–106

border and control plane collocation, 99–100

border automation, 98–99

Cisco ACI policy extension, 252–253

components, 28–29, 245–246

corporate network access use case, 149–159

design considerations, 240

fabric border node, 248–249

fabric control plane node, 248

fabric wireless integration, 249

infrastructure services, 249

large sites, 243

medium sites, 243

mixed SD-Access wireless and centralized wireless option, 250

security policy, 251–252

single-site versus multisite, 244–245

small sites, 242

very small sites, 241–242

wireless guest deployment, 250–251

wireless over-the-top centralized wireless option, 250

DHCP, 172–175

debug on fabric switch, 174

request process, 173

for distributed campus deployments, 228–229

Cisco SD-Access transit, 232–234

fabric multisite or multidomain with IP transit, 230–232

IP transit, 229–230

multisite Cisco SD-Access transit, 234–237

policy deployment models, 238–240

external connectivity, 104

fusion router, 104–105

fabric encapsulation, 167–168
  LISP, 168–170
  VXLAN, 171–172
Fabric in a Box (FiaB) deployment, 227–228
fabrics, 24–25
  border node, 96–98
  control plane, 95–96
  creation, 92
  device roles, 94–95
  edge nodes, 100–102
  host onboarding, 105
  intermediate nodes, 103–104
  MTU considerations, 172
  placement, 93
  roles, 170
  SSID to IP pool mapping, 108–109
  VN to IP pool mapping, 106–108
  VNs, 94
  VXLAN, 26
fusion router, 91
guest access use case, 159–164
host operation and packet flow, 172
IoT extension, 196–197
  extended node configuration, 200–203
  extended nodes, 198
  hosts communicating with hosts connected outside the fabric, 205–206
  onboarding the extended node, 203–205
  policy extended nodes, 198–199
  traffic flow within a policy extended node, 207–208

  traffic from clients connected to policy extended node, 206–207
  traffic to clients connected to policy extended node, 207
latency considerations, 240–241
Layer 2
  border, 221–223
  flooding, 218–221
  intersite, 224–227
multicast, 208
  configuration in Cisco DNA Center, 216–218
  fabric native, 214–216
  PIM ASM with head-end replication, 211
  PIM SSM with head-end replication, 213–214
network profiles, 269–270
network topologies, 81–82
overlay, design considerations, 247–248
segmentation
  macro-, 144–145
  micro-, 145–146
  outside the fabric, 164
  policies, 148
shared services, 90–91
switchport override, 109
transit networks, 91
  IP-based transit, 91–92
  SD-Access transit, 92
troubleshooting, 181–182, 188
  authentication, 188–190
  fabric control plane, 186–187
  fabric edge, 182–186
  policy, 190–191
  SGTs, 191–192

underlay, 82–83, 246

automated, 84–89

design considerations, 246–247

manual, 83–84

wired host onboarding and registration, 175–176

wired host operation, 176

inter-subnet traffic in the fabric, 179

intra-subnet traffic in the fabric, 176–178

traffic to destinations outside the fabric, 180

wireless host operation, 180–181

initial onboarding and registration, 180–181

WLCs, 89

Cisco SD-Access Fabric Network Health dashboard, Cisco DNA Assurance, 296

Cisco SD-WAN, transit, 237–238

Cisco Stealthwatch, 11

Cisco TrustSec, 54

functions

classification, 55

enforcement, 57–58

propagation, 55–57

SGTs, 54

Cisco Zero Trust, 128

claiming devices, 276–279

classification

Cisco TrustSec, 55

endpoints, 40

CLI (command-line interface), 3

Cisco DNA Center, 115

Client Health dashboard, Cisco DNA Assurance, 297–298

Closed Authentication template, 140–141

closed mode, IEEE 802.1X, 134–136

cloud computing, 4, 11

clustering, Cisco DNA Center, 258–259

CMX (Cisco Connected Mobile Experience), 300

COA (Change of Authorization), 38–39

Command Runner, 281–282

commands

ip helper-address, 172

show authentication sessions, 189

show authentication sessions interface, 154

show client detail, 190

show cts environment-data, 191–192

show cts rbacl, 191

show cts role-based permissions, 191

show device-tracking database, 182–183

show ip dhcp snooping binding, 182

show lisp instance-id, 187

show lisp instance-id ethernet database, 183

show lisp instance-id ethernet server, 186–187

show policy-map type control subscriber, 139, 141

show running config, 188

show template interface source user, 139

write erase, 203

Compliance, Cisco ISE, 46–48

configuration changes, 266–267

configuration files, copying, 60

configuring
    extended nodes, 200–203
    Layer 2 flooding, 219–221
connectivity, Cisco DNA Center, 256–257
context, endpoints, 48
contracts, 123–124
control plane, 3, 24–25
    border node collocation in Cisco SD-Access, 99–100
    in Cisco SD-Access, 95–96
    Cisco SD-Access, 29
    show cts rol-based permissions, 156, 163
controllers, 23
corporate network access use case, 149–159
creating, templates, 267–269

D

data collection points, Cisco DNA Assurance, 289–291
data plane, 3, 24–25
dedicated distributed deployment, Cisco ISE, 52
delivery modes, multicast, 210
deployment options
    Cisco ISE
        dedicated distributed, 52
        distributed, 51–52
        standalone, 51
    Cisco SD-Access
        distributed campus, 228–233, 233–237
        FiaB (Fabric in a Box), 227–228
        policies, 238–240
    templates, 270–272

design considerations
    fabric border node, 248–249
    fabric control plane node, 248
    fabric wireless integration, 249
    infrastructure services, 249
    large sites, 243
    medium sites, 243
    mixed SD-Access wireless and centralized wireless option, 250
    overlay network, 247–248
    security policy, 251–252
    single-site versus multisite, 244–245
    small sites, 242
    underlay network, 246–247
    very small sites, 241–242
    wireless guest deployment, 250–251
    wireless over-the-top centralized wireless option, 250
Design tool (Cisco DNA Center)
    Network Hierarchy, 64–68
    Network Settings, 69
    wireless deployments, 70–72
device upgrade process, Cisco DNA Center, 263–266
DHCP (Dynamic Host Configuration Protocol), 90
    in Cisco SD-Access, 172–175
        debug on fabric switch, 174
        request process, 173
digital transformation model, 7
Discovery tool (Cisco DNA Center), 72–75
distributed campus deployments, 228–229
    Cisco SD-Access transit, 232–233
        multisite, 233–237
    fabric multisite or multidomain with IP transit, 230–232

IP transit, 229–230

policy deployment models, 238–240

distributed deployment, Cisco ISE, 51–52

DMVPN (Dynamic Multipoint Virtual Private Network), 24–25

DNS (Domain Name Service), 90

E

Easy Connect template, 141–144

EasyQoS, 63

editing, authentication templates, 142–144

EID (endpoint identifier), 26

encapsulation protocols, 167–168

LISP (Location Identifier Separation Protocol), 168–170

VXLAN (Virtual Extensible LAN), 171–172

endpoints, 112

classification, 40

context, 48

posture checks, 45–48

profiling, 40–41, 43–45

ERS (External RESTful Services), 113

enabling in Cisco ISE (Identity Services Engine), 118

ETA (Cisco Encrypted Traffic Analytics), 12

extended nodes, 197, 198

configuration, 200–203

onboarding, 203–205

external connectivity, Cisco SD-Access, 104–105

F

fabric border node

Cisco SD-Access, 29

design considerations, 248–249

fabric edge node, Cisco SD-Access, 29

fabric WAN controller, Cisco SD-Access, 29

fabrics, 82, 112

architecture, 24–25

Cisco Campus Fabric, 25–28

Cisco SD-Access

access points, 89

automated underlay, 84–89

border node, 96–98

device roles, 94–95

edge nodes, 100–102

host onboarding, 105

intermediate nodes, 103–104

manual underlay, 83–84

SSID to IP pool mapping, 108–109

VN to IP pool mapping, 106–108

VNs, 94

control plane, 95–96

design considerations, 248

troubleshooting, 186–187

creation in Cisco SD-Access, 92

edge nodes

displaying ip addresses, 184

troubleshooting, 182–186

encapsulation

LISP, 168–170

VXLAN, 171–172

encapsulation protocols, 167–168

MTU considerations, 172

placement, 93

roles, 170

segmentation outside, 164

VXLAN, 26

FHRPs (first hop redundancy protocols), 13

FiaB (Fabric in a Box) deployment, 227–228

full BYOD (bring your own device), 45

fusion router, 91

G

Golden Image, 68, 84, 262

GRE (Generic Routing Encapsulation), 24–25

group-based access control, 122–126

guest access

Cisco ISE, 38–40

use case, 159–164

GUIs, 62

H

HA (High Availability), Cisco DNA Center, 258

health dashboards (Cisco DNA Assurance), 292–293

Application Health, 299–300

Cisco SD-Access Fabric Network, 296

Client Health, 297–298

Network Health, 294–296

Overall Health, 293

HIPAA (Health Insurance Portability and Accountability Act), 112

history, of automation tools, 60–62

host onboarding, 128

Cisco DNA Center, 136–137

Cisco SD-Access, 105

Hotspot Guest portal, Cisco ISE, 40

I

IaaS (Infrastructure as a Service), 4, 18

IBN (intent-based networking), 8, 63, 286

problem isolation, 9

IEEE 802.1X, 35–37

endpoint host modes, 128

multi-auth, 129–130

multi-domain, 129–130

multi-host, 128–129

single-host, 128–129

phased deployment, 130-, 131

closed mode, 134–136

low-impact mode, 133–134

monitor mode (visibility mode), 132–133

IGMP (Internet Group Management Protocol), 209

image repository, Cisco DNA Center, 261

infrastructure services, design considerations, 249

inline tagging, 55–56

insights, 9

integrating, Cisco DNA Center and Cisco ISE (Identity Services Engine), 116–122

Intelligent Capture, 300–301

intermediate nodes, 103–104

Inventory tool, Cisco DNA Center, 74–77

IoT (Internet of Things), 4, 112

Cisco SD-Access extension, 196–197

extended nodes, 198

configuration, 200–203

onboarding, 203–205

policy extended nodes, 198–199

security, 196

use cases for Cisco SD-Access

hosts communicating with hosts connected outside the fabric, 205–206

traffic flow within a policy extended node, 207–208

traffic from clients connected to policy extended node, 206–207

traffic to clients connected to policy extended node, 207

IP addresses, displaying in LISP, 184, 185

ip helper-address command, 172

IP multicast. *See* multicast

IP pools

mapping to SSID, 108–109

mapping to VNs, 106–108

IP transit, 84, 91–92, 229–230

fabric multisite or multidomain, 230–232

IT industry, 22

advances in, 1–2

analytics, 9

automation, 2–3, 7

cloud computing, 18–20

history of automation tools, 60–62

IaaS, 4

IBN, 8

multidomain, 16–18

overlay networks, 24–25

SDN, 3

trends, 4

IWAN (Cisco Intelligent WAN), 63

L

LAN Automation, 84–86

configuration, 87–88

first phase, 86

second phase, 87

large sites, design considerations, 243

latency considerations for Cisco SD-Access, 240–241

Layer 2 networks

border, 221–223

flooding, 218–221

intersite, 224

design and traffic flow, 224–227

Spanning Tree, 13–14

Layer 3 routed access, 14–15, 102

benefits, 15–16

lig (LISP Internet Groper), 186

LISP (Location Identifier Separation Protocol), 24–25, 26, 27, 96, 168–170

IP addresses, displaying, 184

map-register debug, 176

low-impact mode, IEEE 802.1X, 133–134

M

MAB (MAC Authentication Bypass), 35

macro-segmentation, 112, 144–145

malware, 112

manual underlay, Cisco SD-Access, 83–84

manually configuring networks, 7, 14–15

risks of, 2–3

medium sites, design considerations, 243

micro-segmentation, 112, 145–146

monitor mode (visibility mode), IEEE 802.1X, 132–133

MPLS (Multiprotocol Label Switching), 24–25

MTU (maximum transmission unit), 172

multi-auth mode, IEEE 802.1X, 129–130

multicast, 208–209

bidirectional PIM, 210

in Cisco SD-Access

configuration in Cisco DNA Center, 216–218

PIM ASM with head-end replication, 211

PIM SSM with head-end replication, 213–214

delivery modes, 210

fabric native, 214–216

IGMP, 209

PIM sparse-dense mode, 209

PIM-DM, 209

PIM-SM, 209

multidomain, 16–18

multi-domain mode, IEEE 802.1X, 129–130

multi-host mode, IEEE 802.1X, 128–129

multisite Cisco SD-Access transit, 234–237

multisite design, 244–245

N

network access, 34

network access control (NAC), 30, 33, 128

need for, 31

network controllers, 3

Network Health dashboard, Cisco DNA Assurance, 294–296

network operations workflow, 9

network profiles, 269–270

networks. *See also* software-defined networking

challenges of traditional implementations, 285–286

corporate access use case, 149–159

guest access use case, 159–164

isolating, 112

planning, 59–60

redundant, 6–7

topologies, 81–82

transit, 91

zero trust, 128

No Authentication template, 137–138

nodes

Cisco SD-Access fabric, 94–95

extended, 197, 198

configuration, 200–203

onboarding, 203–205

policy extended, 198–199

NTP (Network Time Protocol), 90

O

onboarding, extended nodes, 203–205

onboarding templates, 273–274

Open Authentication template, 138–140

Overall Health dashboard, Cisco DNA Assurance, 293

overlay networks, 24–25, 112

design considerations, 247–248

P

Path Trace, 303

PCAPs (anomaly-triggered packet captures), 301

PCI (Payment Card Industry), isolating point-of-sales machines, 112

phased deployment, IEEE 802.1X, 130, 131

closed mode, 134–136

low-impact mode, 133–134

monitor mode (visibility mode), 132–133

PIM sparse-dense mode, 209

PIM-DM (PIM dense mode), 209

PIM-SM (PIM sparse mode), 209

PKI (Public Key Infrastructure), 114–115

placement, of fabrics, 93

planning, networks, 59–60

PnP (plug and play), 62

Cisco DNA Center, 272–273

claiming devices, 276–279

PnP Agent, 275–276

PoE (Power over Ethernet), 196

point-of-sales machines, isolating, 112

policies, 112, 124

deployment models in Cisco SD-Access distributed deployment, 238–240

segmentation, 124–126, 148

troubleshooting, 190–191

policy extended nodes, 198–199

policy sets, 146–148

posture checks, 45–48

private key certificates, 115

probes, Cisco ISE, 41, 42–43

problem isolation, 9

profiling, Cisco ISE, 40–41, 43–45

propagation, Cisco TrustSec, 55–57

Provision tool, Cisco DNA Center, 77–78

pull model, 26

pxGrid (Cisco Platform Exchange Grid), 48–49, 113, 115, 120

Personas, 116

R

RADIUS, 37

for Cisco DNA Center, 126–127

and TACACS+, 33

reactive notifications, 9

redundancy, 6–7

REP (Resilient Ethernet Protocol), 199

risks of manually configured networks, 2–3

roles

in Cisco SD-Access, 94–95

fabric, 170

S

SaaS (Software as a Service), 4, 18

scale numbers, Cisco DNA Center, 256

SD-Access transit, 92

SDN (software-defined networking), 3

SD-WAN (Software-Defined WAN), 17, 18

security, 11, 22
  BYOD, 31
  design considerations, 251–252
  IoT, 196
  shadow IT, 18

Security Advisories, 283

segmentation, 26, 112
  Cisco TrustSec, 54
  macro-, 112, 144–145
  micro-, 112, 145–146
  outside the fabric, 164
  policies, 148

segmentation policies, 124–126

Self-Registered Guest portal, Cisco ISE, 40

self-signed certificates, 113

sensor tests, 303–304

sensors, 287

ServiceNOW, 9

SGTs (Scalable Group Tags), 26, 122, 123, 145–146
  classification, 55
  inline tagging, 55–56
  propagation, 55–57
  troubleshooting, 191–192

shadow IT, 18

shared services, Cisco SD-Access, 90–91

show authentication sessions command, 189

show authentication sessions interface command, 154

show client detail command, 190

show cts environment-data command, 191–192

show cts rbacl command, 191

show cts rol-based permissions command, 163

show cts role-based permissions command, 156, 191

show device-tracking database command, 182–183

show ip dhcp snooping binding command, 182

show lisp instance-id command, 187

show lisp instance-id ethernet database command, 183

show lisp instance-id ethernet server command, 186–187

show policy-map type control subscriber command, 139, 141

show running config command, 188

show template interface source user command, 139

simple BYOD (bring your own device), 45

single-host mode, IEEE 802.1X, 128–129

single-site design, 244–245

small sites, design considerations, 242

SNMP (Simple Network Management Protocol), 9

software image management, Cisco DNA Center, 259–261

software-defined networking, 22–23

solutions for campus networks, 5–6

SPAN (Switched Port Analyzer), 9

Spanning Tree, 15–16
  drawbacks, 13–14
  three-tier campus networks, 14
  versions, 13

Sponsored-Guest portal, Cisco ISE, 40

SSID, mapping to IP pools, 108–109

SSL (Secure Sockets Layer), 113

standalone deployment, Cisco ISE, 51

STOMP (Simple Text Oriented Message Protocol), 49

storage, multidomain, 16–18

streaming telemetry, 290–292

supplicants, 35, 37

SWIM (Software Image Management), 261

　Golden Image, 262

　image repository, 261

　upgrading devices, 263–266

switchport override, Cisco DNA Center, 109

SXP (SGT Exchange Protocol), 92, 164, 228

sync process, Cisco DNA Center, 74

T

TAC (Cisco Technical Assistance Center), 2–3

TACACS+, 37, 38

　and RADIUS, 33

telemetry, traditional versus streaming, 292

templates

　assigning, 269–270

　Cisco DNA Center, 266–267

　　creating, 267–269

　deploying, 270–272

　onboarding, 273–274

three-layer network topology, 82

three-tier campus networks, Spanning Tree, 14

tools

　Cisco DNA Assurance

　　Anomaly Capture, 301–302

　　Cisco AI Network Analytics, 304–306

　　Intelligent Capture, 300–301

　　Path Trace, 303

　　sensor tests, 303–304

　Cisco DNA Center

　　Command Runner, 281–282

　　Security Advisories, 283

　　Topology, 280–281

topologies, LAN Automation, 84–86

　configuration, 87–88

　first phase, 86

　second phase, 87

Topology tool, 280–281

transit networks, 91

　IP-based transit, 91–92

　SD-Access transit, 92

troubleshooting

　Cisco SD-Access, 181–182, 188

　　authentication, 188–190

　　fabric control plane, 186–187

　　fabric edge, 182–186

　　policy, 190–191

　　SGTs, 191–192

　replicating the issue, 9

trunking, 14–15

U

UADP (Unified Access Data Plane), 287

underlay networks, 24

　Cisco SD-Access, 82–83

　　automated, 84–89

　　manual, 83–84

design considerations, 246–247

upgrading devices, in Cisco DNA Center, 263–266

V

verifying, Cisco DNA Center and Cisco ISE (Identity Services Engine) integration, 121–122

very small sites, design considerations, 241–242

VLANs, 14–15, 26

VNs (virtual networks)

macro-segmentation, 144–145

mapping to IP pools, 106–108

micro-segmentation, 145–146

VRF (virtual routing and forwarding), 104–105, 144

VSS (Cisco Virtual Switching System), 7

VXLAN (Virtual Extensible LAN), 26, 168, 171–172

VXLAN-GPO, 26

W

WAN environments, bandwidth, 19

wireless deployments, Cisco DNA Center, 70–72

WLCs (wireless LAN controllers)

Cisco SD-Access, 89

displaying wireless endpoint MAC addresses, 185

write erase command, 203

X-Y-Z

X.509 certificates, 115

YAML (Yet Another Markup Language), 60

zero trust networks, 128

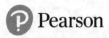